ONE FOOT IN ATLANTIS

THE SECRET OCCULT HISTORY OF WORLD WAR II AND ITS IMPACT ON NEW AGE POLITICS

William Henry

Earthpulse Press
P.O. Box 201393
Anchorage, Alaska
99520 U.S.A.

ISBN – 1-890693-49-9

ONE FOOT IN ATLANTIS: THE SECRET OCCULT HISTORY
OF WW II AND ITS IMPACT ON NEW AGE POLITICS.

Earthpulse Press
P.O. Box 201393
Anchorage, Alaska 99520
http://www.earthpulse.com
907-249-9111
888-690-1277

First Printing
Printed in the U.S.A.

To all who perished in WW II (or any war).
With all due respect.

Acknowledgements

Without the inspiration of Laura Lee, her husband Paul, and her listeners it is unlikely that I would have written this book. (Thank you, Laura, for your encouragement and editorial assistance.)

Thanks to Mom, Dad and Diane for your support and love.

Special thanks to my sister and brother-in-law, Kim and Donny Hinkle for holding my other foot in Atlantis for me.

To Jim Roderick, thanks for handling the editing. But thanks most of all for your sense of humor.

To Dr. Nick Begich and Shelah Slade, and family, thanks for having me in your home while we finished this work. Thanks too for being my angels.

Peace to you.

William Henry

TABLE OF CONTENTS

INTRODUCTION:

MORNING AT THE INTERSECTION OF GOOD AND EVIL

I was reading a book on lost civilizations as I recall it.1
Suddenly, a startling fact leaped from the page. In 1934, at the height of the Great Depression, President Franklin D. Roosevelt and his Secretary of Agriculture, Henry A. Wallace, sent agents to Central Asia. They claimed they were seeking drought-resistant grasses. However, as reported in *Newsweek* magazine, in the Roosevelt Administration, it was common knowledge that F.D.R. and Wallace were actually looking for the reincarnated Jesus in Shambhala,2 the Buddhist paradise.

F.D.R. looking for Jesus in Mongolia? This was surely one of the boldest missions in history! If successful, it would be the tantamount event of modern history. Everything would change.

Further investigation revealed inside occult details of this secretive research project. Wallace, who became F.D.R.'s third-term vice-president, was a disciple of a Russian guru and acclaimed artist and visionary named Nicholas Roerich. He was the ringmaster in the search for Jesus. Roerich had been preaching the gospel of the Second Coming ever since 1927 when he saw a huge, shiny oval object (a UFO?) racing across the Tibetan sky while dedicating a temple to Shambhala.2

For Roerich, Shambhala was the archetypal paradise the world was on the brink of becoming. He knew it was going to be a tough fight to make it happen, but Roerich had deep faith. With Wallace's help, and his high placed connections, he sought to bring peace to the world.

Their plan was to connect America with a group of spiritual masters whom they believed survived the cataclysm of Atlantis and who lived in Shambhala, secretly influencing world affairs. This race of Atlanteans were the spiritually actualized human beings who would usher in the new Golden Age, the prophesied kingdom of heaven on earth.

If anyone could bring Jesus to F.D.R. it was Roerich. A renowned mystic and flamboyant peacemaker with a bald head and long, pointed goatee, his influence on world affairs began in World War I when he was associated with the formation of the controversial League of Nations and its purpose of creating a New World Order.

At that time Roerich made the bold claim that he was in possession of a piece of a mysterious stone from another world. A divine messenger, Roerich claimed, had sent the stone to earth from the star system Sirius. It had previously been given to the emperor of Atlantis and then to King Solomon in Jerusalem (c. 1000 B.C.).3

The stone had been hidden in a tower in Shambhala, broadcasting rays that influenced the destiny of the world. In 1921, Roerich acquired possession of it to aid in the formation of the League of Nations. He returned the stone to Tibet shortly after his UFO sighting in 1927.

Whether or not Roerich was successful in locating Jesus is uncertain. However, in 1935, Roerich did bring forth two major accomplishments. He persuaded twenty-two countries, including the U.S., to gather at the White House to sign the Roach Peace Pact, which created a "Red Cross of Culture." The Roerich pact, which is still in effect today, sought to protect cultural treasures from destruction by means of a special flag of three dots in a red circle on a white banner.4

He also, along with Wallace, persuaded F.D.R. to place the Great Seal on the back of the one dollar bill. The Great Seal, which is America's symbolic coat-of-arms, was commissioned on July 4, 1776 and designed under the watchful eye of Benjamin Franklin, John Adams and Thomas Jefferson.5 Its purpose was to represent the inspiration for the American Revolution and the divine destiny of the American people. It is the logo for the American enterprise.

The reverse side of the Great Seal features an Egyptian-style pyramid with its capstone. Within the capstone is a picture of the single All-Seeing Eye of God and a gleaming sunburst behind it. Surrounding the truncated pyramid is the inscription, "Annuit Coeptis" and "Novus Ordo Seclorum." "Novus Ordo" is Latin for New Order or New Deal of the Ages, a phrase made popular by F.D.R.

The average American likely does not stay up nights trying to figure out the significance of this exotic symbol. However, its mystical meaning is profound.

To occultists, the Seal represents the spiritualization of the world. The Great Seal points to America as the leader in the transition from the Piscean Age that began with Jesus to the New Age of Aquarius. Some believe this symbol represents the Second Coming of Jesus. However, a similar symbol was worshipped as the symbol of the Egyptian gods Isis and Osiris, whom the Egyptians claimed came from Sirius (and with whom we shall meet again shortly).

According to Egyptian legend and popular lore, the survivors of a cataclysm built the Great Pyramid of Giza, which is the model for the pyramid on the one dollar bill. No one can say for certain why this profound structure was built or by whom. Among other uses it has been proposed it was constructed as a star clock, a landing beacon, a resurrection machine, and, most interesting to us, as a book in stone.[6,7,8,9]

Originally, the Pyramid was sheathed in shiny, tura limestone. A few precious pieces of this stone cling to the structure today. Gleaming too brightly to look at in the morning Sun, the immense limestone-covered temple would have looked to the ancient observer like a great, silvered mirror.

The Greek historian, Herodotus, claims hieroglyphics or holy inscriptions of the lost arts and sciences of the advanced civilization that built the pyramid once covered its surface. Pilgrims would stand in front of the pyramid and read it like a book. It also had a capstone, said to have been made of pure crystal, "the priceless gem of Egypt." This capstone was believed to have attracted and transmitted cosmic rays.

Archaeologists are now beginning to present proof (the existence of fossilized sea shells embedded in the masonry at the base of the Pyramid and water erosion on the Sphinx, for example) that the construction of the Great Pyramid complex was started, but not finished, before the biblical Flood.[10]

Mainstream scholars are reticent when it comes to using the dreaded "A word," as in Atlantis, to point to the land of origin of the contractors responsible for the building of the Great Pyramid. However, this possibility is the subject of intense speculation and must be considered.

Like the Great Pyramid, conservative scholars, and some religious authorities who lazily label it Satanic, wish the Great Seal did not exist. After being suppressed since 1776, the Seal was making a comeback in 1935.

Symbolically, it puts us face to face with a priesthood which thrived in Egypt, but which originated in deepest antiquity.

The Great Seal and its ancient variations symbolize both the prophecy and goal of this ancient priesthood. As Roerich and Wallace intended, its placement on the back of the one dollar bill symbolically places America in the continuation of a vast evolutionary spiritual enterprise which originated in ancient times -- in Atlantis, according to the mystics.

With F.D.R's stamp of approval, was this project now off and running in twentieth century America?

If Atlantis was rising again, this would make sense. The harrowing destruction of Atlantis (about 10,000 B.C.) is said to have taken place during the Age of Leo, the sign of the zodiac directly opposite that of our New Age of Aquarius. The Sphinx of Giza, which guards the entrance to the Great Pyramid and its secrets, is half-lion and half-man, indicating to astrologists that the Ages of Leo and Aquarius are connected (coincidentally, F.D.R.'s aides called him "the Sphinx").

Mystically speaking, did the placement of the Great Seal on the one dollar bill indicate to those "in the know" that the long anticipated march to the Golden Age had begun? Did its appearance represent a major paradigm shift in world affairs?

With the Great Seal of the Atlantean enterprise on the back of the one dollar bill did America now have one foot in Atlantis?

"DEAR GURU"

If, in fact, F.D.R. did have an Atlantean muse, the world remained largely unaware of it until 1948. During a political battle in his bid for the Presidency, Wallace was discredited for his spiritual beliefs and his association with Roerich. His letters to Roerich, which began with the salutation "Dear Guru," were sensationalized. (Wallace's private papers show he completely severed his ties with Roerich in 1935.)

We are the losers of this smear campaign. As Wallace's biographers Graham White and John Maze state; "If he, rather than Harry Truman, had become president on Franklin Roosevelt's death, his policy of accommodation with the Soviet Union as against the Truman Doctrine of containment might have spared the world some forty years of cold war."[11]

Here is the point of our investigation.

In 1934 the world was awakening to the dawn of an apocalyptic battle, and the morning of the intersection of good and evil. For Roerich, Wallace, and possibly even F.D.R., the chaos of WW II was seen as the preamble to the final battle when the entire earth would be transformed into Shambhala, the Christian New Jerusalem, or the New Atlantis and Jesus would return.

Out of the loop of secretive Oval Office conversations, most Depression-era Americans had no inkling of the bizarre, occult wonderland their leaders had tapped into, the utopian fantasies that filled their heads, nor the arcane myths that guided and inspired them. (Does the fact that F.D.R. named the Presidential hideaway in Maryland "Shangri-la," suggest that he was captivated by Roerich's mystic myths? Eisenhower later renamed the retreat Camp David.)

Fifty years after the deconstruction of the world, we stand on the far nimbus of this apocalyptic intersection. As a global civilization on the brink of a new millennium, we *think* we are safely removed from the events of WW II.

As millennial children of the American warriors of WW II we buy cars from Germany and electronics from Japan. We routinely adopt babies from our WW II ally and Cold War enemy, the Evil Empire. All without giving a second thought as to why the Soviet Union lost 20 million people, China at least 10 million, Poland 5.8 million, Germany 4.6 million, Japan 2 million, Yugoslavia 1.7 million, France 600,000, Great Britain 400,000, and the United States 300,000 people just a generation ago.

Although it is painful to consider, have we become complacent when it comes to systematic mass murder and organized killing? Are we just plain asleep when it comes to awareness of the archetypal drama of which each of us are players and the mythological linkages that guide and unite our civilization?

F.D.R.'S WORLD

The fact of the matter is, as *Time* magazine recently proclaimed,[12] we live in F.D.R.'s world. What a wondrous world it is. In a mere fifty years, have we not traveled from being a world of disconnected peoples at war to a world that seems like science fiction to the children of the 30's and 40's? We've gone to the Moon and Mars, and back. We've rebuilt Atlantis (the space shuttle anyway); we're mapping the human genome, and are reshaping and redesigning our world with genetic technologies. Through the eye-popping images provided by the Hubble Space Telescope, and other awe-inspiring technologies, we are getting a bird's eye view of the deepest recesses of space and reconnecting with creation.

Yet, in the course of our progress, have we come to take the wide-eyed guiding myths and legends of our ancestors for granted? How many of us know or appreciate where we came from, or for that matter, where we are going? Today, as Generation Y, (those born during and after the Reagan/Bush years) hurtles through space gobbling Skittles and drinking Mountain Dew, do they realize they are on the edge of a powerful new era; an era that will return us and them to our origins? This book is for Generation Y. They too have one foot in Atlantis. It is high time this is widely known.

This book is also for the generation that lived during WW II. For them this book will offer rare and startling insights into the unreported occult beliefs which guided, provoked and inspired the political leaders of WW II. It could forever smash their view of the past and change their future, for it will suggest that the most powerful force in WW II was not goosestepping monsters, the atom bomb or radar. It was an idea. Perhaps the most glorious idea of all time: *Atlantis*.

This study will show that Atlantis is the guiding myth of not just WW II, but of human civilization. It is the great Phoenix-bird of myths -- immolating and reconstituting, over and over again. Like a psychological demon relegated to the deepest recesses of the subconscious, it will rise again. The question is when.

The answer is; sooner than later. Since 1626, with the publication of Sir Francis Bacon's utopian novel *The New Atlantis*, America has been viewed by the occult-minded as the New Atlantis. Sir Francis Bacon was an English essayist, philosopher, statesman, and avowed occultist, Hermeticist and Rosicrucian -- both repositories for the ancient, sacred mystery teachings that were preserved and passed down to initiates throughout history. He was the editor of the King James Version of the Bible. Controversy still exists over whether Bacon wrote the Shakespearean dramas.

As a Utopian, Bacon longed for the creation of a Golden Age where humanity lived without war and violence. He formulated a blueprint for this New Jerusalem -- an enlightened civilization with advanced religion, politics education and science. *The New Atlantis* has been called a prophetic dream of the great technological civilization which was to arise on American soil: "a new nation, conceived in liberty and dedicated to the proposition that all men are created equal."

To the Founding Fathers *The New Atlantis* held a place beside the Holy Bible. They subscribed to this concept of America as the long-awaited New Atlantis. This mythos also silently penetrated the Oval Office of F.D.R.

Unfortunately, as we will see, this tireless myth found its loudest, most muscular wheels in Nazi Germany. The same blond gods who were the would-be Masters of Roerich's and Wallace's New Atlantis also fired the imagination of the Nazis.

The magical name "Atlantis," I will contend, refers to more than just a vanished land (bridge) between Europe and America. It is our constant craving, an irrepressible ideal, a word-symbol that conjures visions of ancient glory that was lost. In "a single day and night" thousands of years ago, the

6

mystical land of Atlantis is said to have been destroyed by earthquake and flood.

Despite the fact that nearly two thousand books have been written about Atlantis in the twentieth century, we may never be able to prove that Atlantis existed. Still, Atlantis reminds us of all that was once great about the human race, and can be great again. It is a state of mind, glued together by far-flung ideas and a large measure of hope.

Our ability to grasp the imortance of the new Atlantis myth to the events of WW II (and today's New Age politics) is matched only by our ability to absorb the astounding. Atlantis is the missing piece in the puzzle of WW II, it is the beginning and ending of the war.

If one makes the effort to unearth the myths, symbols and fantasies which comprise the mindsets of F.D.R., Hitler, Churchill and their associates, one will find that WWII was not "just" a war of good over absolute evil. It was a war of one occult "mind set" over another. Viewed this way, WWII connects us with the most ancient of human history, and the most esoteric of concepts. The history we thought we knew is not the whole story at all. The leaders we trusted were enraptured by a mystery and a history they forgot to tell us about.

One thing is certain. Once Nazism is revealed for what it really was -- an occult religion, and WW II is looked at for what it really was -- a Holy War -- the last *and next* fifty years will never be looked at the same again.

Nor will we be fooled by the shallow, manipulative and violence-centered mainstream military history of our world as we contemplate the beginning of the next thousand years of history. Consider a few of the "tamer" occult discoveries that emerge from our search:

• Adolph Hitler believed he was in contact with alleged extraterrestrial creator gods.

• The Nazis spent enormous resources searching for the Holy Grail and other Hebrew artifacts.

• F.D.R. owned shares in a company attempting to salvage a repository believed to contain the gold and spiritual secrets of the Knights Templar.

• General George Patton believed he was a Roman soldier in a past life.

• Winston Churchill suggested America use the previously obscure prophecies of Nostradamus in a pivotal propaganda war against the Third Reich, which also used these prophecies.

• The Nazis believed they shared the same mystic origins as the Japanese race: blond gods from outer space.

These are just a few of the strange occult facts that emerge in our search. These facts calmly inform us that the leaders of WW II were either men of New Age enlightenment, or by today's conservative standards where Hillary Clinton cannot even have an imaginary conversation with Eleanor Roosevelt without being publicly flogged, they were a generation lost in space.

There are plenty of books detailing (if not pathologically glorifying) the carnage of WWII. Dozens of movies re-enact the battles. Slick Hollywood promoters claim their blood-fests fully capture the true feel of war. Strangely absent from these works are references to the occult, religious or quasi-religious beliefs, which drove the mental wheels of the leaders of WW II. This aspect of the War has been buried, its importance summarily dismissed as irrelevant.

I do not attribute this to a conspiracy. I blame closed-minded historians and Winston Churchill.

The idea of occult concepts influencing world leaders is about as believable to an "official" historian as the idea that it was Satan himself who caused the War. Occult is Latin for "hidden." Esoterically, however, it refers to that which we do not want to face. Perhaps this explains why the occult remains hidden outside of the mainstream scholar's mental box, their paradigm. This does not mean we can wink or crinkle our nose and make the occult beliefs of WW II's movers and shakers go away, which is what Churchill attempted to do.

At the Nuremburg trials of the Nazi war criminals, Churchill ordered the occult beliefs of the Nazis kept secret for fear that the jury would not give the Nazis the death penalty on the grounds that they were insane.13 At the close of WW II, the victorious Allies -- the United States, Soviet Union, Britain and France -- captured Hermann Goering and 20 other leading Nazis and set up the tribunal in the Palace of Justice at Nuremberg in southern Germany.

Prosecutors accused them of shattering civilized standards by organizing or abetting atrocities and laying waste to Europe. At its heart Nuremberg helped lay the foundation for the principle that governments must be held accountable for mistreating their citizens.

What was ommitted was the explanation of why the Nazis did what they did. The reason is ideas are the true powers that turn the wheel of fortune of nations.

The Allies feared that if word leaked of the spiritual principles, which guided the Nazis to such a fast rise to power, it might inspire imitators. Churchill may have secretly feared that if this piece of the puzzle were let out, it would reveal, to the masses, what the puzzle of humanity really is. So, he ordered the key piece buried.

Churchill's attempt to make Atlantis go away could not possibly succeed. It is like trying to make the sun disappear by making everyone walk around with open umbrellas. This book will identify and document the ideas and beliefs Churchill was so afraid of releasing and which have been hidden from the public and from history by future leaders. It will bring to the surface the secret occult history of not just WW II, but of humanity: the unseen, the unheard, the unspoken.

NEW AGE POLITICS

As will become evident, many of the myths and beliefs which formed the occult mind-sets and guided the politics of WWII are illuminating millennial consciousness and New Age politics today: UFO's, a belief in extraterrestrial creators, a yearning for a Golden Age, the human drive to develop our mental powers, the goal of creating the "perfect" human, and the heightened anticipation of the beginning of a New Millennium of Peace introduced by a Christ, Messiah, or Earth Teacher.

For this reason it is essential that we study the occult history of World War II. Without an understanding of these concepts the mayhem of WW II will never be completely understood. As history demonstrates, what is not understood by one generation becomes the psychological demon to be exorcised by future generations. If for this reason alone, we must undertake this study.

Since 1945, armies of historians, scholars, journalists, and social commentators have attempted to track down the root cause of WW II and have brought forth astonishing details and information. Through an examination of these works, the highlights of which comprise this book, I discovered a controversial, but profound and powerful, thread: the political leaders of WWII had one foot in one of the most perplexing myths of all time: Atlantis.

And why not? The Atlantis myth is ubiquitous. Her muses kick around in the heads of millions of ordinary people. So, why not world leaders? For many, Atlantis was the greatest triumph in human civilization and also humanity's greatest failure. The failure of Atlantis, I will propose, can and must be transcended.

In part, this book will seek to answer several underlying questions: what made Atlantis so great? How did this highly charged myth get lodged into the global mind? How can we use this myth to guide humanity today? As New Age politics becomes more and more about "spin" (or what used to be called lies) and making people believe something is real even if it isn't, how can ordinary citizens purify the global mind?

Our journey into this subject relies on a willingness to peek beyond the surface and to connect the glaring dots that are already there. The rewards are plentiful. Beyond politics, imagine what would happen to religion if this heretical Atlantis-centered history became orthodoxy. Imagine if the puzzle of humanity were solved. In myths and legends, Atlantis was a technologically advanced civilization. Her technology was based on light. Her scientists mastered (and botched) genetics. As she increased her mastery, she proportionally increased her vulnerability. Strange, that when the warriors of WW II returned home, they swapped their battlefield uniforms for grey flannel suits and fit themselves in the pyramidal chain of command of corporate America.

Driving the booming post-WW II economy were two new technologies: the computer, based on light; and genetics, based on the alteration of the genetic code. Both technologies ushered in a new, otherworldly era: a designer reality, the New Atlantis.

Welcome back, my friends, to the show that never ends.

Notes:

1. David Hatcher Childress *Lost Cities of Asia, China and Mongolia* (Stelle, Ill., Adventures Unlimited Press, 1993)
2. Graham White & John Maze *Henry A. Wallace: His Search for a New World Order* (Chapel Hill, The University of North Carolina Press, 1995).
3. Nicholas Roerich, *Altai-Himalaya:A Travel Diary*, pp. 361-362.
4. J. Saint -Hilair (H. Roerich), *On Eastern Crossroads* (New York, Roerich Museum, 1930).
5. Robert Hieronimus, Ph.D. *America's Secret Destiny* (Rochester, Vermont, Destiny Books, 1989).
6. Graham Hancock *Fingerprints of the Gods* (New York, Crown Publishers, 1995).
7. Zecharia Sitchin *The Twelfth Planet* (New York, Avon Books, 1976).
8. Vivian Davies and Renee Friedman *Egypt Uncovered* (New York, Stewart Tabori & Chang, 1998).
9. Peter Lemesurier,*The Great Pyramid Decoded* (Great Britain, Element, 1977).
10. Colin Wilson, *From Atlantis to the Sphinx* (New York, Fireside, 1997).
11. ibid.
12. *Time Magazine* May 7, 1998.
13. *The New Atlantis*
14. Trevor Ravenscroft, *The Spear of Destiny* (York Beach, Maine, Samuel Weiser, 1973).

CHAPTER ONE

THE THEOSOPHICAL SOCIETY: PLANTING THE SEEDS OF THE ATLANTEAN CENTURY

On a summer day in 1875, Madame Helena Petrovna Blavatksy, the woman *McCall's* magazine called "The Founding Mother of the Occult in America,"1 sits huddled in the study of her apartment at 46 Irving Place in New York City chain-smoking cigarettes. She takes another long drag and spews out a massive cloud of smoke.

Suddenly, the astral bell rings. An incoming message electrifies the ether. With the ease of someone jotting down a toll-free number from a radio commercial she squeezes out another cryptic note:

"Orders received from India direct to establish a philosophic-religious Society & choose a name for it -- also to choose Olcott."2

When the air finally clears, HPB peers into a note that will change the rest of her life, and alter the history of western civilization.

The Society she was to found was the Theosophical Society (TS), the mother of all-American occult societies. Within a few short years global New Age superheroes such as Rudolph Steiner, Thomas A. Edison, Mohandas Gandhi, and Nicholas Roerich would gravitate to her, and orbit her circle. So too would Adolph Hitler.

Through her writings each of these men (and millions of other people), would blast off from the mundane material world, achieve escape velocity, and find themselves with one foot in Atlantis.

"HPB"

It had been a long and winding road to New York and occult superstardom for Helena, or "HPB," to her friends. Born in Russia to an aristocratic father who was in the army, and a mother, who was an accomplished novelist, HPB exhibited psychic gifts -- and her trademark temper -- since childhood. At seventeen, she married General Nikifor Blavatsky, a man twice her age, whom she abandoned without consummating the marriage.

Before her eighteenth birthday, she escaped Russia to the crossroads of Constantinople by enlisting the help of a British steamship captain. From 1848 to 1858, HPB conquered the world, a lone, liberated woman in search of herself and her life's mission. She rode horseback in the circus, served as a companion to elderly noblewomen, and traveled Europe first as the mistress to a Hungarian opera star and then to a famous medium.

In Egypt, she was said to have conducted an esoteric ceremony in the Great Pyramid, raising the spirit of a long dead Egyptian priest. She claims to have studied with the Masters in India and in Tibet for two years, where she cunningly disguised herself as a man to gain entrance into secret monasteries. Included in her contacts were the Great White Brotherhood, the Count Saint Germaine and the Master Koot Hoomi.

By 1858 HPB returned to Russia a grown woman of twenty-nine years. The road to enlightenment had been hard on her. One of her cousins who met HPB at that time wrote that her once beautiful face, "bore all the traces of a tempestuous and passionate life."[3] Further, she had become fat and slovenly. It has been said that Helen of Troy had a face that launched a thousand ships. In the case of our endearing Helena of Russia it was her eyes that would have to be relied upon to launch an occult movement. "Never in my life have I seen anything like that pair of eyes," wrote her cousin.

In July of 1873 HPB sailed into in New York City. At forty-two she was flat broke, and like many of the European immigrants who poured past Lady Liberty, she was subjected to soul-grinding poverty and hardship. However, like the effervescence of shiny pearl, HPB's indomitable spirit rose to the surface. She quickly impressed folks with her psychic talents, and enchanted Victorian New Worlders with her Old World charm and gripping adventure stories.

In 1874 HPB met Colonel Henry Olcott, an aging lawyer, promoter and chronicler of spiritual news for several New York daily newspapers. Olcott had gained HPB's attention when he wrote an article about a haunted farmhouse in

Vermont. HPB went to check this out for herself. Strangely, while she was there Russian ghosts suddenly appeared. Impressed, she and Olcott became friends.4

Within a year of meeting, HPB and Olcott had teamed up with William Q. Judge, a twenty-four-year-old-Irish-born attorney whom James Joyce (author of *Ulysses*) later called "the noblest Roman of them all." Putting the petal-to-the-metal, they quickly formed the Theosophical Society.

The power pack driving this occult club was HPB's insistence that she was in possession of secret teachings and writings, which came from the Masters of Wisdom or Mahatmas. Olcott was practically foaming at the mouth with the possibility of communicating with these Masters. He had heard of the existence of such ultra-evolved beings. Like HPB, he had been deeply influenced by the bizarre romantic novels written by the English statesman and occultist Lord Edward Bulwer-Lytton (1803-1873), the writer perhaps best known for giving us the opening line, "it was a dark and stormy night."

THE COMING RACE: ENTER THE ANA

Today, Bulwer-Lytton's book *The Coming Race*5 is the needle in the haystack of all occult books. In the 1870's, however, it was widely read in England, America and Europe. *The Coming Race* describes the existence of a utopian society of advanced beings who live in tunnels and caverns beneath the surface of the earth in a land called *Vril-ya*. These beings, known as the *Ana*, were forced into the inner earth because of earth changes, specifically a flood, which destroyed their civilization thousands of years before the Biblical cataclysm.

The Ana had the ability to fly with wings attached to their bodies. Of even greater interest to many Victorian readers was the Ana's mastery of the limitless *vril* or Life Force, an energy which the Ana scientists learned to draw from the atmosphere and which instantly bumped the Ana race a few rungs up the evolutionary ladder.

This ineffable and mysterious cosmic energy dramatically enhanced the Ana's psychic powers and was wielded by the inhabitants of the inner earth. It could also produce a laser-like death ray. Its use became so pervasive the Ana changed their name to the *Vril-ya*.

Bulwer-Lytton intended *The Coming Race* and the Ana's matriarchal, democratic utopian society to be a satire aimed at feminists, democrats, socialists, and all others who he believed were deluded into thinking utopia could be achieved. Besides, with vril power, all wishes were instantly materialized, all hurts healed, paradise found. What challenges would remain to make life interesting?

Satire or not, like a turn-of-the-century Luke Skywalker, HPB had no doubts that vril was real. "The name vril may be a fiction," she later wrote in *The Secret Doctrine*,6 but "*the force itself is doubted as little in India as the existence itself of their Rishis, since it is mentioned in all the secret works.*" Secret works you say? In India? *The Coming Race* not only influenced HPB and Colonel Olcott, but also found wide acceptance among European occultists. Most dangerously, it found acceptance among the soon to be goose-stepping German nationalists, including Adolph Hitler, who, once in power, sent expeditions to India and elsewhere in search of the land of the Vrila.

One of the most dangerous of the German mystical political groups called itself the Vril Society. It combined Bulwer-Lytton's fiction with the occult ideas of the Order of the Illuminati, Hindu mysticism, Christianity, Theosophy and the Hebrew Kaballah. The Vril Society was formed in the early 1900's and was an incubator of Nazism, being the first group to use the swastika as a political emblem linking Eastern and Western mysticism.

THE RESURRECTION OF THEOSOPHY

The notion of an "ancient wisdom," guarded by hidden Masters, was irresistible to Olcott. In short order he wrote an article in a spiritualist newspaper which in very general terms described HPB's encounters with the Masters of India and Tibet. Soon, the two friends had a small, but dedicated group of seekers of Ancient Wisdom gathered around them. From these inauspicious beginnings the Theosophical Society was born in September 1875, in Manhattan.

Theosophy comes from the Greek words *theos*, "God," and *sophia*, "wisdom." The name was proposed by founding member Charles Sotheran. However, according to HPB, the word "theosophy" originated in the third century A.D. when Ammonius Saccas and his disciples attempted to purify their souls, and connect with the Source, so as to receive divine secrets.

Saccas and his disciples were descendents of Pythagoras (the first "philosopher" and personal friend of Buddha) and Plato (the Greek "father of Atlantology"), and were highly influenced by the Orphic and Egyptian mystery schools. (The Nazis later spent enormous sums attempting to develop Pythagoras' theory of vibration into weapons systems.)

The basic premise of Theosophy is the belief that wisdom is accessible to the human soul through direct intuition or transmission. HPB believed that ancient civilizations, such as Greek and Egyptian, had a far greater understanding of the relation between the soul and the Source. She considered the ancient teachers to be considerably more spiritually advanced than modern scholars and "men of God" who were blinded by the modern school of materialism and warped by its twin pillar, bigotry.

These Masters, or "Mahatmas," as they are known in India, reincarnate continuously throughout history, said HPB, preserving their knowledge, and sharing it with certain deserving initiates.

Most of these Masters, she claimed, lived in spa-like retreats in India, Tibet and Mongolia, and are members of a Brotherhood of Adepts. Pythagoras and his followers, the alchemists, the Freemasons and Rosicrucians are all exemplary Theosophists. All claimed to possess teachings that would assist in the purification of the human soul and the elevation of the soul from earth.

While HPB and her growing band of disciples were its spokespersons, HPB believed the Masters Koot Hoomi (or Kuthumi), Lal Singh, and Morya were the true founders of the Theosophical Society. Late in the spring of 1875, just before the TS was founded, HPB claimed she had a profound mystical experience in which she said was overshadowed by Master Morya, or Master M. They "mind-melded." Morya began to speak through her.[7]

El Morya is one of the assistants of the Manu whose work is primarily concerned with planetary politics, government and the founding and dissolution of races. The Manu's staff spends a great deal of time attempting to influence the minds of earth's statespeople and politicians. The name Manu will return later in our story in a most remarkable way.

Despite its ancient pedigree and impressive roster of founders and members, the Theosophical movement did not exactly take the modern world by storm. It did, however, receive a needed boost of publicity when one of its sponsors died and asked to be cremated. This was America's first cremation service and was well attended by curiosity seekers. The ceremony was lambasted as a pagan ritual by numerous New York newspapers. This humiliating publicity could not stop the indominatable spirit of HPB, however. The wheels of destiny were spinning.

The force, she knew, was with her.

ISIS UNVEILED

HPB's first book, *Isis Unveiled*,[8] which came to be known as her "bible," was published in 1877. Running over a staggering 500,000 words, the text was 1,300 pages long. The first one thousand copies sold out in less than ten days. It is a truly remarkable work.

In the preface to *Isis Unveiled,* HPB stated that the book was "a plea for the recognition of the *Hermetic* philosophy, the ancient universal wisdom."

Hermes was the Greek name for *Thoth,* the Egyptian Peacemaker who, according to legend, was the supervisor of the construction of the Great Pyramid. He was known as the guardian of the gateways to higher dimensions and a transmitter of teachings centered around the creation of peace (the uniting of heaven and earth), the acceleration of consciousness and the transmutation of the soul from a lower, human form, *homo sapien,* to higher, angelic beings, *homo angelis.*

We will encounter Thoth repeatedly in the pages to come. His teachings were the guiding light of the mystic Founding Fathers of America, as well as the source of the ancient Nordic legends which also inspired the Nazis.

THE ANCIENT SHINING ONES

Isis Unveiled tantalized the Victorian mind with its tale of a vast inland sea that once existed in Central Asia, where is found the fabled Shambhala, the beautiful island home of the "last remnant of the race which preceded ours," who were masters of the universe. These beings were the "Sons of God," or the *Elohim* of the Old Testament, the teachers of humanity.

The Elohim are shrouded in mystery. *El* means "shining one," and is the name given to God in Genesis 1:1, "In the beginning, God created the heavens and the earth." Or in Genesis 1:26: "God said, Let us make man in our image, in the likeness of ourselves...."

This is strange. If El means "God" or "shining one," then Elohim (plural) must mean "the Gods" or "the shining ones." Thus, "In the beginning, the Shining Ones created the heavens and the earth"; or, "The Shining Ones said, Let us make man in our image, in the likeness of ourselves..." They called their offspring human because "Hu" means "shining one," "effervescent one," and "God." Thus, hu-mans are technically hybrids or god-men.

This odd plural description of God appears thirty times in the first five books of the Old Testament and is one of the greatest unexplained mysteries of the Bible. We'll be meeting the Shining Ones again and again as we proceed.

Isis Unveiled is a monumental work by any standard, especially considering HPB's native tongue was Russian. Put yourself in her shoes. Writing in English had to have been an immense challenge. This led readers to ponder exactly how HPB single-handedly amassed the enormous vocabulary and expansive knowledge contained in the work.

Later, sleuthy literary critics discovered hundreds of passages in *Isis Unveiled* bore striking resemblance to other published works. Accusations of plagiarism caused HPB to comment in a follow-up work, *The Secret Doctrine,* that she merely provided the string that tied together the disjointed and unconnected ideas of other scholars.
She invited everyone to pull the string.
This was important. As we'll see, the reigning scholar at the time was Charles Darwin, whose *Origin of Species* was an international phenomenon. HPB intended *Isis Unveiled* to be a direct attack on the "machine man" premise of Darwin.

Notes:

1. Sylvia Cranston, *H.P.B. The Extraordinary Life and Influence of Helena Blavatsky* (Jeremy P. Tarcher, New York, 1993)
2. H.P. Blavatsky, *H.P.Blavatsky Collected Writings,* p. 95; Gomes, *The Dawning of the Theosophical Movement,* p. 79
3. ibid
4. ibid.
5. Edward Bulwer-Lytton, *The Coming Race.*
7. Peter Washington, *Madame Blavatsky's Baboon* (New York, Schocken Books, 1995).
8. H.P. Blavatsky, *Isis Unveiled*

CHAPTER TWO

ATLANTIS: THE ANTEDELUVIAN WORLD

For many, HPB's work was their first introduction to the idea of Atlantis and the concept of a hidden Master Plan for humanity. In hindsight, it was but a drop that helped open the flood-gates to the ocean of Atlantis books to follow. In 1882, one of the most important books in the history of Atlantean research since Plato's time was published. *Atlantis: The Antediluvian World*₁ was the tour d'force of former U.S. Congressman Ignatius J. Donnelly. When not attending to his Congressional duties, Donnelly prowled the hallowed halls of the Library of Congress answering the siren song of his Atlantean muse. 2,200 years after Plato gave his account of the lost land and introduced Atlantis to the Greek mind, Donnelly took up the mantle as the "Father of Atlantology" in modern America.

In chapter one of his *Atlantis* Donnelly presents a cluster of ideas which represent the ripe fruit of his many years of Atlantis research. Twelve thousand years ago, he concluded, there was a large island in the Atlantic Ocean which was known to the ancient world as Atlantis.

That's not all. According to Donnelly:

• The description of Atlantis given by Plato is not fable, but history.

• Atlantis was the true site of the Garden of Eden and all other mythical earthly paradises, and home to the first human civilization.

• The gods and goddesses worshippped by the ancient Greeks, the Phoenicians, the Hindus, and the Nordics were the kings, queens and heroes of Atlantis.

• The children of Atlantis were the founders of Egypt, Mexico, America and Peru.
• Egyptian and Peruvian religions are remnants of Atlantean sun worship.

By Donnelly's reckoning, no civilization had matched the beauty, elegance, sophistication or spiritual achievements of this island world. He gave the Atlanteans credit for creating the alphabet, medicine and nearly all the arts and sciences.

Despite its very advanced science, Atlantis suffered a cataclysmic destruction in which the entire island sank with nearly all its inhabitants. However, a few lucky Atlanteans escaped in ships. These culture bearers spread throughout the world telling the tale of their paradisiacal homeland.

THE GOLDEN THREAD

"I give you the end of the golden thread
only wind it into a ball,
it will lead you in at heaven's gate
built in Jerusalem's wall."

William Blake, *Jerusalem*

Shortly after its American debut Donnelly's *Atlantis* was published in England and Germany. In both countries it exerted enormous influence.

William Gladstone, Prime Minister of Britain, was so overwhelmed by Donnelly's proposition that in 1882 he asked the Cabinet for cash to send a ship to trace out the outline of Atlantis in the Atlantic.

The Atlantis archetype had been close to the hearts of Britons ever since the time of the poet, artist, mystic, and radical prophet William Blake (1757-1827).

Blake, principally known for his poem *Jerusalem*, was a disciple of British scholars who thought the early Celts of the British Isles, and particularly their Druid priesthood/wisdom keepers, were the source of Ancient Wisdom, which they shared, with the rest of the world.

Blake was a one time Grand Master of the Rosicrucian Order (who took their philosophies from Moses -- whom they believed was the Egyptian heretic king Akhenaton -- and King Solomon). He subscribed to the belief that early Britain was called *Albion* (Scotland in Gaelic is called Alba) and was the home of "Albion the giant."

Blake identified Albion with *Atlas*, the first priest-king of Atlantis and leader of the *Titans*, for whom Atlantis is named. Atlas, we all know, was the god who held the world upon his shoulders. (Actually, it was the word, the life force energy upon which the world is built.)

If Albion is Atlas, it sounds as though Blake thought Britain was a part of Atlantis. In Celtic tradition the "Scilly Isles" or "the Blessed Isles" are names applied to the surviving islands of Atlantis, which are located in Britain and Ireland.

UR-LANGUAGE: UR-RELIGION

In Germany, Donnelly's *Atlantis* struck an equally powerful chord.

This was due to its premise that Atlantis was the original land of the Aryan and Indo-European family of nations. In the 1890's and early 1900's many Germans were involved in a single-minded pursuit of a particular kind of knowledge: a quest for their Aryan origins.

Of utmost importance to the Aryans of Germany and Europe was the recovery of the Aryan *Ur-religion* (ur meaning ancient, primordial, elemental, archetypal), the religion of prehistory in which the direct experience of God could be attained through initiation rituals involving the sun, stars and nature.2

They also sought the *Ur-language*, the original power language spoken by humanity in the Garden of Eden (aka Atlantis) which was thought to have been lost when Adam and Eve were evicted from paradise.

"There is," said HPB, "a natural connection between language and religion."3

German scholars and linguists were hot on the trail of the golden thread of the "secret doctrine" and the original prehistoric religion and language, which since the Middle Ages they were convinced, was German.

They traced this thread as it wove itself through India, Iran, the mystery religions of Greece and Rome, the Gnostics, the alchemists, Freemasons and the Rosicrucians.

The Germans were not conducting this search out of pure self-interest.

It was widely thought that an Aryan or Germanic Christ or Messiah would soon appear who would lead the Germans to the gods of antiquity, but more importantly, to the teachings that would enable the German people to transform themselves into gods.

With this return imminent, it was a good idea to learn the language of this Messiah.

Briefly informing ourselves of the stunning advances in archaeology which led to the possible recovery of this language at the turn of the twentieth century will be helpful.

THE RETURN OF EZEKIEL AND THE RACE TO BABYLON

On a quest for their origins, eager German archaeologists began tearing up the lands of Babylon (present day Iraq) and Assyria in search of answers and for the ur-language. Another favorite digging ground was Ur (which is also in Iraq), the birthplace of Abraham, the great patriarch of the nation of Israel.

A race to Ur and Babylon was on. It began in the 1840's, when French and English archaeologists uncovered the ruins of an ancient palace of the Assyrian king Ashurbanipal (ruled 883-859 B.C.) in the village of Nimrud in what is now northern Iraq, and the palace of Assyrian king Sargon II (ruled 721-705 B.C.). There, they found inscribed stone slabs and colossal, sphinx-like, human-headed winged bull and lion statues guarding doorways.

Scholars were struck by the similarities of these antiquities to Biblical references. Especially those in Ezekiel 1:10, which describes extraterrestrial winged figures with the features of a man, a lion, a bull, and an eagle, and Ezekiel 23:14-15, which details images on the wall of an Assyrian palace. Generations of theologians had considered Ezekiel's vision purely a symbolic fantasy. But now, was there proof that it was real?

Ezekiel (600 B.C) was a young Hebrew prophet who was captured, along with the Children of Daniel, by King Nebuchadnezzar and taken to Babylon, home of the Tower of Babel and the site of important Biblical happenings. While there, he had a vision, which he described as a vision of God or Elohim.

The Bible describes Ezekiel's vision as a great cloud, with fire flashing through it, and a radiant glow around it. Something gleamed like metal in the middle of it. Ezekiel heard "the noise of great waters." From the cloud descended what appeared to be four extraterrestrial men who each had four faces: a lion, bull, man and eagle (the same four beasts that comprise the Sphinx).

When these sculptures and carvings depicting Ezekiel's vision were displayed in London and Paris museums, they caused a worldwide sensation. Could it be these exotic sculptures provided concrete proof of Biblical events?

Many of these sculptures were purchased by John D. Rockefeller, Jr., who later donated them to the Metropolitan Museum of Art in New York City (where they are found today). The only other collections of comparison are found in the British Museum and the Louvre. Appropriately, the University of Pennsylvania in Philadelphia, the birthplace of America ("the New Atlantis"), was a third repository for these powerful stone antiquities.4

As a result of the unexpected finds in Iraq, in 1842-43 the American Oriental Society was founded. The German Oriental Society was founded in 1844. These societies spawned a new breed of scholars who pulled from the fields of speculative history, Old Testament studies and personal observation to create dramatic new theories of humanity's past.

THE FIRST AMERICAN INVASION OF BABYLON

Inspired by the discovery of statuary possibly proving Ezekiel's vision true, from the 1880's through the 1920's the greatest collection of American scholars, soldiers of fortune, institutional bureaucrats and financiers invaded Babylon.5 These forces were not matched until the Gulf War coalition stormed this area in 1991.

In contrast to the Atlantis-seeking Germans (and the Gulf War coalition), turn-of-the-century American scholars were more interested in proving the Bible true and bringing home trophies then in finding secret teachings, bumping themselves up the evolutionary ladder or bumping off Saddam Hussein, a thug who believed himself to be the reincarnation of Nebuchadnezzar, and who in the 1980's spent more than $500 million attempting to rebuild Babylon.

In the early 1900's, the center of American intelligentsia was in New England: Yale, Johns Hopkins, Princeton, Colombia, and Harvard universities. The University of Chicago (a Baptist college newly funded by John D. Rockefeller and later involved in the development of the atom bomb and esoteric Tesla weapons technology) and the University of Pennsylvania (run by a man who was proclaimed the Benjamin Franklin of the nineteenth century) were also prominent centers of Biblical archaeology and its scholarship.

American scholars had recently broken away their ties to European, particularly German, scholarship and now were in competition with the Germans for dominance in the field of Near Eastern or Oriental studies. The Europeans, especially the German *doktors* who felt teaching in the United States to be beneath them, considered American universities, and their scholars, second-rate.6

In America, Bible stories were the root of the academic and popular mind. If an American could read he likely read the Bible. To a large extent these stories defined the limits of the possible by which the people at the turn of the 20th century lived. American universities showed an inclination toward supporting researchers who upheld the Judeo-Christian theology and the idea that the creation of the New Jerusalem was imminent.

"LIKE BIRD TRACKS ON WET SAND"

The spadework of these scholars revealed tens of thousands of *cuneiform* (from "cuneus", Latin for wedge) tablets, part of the libraries of ancient palaces. These documents supplied vital information about Assyrian history, religion and society, including many with myths and hymns about the gods and goddesses worshipped there.

Cuneiform is a triangular, pyramid-shaped language. "Like bird tracks on wet sand." This is how cuneiform script struck the first Europeans to lay eyes on it

The tablets remained undeciphered until the mid 1800's when Georg Grotefend, a German high school teacher, began the decipherment of cuneiform.[7] He studied the cuneiform inscription cut into the Rock of Behistun, a giant sculpture carved so that it projected a near 3-D image from a cliff face 300 feet above the ground. A tall figure raises his hand toward ten standing men, and two others behind him. A god in a flying disk hovers above them. No one has identified who they are (some said it was Jesus and the Apostles). Englishman Henry Rawlinson later solved the full text of this inscription.

Sanskrit, the ancient language of India (home of the Aryans), was also becoming popular among academics. This led to an enthusiasm for ancient India and the Vedas, the sacred books of knowledge of Hinduism.

Many scholars were interested in comparative philology or linguistics, which essentially tries to connect long-extinct languages. What are the connections between the world's oldest languages, they wondered? How had they evolved?

It was widely concluded that unknown or undiscovered texts, cultures, species and languages existed before the present civilization of humanity.

ENTER THE SUMERIANS

In the 1870's the story of an Assyrian Noah and the Babylonian *Epic of Gilgamesh* were discovered which pre-dated the Hebrew story by millennia. Scholars noted that both the Assyrians and the Babylonians had borrowed their stories and their language and scripts from an older source.

By 1880, archaeologists discovered this older source: the *Sumerians*, who lived in the Biblical *land of Shinar* or *Sumer*, which is also underneath present day Iraq. This discovery pushed the date of the first civilization back 2,000 years.

Another text contained an astonishing statement made by Ashurbanipal himself that said: "I can read the intricate tablets of Sumerian. I understand the enigmatic words in the stone carvings *from the days before the Flood*."

Which stone carvings were these?

The realization that Sumer was the origins of ancient languages and mythology suddenly opened the floodgates to ancient Mesopotamia. Obsessed with finding the origins of their ancestors, the Germans swarmed on this area. In Sumer, they found the oldest example of the use of the word "Nazi." Sumerian scholar Samuel Kramer reveals that in this paradise or creation myth the mother Goddess Ninharsag brings forth eight gods, including one who is named *Nazi*.8

The Sumerian Nazi was created to heal *Enki*, or literally Lord Earth, who was the leader of a group of space beings, called *An-nun-aki*. The Egyptians called Enki Osiris. Author and linguist Zecharia Sitchin upholds Enki/Osiris as an extraterrestrial bio-engineer who genetically altered the human race and taught humanity spiritual secrets.9 We shall have much to say about Enki/Osiris momentarily.

Sumer (specifically Eridu, or "home in far-away built," in present-day Kuwait) was Enki's original landing place and was the special domain of the An-nun-aki.

Sumer also had a special place in the heart of the academic mind of Americans and Germans. It soon became a battle ground for American and German scholars. Many of the American scholars who went to Sumer at the turn of the century did so with an attitude of imperialism. They believed the torch of civilization had been passed from:
- *Egypt*
- to *Greece*,
- to *Rome*,
- to *Britain*
- and now to *America*.

Further, they believed they were connected to these ancient cultures.

This progression or evolution stands in contrast to that of the Germans, who traced their lineage from:
- *Germany*,
- to *India*,
- to *Sumer*,
- to *Atlantis*.

Both sides sought trophies to prove their dominance.

High stakes were involved.

Philologists (those who connect ancient languages) who unearthed the "dead" language of Sanskrit, were not just looking for the ur-language -- the original language that human beings had spoken in the Garden of Eden -- they were also looking for the first group of people who spoke this language.

24

The Nazis, and more than a few German scholars, equated Eden with Atlantis. They also believed its inhabitants were extraterrestrial blond gods.

American scholars, on the other hand, believed in the reality of Eden, but not in the myth of Atlantis. To them, connecting these dots was absurd.

Little did they know that these two mythological threads would be connected in a tapestry of intrigue concerning the return of Jesus woven by the occult-minded Administration of F.D.R.

THE LANGUAGE OF THE BIRDS

The Ur-language -- also known as the Language of the Birds because the Latin *ave* is the root for *angel* and *bird* -- was known to King Solomon (who at one time was said to have possessed the mysterioius supernatural stone which was more recently in the possession of Roerich).

The Knights Templar (who claimed they guarded the secrets of Jesus) spent nine years excavating the site of Solomon's Temple, recovering its treasure. The Templars also claimed they knew this ancient occult language.

As we shall see, they may have transferred this secret to North America. According to the Koran, this language was the source of Solomon's immense wealth and wisdom. Solomon built his renowned temple of wisdom atop Mount Moriah in Jerusalem (c. 1000 B.C.), encoding the Language of the Birds within it.

For more than five thousand years, the bloodiest game of king-of-the-hill has been for the supremacy of the Temple Mount in Jerusalem, the site of Solomon's ancient Temple. Here resides one of the most sought after treasures of history. Yet no one seems to agree exactly what it is.

It is worth noting that the "tunnel flap" of 1996 was just the latest in a string of agitations to the Arab people who fear the recovery of whatever is stored underneath the Temple Mount. Students of Judeo-Christian prophecy claim that the secret within Solomon's Temple will be instrumental in the creation of the New Thousand Years of Peace.

What's the best guess for what this secret is?

A rock. Perhaps even a meteorite like that which Roerich claimed was once given to the King of Atlantis (whom we now know was Atlas) and then to King Solomon, or the Black Stone of the Kaaba in Mecca, which is the Holy of Holies of the Islamic religion.

In a moment we shall see why just a "rock" or "stones" can contain powerful secrets.

25

WHOSE HISTORY IS THIS ANYWAY?

With the recovery of ancient languages and the dramatic decipherment of Assyrian and Sumerian tablets, it became apparent that the Old Testament bore striking resemblance to older stories. Even mainstream scholars had begun to treat the Bible like it was any other book instead of as the Word written by the hand of God.

A major blow came in the 1880's when Americans were stunned by the work of German Julius Welhausen whose *Prolegomena to the History of Israel* boldly presented proof that Moses did not write the Pentateuch, the first five books of the Bible. He argued that these stories, including those of the Elohim, the Shining Ones, came from older sources -- many of which had not yet been found (but which were shortly identified as Sumerian).

Even the miracles and divinity of Jesus were beginning to be called into question, threatening the Judeo-Christian world order.10

Another popular work, James Frazier's *The Golden Bough*, published in 1890, presented an accumulation of primitive myths of magic and the ancient gods. It became an instant classic, hinting that, like the stories in Ezekiel, the god beings of the ancients were real.

At the same time Charles Darwin's *The Origin of Species* -- while widely hailed in Germany -- was negatively affecting the American brand of Judeo-Christian theology and its literal interpretation of the book of Genesis' tale of creation and the origins of humanity.

Notes:

1. Ignatius Donnelly, *Atlantis: The Antediluvian World*
2. Bruce Kuklick, *Puritans in Babylon*. (Princeton, NJ, Princeton University Press, 1996).
3. H.P. Blavatsky, *The Secret Doctrine*
4. Andrew Robinson, *The Story of Writing* (London, Thames & Hudson, 1995) p. 76-77
5. Samuel Noah Kramer, *History Begins at Sumer* (London, Thames & Hudson).
6. Zecharia Sitchin, *The Twelfth Planet* (New York, Avon Books, 1976).

CHAPTER THREE

ROAD WARRIORS

Each of us is a spiritual warrior on the road of life. Our awareness of our cosmic predicament is what separates us from the beasts. We are the only species on earth that is aware of its mortality. The realization that we will die is what propels some of us on the search for ancient languages and advanced spiritual knowledge. For others, our mortality causes us to seek beings who can assist us in achieving our maximum spiritual potential to become angels or gods. For it is gods and angels, we all know, who live in heaven.

Seeking the Ancient Wisdom of the gods, soon after the publication of *Isis Unveiled*, HPB and Olcott traveled to India. She was in search of the sanctuaries of the gods and their immense libraries of wisdom beneath the sands of the Gobi desert. These sanctuaries, she wrote, were connected with similar outposts in South America.1 They were joined by tunnel systems constructed by Atlantean magicians. When he came to power, Hitler ordered the recovery of every German folk tale and myth that spoke of these cave systems. *The Pied Piper of Hammelin* was particularly instructive.2

THE SECRET DOCTRINE

In 1888, while Moses was undergoing a debunking by German scholars, HPB published her master work, *The Secret Doctrine*, which she described as an outline of the True History of the cosmos. This history, she said, had been revealed to her not in Moses' book of Genesis, but in the *Stanzas of Dyzan*, one of the world's oldest and rarest books, written in a pre-flood symbolic language.

HPB claimed the *Stanzas* came from a secret and precious subterranean library far beneath the sands of a subcontinent far from Western capitals and even farther from Western

27

understanding. This Indian library was bigger than the British Museum (a real slap in the face to British Imperialism) and belonged to the Masters of the Aryan race. Its secret contents represented the essence of the ancient wisdom religions of all traditions which, said HPB, belong to everyone, but had been lifted from the earth so as to be concealed from the profane.

In fact, HPB said, the *Stanzas* are the secret metaphysics of Buddha. This one small, powerful work was but a droplet in the ocean of esoteric Buddhism HPB was blessed to possess.

THE CHILDREN OF AN

In *The Secret Doctrine*, HPB provided a gleaming insight into the origins of the *Stanzas of Dyzan*, which illuminates the linguistic path on our odyssey.

"*Dyzan*," said HPB, is phonetically "*Dan*" or "*Janna.*" *Dan*, in modern Chinese and Tibetan phonetics, is *ch'an*, the Chinese term for esoteric schools. *Janna* is defined as "to reform oneself by meditation and knowledge."

Each of these traditions tells of an esoteric school or group of beings, road warriors, whose name features "an" or "ann." This is noteworthy, for, as we have seen:

• *Ana* was the name of the fictional master race in *The Coming Race.*

•*Tuatha de' Danann*, is the name of the original Celts, the former Atlanteans who were forced to live in the inner earth (*Tuat* is the Egyptian name for the inner earth).

• *An-nun-aki* is the Sumerian name for the Elohim.

• *The Children of D'an* guarded the treasures of the Temple of Solomon.

Will following the legends of the Children of An in their various forms, put us on the way to finding their home? Our predecessors certainly believed so.

THE FOUR TREASURES OF THE AN

Legends claim the Children of An, or Shining Ones of An, possessed advanced spiritual knowledge which they shared with humanity.3 For example, according to Celtic tradition the Tuatha de' Danann brought with them four treasures:4

• A magic cauldron (which may be the Holy Grail) called the Cup of Destiny;

• A magic sword called the Sword of Destiny;

• A magic spear or staff (which Hitler later claimed to have acquired) called the Spear of Destiny;

• A magic rock called the Stone of Destiny. (This Stone was believed to be the same stone that the Biblical patriarch Jacob, the father of Dan, had used as a pillow when he had his vision of "Jacob's Ladder" which transported angels from heaven to earth.)

"It was the special duty of the Druids," writes W.Y. Evans-Wentz in *The Fairy Faith in Celtic Countries*, "to act as intermediaries between the world of men and the invisible or underground world of the Tuatha de' Danann." In the Old Testament this role is assigned to the *D'an* or *Dani-el* the Hebrew tribe which preserved and transmitted the secrets of the Ark of the Covenant and the other holy relics which were stored in Solomon's Temple in Jerusalem.

Because of their obvious and striking phonetic and mythological correspondences, it is tempting to link the biblical children of Dan or Daniel and the Tuatha de' Danann with the fictitious Ana and the alleged survivors of the cataclysm of Atlantis (which phonetically is *At-El-An-Ti*). However, we must be careful with these language connections, warn mainstream scholars.

Likewise, warn scholars, even though the mother of both Thoth and Buddha was *Maya* ("illusion") and the mother of Jesus was Mary (from *Mare*, the Sea, and symbolically illusion), and, Jesus' grandmother's name was *Ann*, this too is simple coincidence.

Or is it? Could it point to a continuous thread of tradition beginning in Egypt and winding through Asia to Palestine? (A thread which we are all seeking to understand.)

The Maya of Mexico, who claimed they were the survivors of a cataclysm which sank their homeland called *Atlan*, aligned their temples with the Pleiades, a cluster of seven stars in the constellation Taurus the Bull. This cluster features a star called Maya. Is there a connection? Or, is this too merely coincidence?

Further, what are we to make of the fact that the Greeks called the Pleiades the *Atlantides*, naming them after the daughters of Atlas, the priest-king of Atlantis (who is believed to be one and the same as Thoth)?

It's all just linguistic coincidence and circumstantial evidence, say scholars. Agreed. Still, are these not interesting connections and hints of possible linkages between Egypt, the early Christian community, the Maya and the myths of Atlantis?

THE OCCULT, THE FOURTH DIMENSION AND THE AWAKENING OF THE COLLECTIVE UNCONSCIOUSNESS

From the *Stanzas* and other Tibetan temple-literature, HPB learned that the creation of the material world and the evolutionary master plan for humanity were linked in an unimaginably long series of advancements. Further, all life pulses out of the hidden astral level, into the material, and back into the astral again. The universe, or God, appears to have a strange mentality: "Create it, to destroy it, to create it again."

The word *occult* comes from the Latin for *hidden*. In the 1890's the alluring bells of this hidden, astral realm were ringing in millions of ears, almost as if the universe was on the verge of recreating, or at least, revealing itself.5 All of intellectual and spiritual Europe was involved in an immense, public debate about something that had till then been concealed: the fourth-dimension, the astral realm of creation according to HPB.

The fourth dimension locked onto the imagination of Europe in 1877, when a scandalous trial ignited in London. The events centered on American psychic Henry Slade who visited London and held seances for high society Londoners. He found himself arrested for fraud and charged with using "subtle crafts and magic" to deceive his clients. Slade claimed he could summon spirits living in the fourth dimension. Sparks began to fly when Slade was defended at his trial by several of Britain's greatest scientists, including several future Nobel Prize winners.

In 1896, the French scientist Henri Becquerel discovered radioactivity. That same year Madame Curie discovered radium. French and German literary circles found themselves embroiled in a ferocious philosophical debate. Matter, they discovered, could disintegrate in one form and appear in another as radiation. How could this be? After all, they were living in the Greek model that considered everything was eternal. But now, matter was disintegrating and reappearing right before their eyes!

For some, including famed physicist Frederick Soddy, mankind was simply rediscovering what the ancients knew long ago. In his *Interpretation of Radium*,6 which hit the bookstores in 1909, he commented on the ancient accounts he found in the Hindu (Aryan) literary work the *Mahabharata* (which was written in Sanskrit in 500 B.C. that describes events that occurred thousands of years earlier). This epic poem describes god-beings travelling in flying aircraft and engaging in atomic warfare.

Soddy asked:

"Can we not read in them some justification for the belief that some former forgotten race of men attained not only to the knowledge we have so recently won, but also to the power that is not yet ours? ...I believe that there have been civilizations in the past that were familiar with atomic energy, and that by misusing it they were totally destroyed."

J. Robert Oppenheimer, the "father of the atom bomb," also caught the Sanskrit bug and was an avid reader of the *Mahabarata*. Is it possible, as Oppenheimer claimed, that we didn't invent the bomb either, we reinvented it?

WHERE HAVE ALL THE COWBOYS GONE?

Astrologically, the focal theme of the New Age of Aquarius is communication (especially communication with the "gods"). The souls who dwelled in America during the period from 1890 to 1935 began to express this theme in a remarkable way. The wild, wild west world of cowboys and western expansion (and Indian genocide) gave way to the eastern world of art, literature, and philosophy, whose denizens were all deeply probing the world of the fourth dimension (which ironically the American Indians were expert on).

The *real* Aquarian fun began with the laying of miles and miles of telegraphs and telephone wires, transatlantic cables, interstate highways and transcontinental railroads. Cowboys and cowgirls were coming closer together, uniting themselves with a spider's web of copper, steel and concrete. The earth was becoming smaller by the day. The pace of life was speeding up.

As if some cosmic light switch had suddenly been flipped, human consciousness was rapidly switching from the pastoral and agricultural world known since the stone age to the material world of the city and its new, unlimited possibilities and comforts. Wizards were appearing left and right bringing technological wonders forth.

• The use of electricity was becoming widespread.

• The tape recorder was unveiled in 1900 at the Paris Exposition.

• The Wright Brothers journeyed to Kitty Hawk with their fragile gliders.

• Nikola Tesla was attempting to build a stargate.

• Thomas Edison was trying to construct a machine for communicating with the dead.

• Tesla's former assistant Marconi thought he had intercepted messages from Mars.

With the global mind awakening and all the technological hoopla going on it could only be a matter of time before God appeared. The fact is; for many, God did appear.

In 1898, Secondo Pia, an amateur Italian photographer was appointed to take the first-ever official photograph of the Shroud of Turin. When he developed the photographs he found, to his amazement, that there appeared a photographic likeness of Jesus. The Shroud, it appears, was a photographic negative that had been waiting, like an explosive time capsule,

31

for the right moment, the invention of photography at the beginning of the Age of Aquarius to unmask its hidden true "positive".
One of the first to recognize the significance of this was HPB. Another was Russian mystic Gurdjieff, an alleged former Russian spy, friend of Joseph Stalin, tutor of the Dahli Lama, and founder of a group devoted to uncovering the original earthly religion. Another was Rudolph Steiner, who was Hitler's most feared occult opponent.

Notes:

1. Alec Maclellan *The Lost World of Agharti* (London, Souvenier Press, 1982) p. 112
2. Sylvia Cranston, *H.P.B. The Extraordinary Life and Influence of Helena Blavatsky* (New York, Jeremy P. Tarcher, 1993)
3. Walter Kafton-Minkel *Subterranean Worlds* (Port Townsend, WA., Loompanics, 1989)
4. John Matthews *The Grail Tradition* (London, Element, 1990) p.5
5. Michio Kaku, *Hyperspace* (New York, Oxford University Press, 1994) p. 49
6. Frederick Soddy, *Interpretation of Radium*

CHAPTER FOUR

DR. JUNG

While the rapidly changing world clamored around the alleged photographic image of the son of God, the one who believed he was perhaps closest to actually talking with God was Dr. Carl Jung, the famed Swiss psychologist. Jung is best known as the archrival of Sigmund Freud, whose plumbing-based, libido-centered psychological theories left millions wondering what to do with their sexual hang-ups (and who wrote an explosive book claiming Moses was indeed the Egyptian king Akhenaten).[1]

No matter what he called himself, Dr. Jung was an avid occultist whose works explored the mystic gamut from UFO's and psychic phenomenon to sex magic. According to Jung biographer Richard Noll, Jung believed he was a prophet, if not *the* prophet of the Age of Aquarius.[2]

As a young man, Jung had a recurring dream in which he was the overlord of a town and lived in a medieval castle with a tower.

Hidden in this tower was the source of his power, *a thick copper column* whose top, branching into a network of tiny capillaries, *drew from the air an ineffable spiritual substance*.[3]

Now, we have seen this substance described as *vril*. From his testimony it appears Jung had either read *The Coming Race* or had tapped into the same source of inspiration as the other prophets of the New Age. (As we shall see, Moses also had an encounter with an identical copper column that spewed magic energy).

As the patron saint of the unconscious mind (his disciples exist today and form the basis of the powerful global Jungian psychotherapy school), Jung was a consciousness cowboy. His theories provided a big chunk of pages in the psychological "how to" instruction manual for the occult world of HPB, and important food for thought for the Nazis in their quest to connect with the ancient Atlanteans. Jung's top three occult ideas, as far as the Nazis were concerned, were his groundbreaking theories of ancestor possession, the collective unconscious and archetypes.

ANCESTOR POSSESSION

Jung believed it was possible to summon the spirits of the ancients. In 1925 he laid out his own ideas and beliefs concerning the idea of "ancestor possession." We each have a cluster of parts of our ancestors within us, Jung speculated. At certain times we could enable these parts to command the ship for a while, so to speak.

Hitler and certain Nazis believed they were in contact with the survivors of Atlantis and other god-beings who were the ancestors of the Nazis. And why not? Jung believed his primary personality was an avatar, a spiritual prophet, perhaps even *the* Aryan Christ.4 This personality was wiser and older than Jung. Further, it was directly connected with the ancient ancestors, with the dead, and with spiritual Mysteries. All Jung had to do was learn to make the cosmic connection with this being and, faster than you can say lightning rod, the wisdom of the ancients would be his.

In his *Memories, Dreams and Reflections*, Jung stated that by the age of nineteen he had become aware of additional personalities surrounding him. One of the secondary parts Jung claimed he could draw from was the German mystic poet Johann Wofgang von Goethe. It was Goethe who, in his *Faust*, anchored the idea of the reality of true evil. Jung called Goethe a prophet who explained "the mysterious role it (evil) played in delivering man from darkness and suffering."

THE COLLECTIVE UNCONSCIOUS

Jung was obsessed by a search for a language or vocabulary that would reveal "that deeper layer common to all men,"5 and deliver humanity from suffering. When books failed to adequately reveal this deeper layer, Jung began conducting seances, galloping headlong into the wild, wild west of the consciousness frontier where physicists Einstein and Heisenberg only dreamed of going.

Jung soon emerged with the concept of the "collective unconscious." He theorized that this was a universal "force" which "not only binds individuals together into a nation or race, but unites them with the men of the past and with their psychology." In 1917 he defined this as "the deposit of all the world's experience in all times, and hence an image of the world which has been built up through the aeons."6

Jung viewed the collective unconscious as having its own independent existence, which was not even limited to the human species in its expression. Jung claimed it went as far back as the era of the dinosaurs.

This is important. As in HPB's model, it suggests the collective unconscious existed in a hidden realm before it appeared, or "pulsed," in the blood of the dinosaurs. With the extinction of the dinosaurs the collective unconscious (or is it a collective *soul*?) possibly went into dormancy and then reappeared with man.

"We carry within us in the *structure* of our bodies and of our nervous system all our genealogical history," wrote Jung. "The same is true of our souls which likewise reveals the traces of its ancestral past and of its future . . . all that which once existed is still present and operative within us."

ARCHETYPES

This idea propelled Jung on to his theory of *archetypes*, or constantly repeating figures that appear in the myths of all cultures and are communicated through genes. Examples of archetypes are the savior (Jesus), magician (Merlin), the wise old man (Einstein), the princess (Diana), the king (Arthur), the goddess (Madonna), the warrior (Lt. Warf), and the destroyer (Hitler).

Jung was particularly interested in the occult archetype of the dragon, (which was the focal occult image of the Japanese nation and also the primary end times antagonist in the Christian book of Revelation).

The "dragon" is a universal symbol found in the myths of virtually every culture. Whether cast as a cuddly, purple good-guy bringing wisdom to children (*Barney*), as the guardian of occult gold (*Puff the Magic Dragon*), or as the havoc-wreaking monster (*Godzilla*) with a fetish for kidnapping virgins (as in *King Kong*, which happened to be Hitler's favorite movie), the dragon archetype is ubiquitous in the mythology and collective brain of the past and present.

This archetype, Jung speculated, was due to "nature having passed through two great experiences," through the successive creation of invertebrates and vertebrates.

For this reason, said Jung, "we are both crustacean (through the sympathetic nervous system) and sauri (through the spinal cord)...."7

ONTOGENY RECAPITULATES PHYLOGENY

Jung's work also proposed that this unconscious mind was the product of an ancient, phylogenetic, evolutionary process. Further, Jung speculated there was a Jewish unconscious and a separate Aryan unconscious.8

Jung's teacher was Ernst Haeckel, a German zoologist who is given credit for introducing Darwinism to Germany. Like HPB, Haeckel was convinced that evolution was based on a Master Plan. While HPB and Jung based their ideas on contact with ancient god-beings, Haeckel derived his ideas from the historical study of biology. He formulated a biogenetic law – "ontongeny recapitulates phylogeny" -- which states that the evolutionary stages of human growth and development (ontogeny) replicate, in order, the stages of the development of the human race from lower forms of life (phylogeny).

Haeckel observed that in its embryological unfoldment, an animal tends to repeat or recapitulate the sequence that its ancestors followed during their evolution and integrate them into its own higher form.

This is most dramatically apparent in human intrauterine development. In our own unfoldment each of our bodies went through stages very much like fish, reptiles and nonprimate mammals before we morphed into human form.

THE ATLANTEAN MOMENT

If indeed there is a collective unconscious (or even a collective soul), isn't it also a living entity on its own spiral of ascension? If so, it can be expected to follow this evolutionary model.

The laws of evolution state that all life, be it the dinosaurs or a group soul, had to diversify along the successive stages of development. Man happened to be the most recent stage.

As Plotinus once stated, "Mankind is poised midway between the gods and the beasts." Put another way, we are midway between earth and heaven. Or, as the book of Job (30:29) says: "I am a brother to dragons, and a companion to owls." (Interesting, isn't it, that birds evolved from the dinosaurs?)

Let us suppose Atlantis was the last great civilization in which this group soul or consciousness mutated or incarnated. Were it to reincarnate in modern times, in Nazi Germany for instance (or in America), then as it seeks to re-create itself, evolutionary law requires that it must re-experience Atlantis. It must re-experience what I'll refer to as the Altantean moment. Only then can it transcend it. (Which is apparently easier said than done.)

By this conjecture, suppose when *homo erectus* turned into *homo sapien* it created a mutation, *homo Atlantean*, which because of a thinking problem destroyed itself. Now, it reappears. According to evolutionary law, this collective soul must pass through another Atlantean moment.

What's next? For some occultists the next evolutionary step for *homo Atlantean* is *homo christos* or *homo angelis*, a race which harnesses the power of spirituality and moves into the stars.

For a small group of fanatics living in Germany in the 1930's the next level above human was clearly *homo Nazi*.

As we all know, *homo Nazi* was a miserable failure, a grotesque mutation. While the Nazis believed they inherited all that is great about their ancestors, their failure possibly left succeeding generations of Germans holding the bag for their horror. It is unfair to hold innocent people accountable in this way. It is hoped this book will assist in releasing the German people from any residual shame or responsibility.

Notes:

1. Sigmund Freud, *Moses and Monotheism*, London, 1951
2. Richard Noll, *The Ayran Christ: The Secret Life of Carl Jung*, (Random House, New York, 1997).
3. Carl Jung, *Memories, Dreams, Reflections* (New York, Pantheon, 1962).
4. ibid. p. 134
5. ibid. p. 288
6. ibid. p. 87
7. ibid. p. 288
8. ibid. p. 105.

CHAPTER FIVE

THE ORIGIN OF SPECIES AND THE BIRTH OF A GENOCIDAL PHILOSOPHY

Jung's collection of ideas could not survive as some New Age occult theory. In order to achieve his goal of raising humanity's standard of living, Jung's ideas had to gain mass acceptance. This meant they had to be molded to conform to the intellectual standard of the turn of the twentieth century.

That standard was not the occult ideas of HPB, Haeckel or Jung. The standard was the laws of evolution expressed in *The Origin of Species* by Charles Darwin (1809-1882), which was probably the most influential book of the nineteenth century.

In *The Origin of Species* Darwin posited the two famous principles of the *survival of the fittest* and the *struggle for existence*. These principles were integrated into the idea of an ascending line of all living beings from lowest to highest that were on an ascending spiral of unlimited turns upon which only the strongest survive.

Originally, Darwin limited his conjectures to the animal kingdom. If he had kept his mouth shut and limited his flawed theories to the animal kingdom he would have been relegated to the back pages of history. Instead, this was one of those historical incidents where one man with one idea altered the collective unconscious of millions and completely altered history.

Darwin extended his animal theories to humankind by combining his ideas with the antisocial population theories of Thomas Malthus (1766-1834), a renowned British big brain economist and demographer. Malthus proposed that human population grows exponentially, while food supply increases arithmetically. As food quantity becomes insufficient, this

38

creates a gulf between the haves (the aristocracy) and the have nots (the lower classes). Therefore, Malthus coldly proposed, wars, conflicts, epidemics and famines could serve as a productive herd thinning mechanism.1

Translation: organized killing is good. Discouraging the poor from procreating and encouraging them to control their "sexual mania,"was another positive step, said Malthus.

When Darwin enthusiastically latched on to Malthus' ideas (which proposed that certain humans were expendable) and combined them with his own Social Darwinism, a disastrous, genocidal philosophy which proposed the lower races would be eliminated by the higher races, was born.

While Darwin got the credit, the leading proponent of this chilling, racial evolutionary theory was not Darwin but Herbert Spencer, whose ideas were based on race. Spencer was more explicit than Darwin in his conclusion. Only one race was capable of ascending to the highest levels of the evolutionary spiral. The others would be left behind.

EUGENICS

The resonant tones of this disgraceful master race theory reverberated through the works of Darwin and his big-brained, little-moraled cousin Francis Galton (1822-1911), the founder of the science of *eugenics* (from the Greek words "eu" -- meaning "well" or "good," and "gennan," or "to reproduce").2

The theory of eugenics states that certain genetic traits are favorable, others not so good. In his book *Hereditary Genius*, Galton proposed that intelligence, like physical characteristics, was hereditary with certain races (read "Aryans") being favored over others.

Galton had some advanced ideas about the brain for his time; he anticipated right brain-left brain research by a hundred years. Also he laid down the ground work for the behavioral theories of Pavlov and Watson (whose behavioral theories formed the basis for the school of American psychology until the 1960's), and was among the vanguard in the understanding how the brain forms images.

Galton was also a devout conspiracy theorist. He blamed the Catholic Church for the degradation of humanity. The enforced celibacy of its priesthood and the extermination of the gnostic Cathars (the "pure ones") and other spiritual superheroes-in-training during the Inquisition, were two examples of the Church's plan to keep humanity perpetually enslaved. If the Church exterminated the most enlightened spiritual groups or prevented them from leaving progeny, there would be no one to carry on their spiritual work, according to Galton.

THE CATHARS

It is notable that Galton would focus on the Cathars. These religious mavericks of 13th century France believed they were a collective or group soul3 which reincarnates throughout history and were sent to earth to show others the way out of earth life.

The Cathars called themselves the Good Christians4 and claimed to have possessed something close to 100% of the world's hidden stock of Jesus' occult teachings.

Included were said to be the secrets for transforming homo sapien into *homo angelis* or even *homo christos*.

The Cathars claimed these works were written in an ancient esoteric language (the Language of the Birds) which they understood.5

For this and other religious reasons, Pope Innocent III exterminated as many as one million Cathar men women and children during the first European holocaust, that began in 1209 and ended in 1240.

In 1934, Hitler sent author and mythologist Otto Rahn into Cathar country in Southern France to recover the Ark of the Covenant and other Cathar secrets. After learning their legends, Rahn converted to Catharism. He proposed the Cathars should be the true role models for the German people and that war was not a good thing. Rahn disappeared under mysterious circumstances soon after voicing his heretical opinions.6

AMOR:ROMA

The other reason the Cathars were exterminated may have to do with their peculiar beliefs concerning Satan which were later adopted and distorted by the Nazis. According to the Cathars, there exist two realms: spiritual and material. God's realm, AMOR, was the spiritual realm of love. The mirror image of AMOR was ROMA, Rome.7

The Cathars believed Roma's material realm was evil, the creation of the devil. As a material object the human body belonged to Satan. The human soul needed to be saved not from sin, but from matter.

To escape imprisonment in matter the soul needed to learn esoteric secrets to enable the return to the astral world. Further, as the prophet of Amor, Jesus could not have been the son of God because God could not enter evil matter.

In accordance with Cathar thinking, modern German Gnostics came to believe the Jewish God, Jehovah or Yahweh, is really the Devil. Further, it was German karma to destroy the Devil.8

HOLY WAR
Long before Hitler, Galton envisioned a time when mankind would master the laws of heredity. Once this occurred, it would be a "fit moment to proclaim a 'Jihad" or Holy War, against customs and prejudices that impair the physical and moral faculties of our race."9

Implicit in this vision is the idea of setting up genetics lab to create an army that could carry out this Holy War. The Nazis carried out this plan with the formation of the SS, Hitler's Order of Knights. Membership in this elite corp required proof of German ancestry going back 200 years.

Similarly, in the book of Revelation, Jesus envisioned a time when he and his "army from heaven" would conquer the dragon ("that old serpent," Satan) and place it under lock and key for a thousand years. When this happened, the Kingdom of Heaven, "the holy city, the New Jerusalem," would come down out of the heavens and humanity would begin a Thousand Years of Peace.

At that time there would appear "a new heaven and a new earth; for the first heaven and the first earth were passed away; and *there was no more sea*" (Revelation 21:1). In occult symbolism "the sea" is a mystical reference to the veil of illusion. Occultists believe during the so-called "end times" humanity will awaken from its sleep, recognize its cosmic predicament (and latent powers) and live perpetually in an altered state of godliness.

The ideas of Jesus, Jung, Galton, Darwin and Spencer were all enthusiastically adopted, and twisted, by the Nazis who incorporated them in their racial theory of history and their plan to create the Third Reich, an altered state if there ever was one.

THE THIRD REICH: THE ALTERED STATE
At the apex of this racial theory is the coming of a new (German) Messiah (Hitler), a descendent of a race of the ancient blond gods. He would pop out of the collective Aryan unconscious and not just save and lead Germany, but the entire human race and create a "Thousand Year Reich" (which lasted a pathetic twelve years).

Within a generation, Hitler would launch the Holy War envisioned by Galton, building death camps in which to imprison the serpent -- which the Nazis believed were the inferior races and all non-Germans.

In planning the Aryan golden age, which as we shall see was envisioned as the New Atlantis, the Nazis realized they needed a lot of room. So, they concocted and implemented:

• A eugenics program aimed at tightly focusing the Reich's gene pool:

• A euthanasia program -- a horrifying program of machine-like mass murder -- aimed at disposing of prisoners; those incapable of working (especially the crippled); and political and racial undesirables including homosexuals, alcoholics, communists, democrats and pacifists;10
• And a global war with control of the entire planet as the goal.

By 1939, Hitler was publicly proclaiming his ghoulish plan to exterminate the Jewish race in Europe (which F.D.R. and other political bosses of the time did nothing about). The Nazis would stop at nothing: arrest, incarceration, torture, murder, extermination by gas chamber to achieve their plan. The Nuremburg Tribunal estimated that 5,721,800 Jews died during this time.11

IN AMERICA

It is important to note that the Atlantis myth was surfacing in America, also. In addition, the gnostic tradition, which represented a threat to orthodox Christianity, was attractive to some of the greatest minds in history including the Founding Fathers of America. Washington, Jefferson, and Franklin all mystically identified themselves with the ancient people and occult traditions -- including the gnostic traditions -- and others dating back to Egypt.12

It is widely known that the Founding Fathers were Freemasons. Less widely known is the occult beliefs which guided them. We will explore those beliefs in detail later. For the moment, it is important to note that the Freemasons are connected with the Knights Templar, a rogue group of warrior monks who claimed to guard the secret teachings of Jesus.

The Templars are connected with ancient holy orders including the Essenes, who called themselves the Sons of Light, and the Cathars. The Essenes and later the Cathars are regarded by many as maintainers and preservers of the original religion of spiritual Israel -- the ur-religion -- (which was not the religion of the Jews), and the Messianic Plan for the salvation of humanity.

The Founding Fathers believed that the founding of America is God's undertaking. It is the continuation of His covenant with Abraham, Isaac, and Jacob ("Israel") and the fulfillment of His promise to "assemble (rather than exterminate) the outcasts of Israel, and gather together the dispersed of Judah from the four corners of the earth" in the process of creating the new heaven on earth. They even baptized their children with Hebrew names: Benjamin, Sarah, and Abraham.13

The United States of America was to be a melting pot society. Its genetic imperative: diversity. "Give us your tired, your poor and your hungry," reads the inscription on the Statue of Liberty. They will be transformed. The model for this civilization; Egypt, a nation founded by a Peacemaker and centered upon the construction of the Great Pyramid.14

MIGHT VS. RIGHT

By the early 1900's, the difference between the two mind-sets of Germany and America was stark. Not only were there competing versions of the New Atlantis: one a pure race, the other a melting pot, but each also had its own messiah and its unique image of God. In America, scholars sought to defend Jehovah or Yahweh and his Jewish son Jesus, who would soon introduce a Thousand Years of Peace. In Germany, Jehovah and his people, the Jews, were standing in the way of the creation of Thousand Year Reich introduced by Hitler.

Only a Holy War would decide who was right. As military strategists have known since the beginning of time, and Darwin's theories gave scientific language to, "might is right."

The two sides were lining up.

Notes:

1. Dr. Thomas Roder, Volker Kubillus & Anthony Burwell, *Psychiatrists - the Men Behind Hitler* (Los Angeles, Freedom Publishing, 1994) p. 11.
2. ibid
3. Arthur Guirdham, *The Cathars and Reincarnation*
4. Clive Prince and Lynn Picknett, *The Templar Revelation* (London, Element, 1998) p. 87
5. Margaret Starbird *The Woman With the Alabaster Jar* (Santa Fe, Bear & Co., 1993).
6. Col. Howard Beuchner *Emerald Cup: Ark of Gold* (Metarie, LA, Thunderbird Press, 1991).
7. Michael Baigent, Richard Leigh and Henry Lincoln *Holy Blood, Holy Grail* (London, Crowns, 1982) p. 25.
8. Dusty Sklar *The Nazis and the Occult* (New York, Dorset Press, 1977) p. 140.
9. ibid.
10. ibid. p. 50
11. ibid. p. 12
12. Michael Howard *The Occult Conspiracy* (Rochester, VT, Destiny Books, 1989).
13. ibid.

CHAPTER SIX

IN GERMANY: THE REDISCOVERY OF RUNES, SWASTIKAS AND NUDE SUNBATHING

Jung could not have picked a better (or worse) time to promote the idea of connecting with the ancient ancestors of Germany. The restless German group soul was preparing to come alive. A revival of the Nordic past was underway.

Feeding this revival was the German reaction to the industrialization of the planet and a sense that the German people had severed their connection with nature. There was a movement to recover the German *Volk* -- the mystical union of the German blood and its sacred soil -- from the steel claws of industrialism and Judeo-Christianity, which was blamed as the source of Germany's industrial disease. (After all, it was Jehovah who inspired man to conquer and subdue nature).1

What was needed was a German messiah to lead Germans back to Eden, the Promised Land. German astrologers claimed to have proof of his coming. This is ironic, given that it was the Jewish prophets who introduced the revolutionary idea of the Golden Age as a *future* event introduced by a Messiah. As this movement progressed, it would be *the* contributing factor leading to the Nazi leadership's trip to the "wild side" of nationalism and a leading factor in the occult roots of WW II.

THE SONS OF THE SUN

Like other prophets of the New Atlantis, Jung rejected the Judeo-Christian idea of a distant, judgmental God. Instead, he sought a God that lived within. Jung was highly influenced by the famous German scholar Ernest Renan, who promoted the idea of sun worship. In *Psychology of the Unconscious*, Jung wrote:

44

"The sun is, as Renan remarked, really the only rational representation of the God.... The sun is adapted as is nothing else to represent the visible God of this world."

In Germany, many gnostics began to believe the only way to conquer the Christian god and escape from the prison-like world of Christianity was to return to the Aryan roots and reclaim the Nordic past. This powerful movement began innocently and simply enough: vegetarianism, abstinence from alcohol, nude sunbathing, and hiking, were popular back-to-nature, self-discovery activities.

As they paraded through the lush Bavarian forests, many of these bohemians did so with copies of the works of Goethe, Haeckel, Hesse and HPB in tow, sporting swastikas and wearing runic jewelry.2

Many gathered in clubs, societies and lodges devoted to the study of the ancient Aryan gods. These associations ran the gamut from the innocuous -- reconnecting with Odin, Thor, and Baldur, or imagining themselves as modern Grail knights charged with protecting the Holy Grail -- to the goofy -- dressing in bear skins and antlers and dancing around campfires -- to the sick -- as in the Society for Racial Hygiene, a driving force behind the Nazi racial hygiene and eugenics program.

The unfortunate truth is that as a result of this movement innocent Germans were on the verge of getting in touch with their inner Nazi, and releasing the most appalling beast humanity has ever seen.

THE SECRET SCIENCE

Let's talk for a moment about the beef the German gnostics had with the Judeo-Christian world order. German occultists like Lanz von Liebenfels, Guido von List and Rudolf von Sebottendorff (founder of the powerful Thule Society, another occult club whose ideas we will explore momentarily) borrowed heavily from HPB. They sought to show that the ancient Germans had been keepers of a secret science (which originated in Eden/Atlantis). They claimed this science had been destroyed by the leaders of Judeo-Christianity (as in the burning of the Library of Alexandria and its 500,000 volumes of ancient, possibly pre-flood texts, for example.)3

The common desire shared by these Volkish groups was that all sought to erase what they considered "the plague of Christianity" from German society and replace it with "the pure Aryan religion" (which was later called Nazism). This required the rediscovery of the Aryan secret super science of Atlantis and its Pandora's Box full of magic, technology and unlimited vril power.

The question: how to do this? Echoing the evolutionary theories of Haeckel, Jung proposed that just as the human body contains a record of all that came before it, so too does the human mind. It is full of ancient ideas. The most powerful ideas are of the religious nature. Therefore, Jung proposed, our focus should be on discovering the primordial symbols of the ancients. Do you have god beings with high ideals floating around in your mind? Why not learn their language and communicate with them?

RUNES

Since at least the time of the rebellious Christian heretic Martin Luther, German scholars had been on a quest for the origins of the German race. Always, race and language were linked. This link was no more evident than in the Ur-Runes or *runes*, carved or engraved symbols. In both German and Celtic language and mythic tradition, runes represent " a Mystery," or a "holy secret" that is "whispered."[4] What message? What secret?

Runes were believed to be magical symbols that directly connected their user with the ancestral spirits of their origin. As they are meditated upon and uttered, the song-names of the runes became keys, which unlock the doors to the spirit world of the ancestors.

Heinrich Himmler, the former chicken farmer turned number two Nazi and head of the SS, believed that the runes of Nordic antiquity resembled Indian runes and Japanese ideograms.[5] This was evidence to Himmler that the Japanese, too, were Aryans or "Nordic Japanese." Himmler also noticed the glaring similarities between the German runes and the Indian runes.

It was likely no surprise to the German scholars how much their Nordic runes resembled the Indian runes. The runes, the Germans believed, concealed the secret revelation of the existence of god beings who lived in India, but who migrated to Europe, and became known as the Indo-Europeans.[6]

Evidence of the use of this ancient script by English, Swedish, Norwegian and German tribes has been found from as far back as the 2nd century AD.[7] These ancestors were not simply primitive, illiterate nature boys carving graffiti on spears, rocks and pieces of wood, as some historians like to think. Runic symbols were their alphabet before they were forced to become Christian and adopt the "barbaric" Roman alphabet.

It may be said that with the introduction of the Roman alphabet, "writing" became mundane. More importantly, Rome took control of the western mind (after all, language is power) by controlling the language system which formatted the brains of its citizens.

Until then, as exemplified by runes and other magical writing systems, "writing" was a means of recording esoteric or spiritual knowledge reserved for "magicians". These shamans, or intermediaries between man and god, had the power to project memories or knowledge into rocks or other objects. The runes were symbols of this knowledge, which was labeled secret, forbidden to the profane.

Of course, it takes a massive mental effort to be able to project sacred knowledge in this manner. Likewise, it takes a complimentary mental effort to be able to "download" this knowledge to one's brain. The Nordic people called the process of interpreting the runes *raeden*, "reading"; the result was *raedels* or "riddles."8

In inner Asia, the reputed home of the Aryan gods, we learn of the *terma* tradition.9 Terma are "concealed treasures," sacred texts that are "hidden" in rocks, and sometimes on hilltops or even in whole valleys. The locations of rocks inscribed with magic knowledge became sacred areas or terma themselves.

The idea that sacred rocks or hilltops may be repositories of immense amounts of advanced magical knowledge may go a long way toward explaining the secret allure of the Dome of the Rock in Jerusalem and other hotly contested or highly guarded areas marked by extraterrestrial stones. The sacred Black Stone of the Kaaba in Mecca, focal point of the Islamic religion of Allah, is another example of this concept.

Like the runes, magicians of ancient times are believed to have projected knowledge into the terma for safekeeping. The big Secret contained within the immense Asian terma library -- hidden in the rocks, rivers and trees of Tibet -- concerned the legends of Shambhala, the homeland of the Sons of the Sun or the Sons of Light (the German ancestors) and the way to enter their world.

THE DESCENT INTO HELL

Learning about the sacred Mysteries and Secrets of the ancient ancestors involved more than just getting back to nature. Although now that we know the wisdom of the ancients was believed to be literally stored in sacred rocks, rivers and trees we can appreciate why this is an obvious first step in the process. In actuality, attaining mastery of this knowledge requires a symbolic descent into the Underworld, or what the Christians called Hell.10

It should be made clear that the Underworld spoken of by the ancients and the Christian Hell are not the same place. The ancients did not hold the view that the underworld strictly was a place of punishment. This secret place was also a place of pleasure where enlightened beings were granted every wish (due to the fact that they wielded the life force energy). The Greeks called it *Tartarus*, from the "tortoise."11 The indiginous American Indians called it Turtle Island. We call it North America.

Why Turtle Island? The Flood which destroyed Atlantis is believed to have occurred circa 10,000 B.C., or during the transition from the Age of Leo the Lion (11,000 B.C. to 9,000 B.C.) into the Age of Cancer (originally the Turtle), an Age which lasted from 9,000 B.C. to about 6,800 B.C.

Most astrologers associated the Age of Cancer with the crab, a sea creature, which like the turtle, a land creature, goes into its shell, symbolizing the going into and coming out of the earth and sea of those who survived the destruction of Atlantis.

As the early American Indian creation legend states, it was "upon the back" of the turtle, the inhabitants of Turtle Island, that civilization began to rebuild and re-establish civilized life.

In Greek myth, Tartarus or Turtle Island is the place where souls live. They live a very different form of existence, one devoid of *blood*, *voices* and *vital energy* (vril). They await rebirth so that they might incarnate in human form to acquire these "tools of the soul." This provocative myth may state the soul's purpose on earth:

• to gain a particular blood;
• to acquire a voice to utter the word of power (the key to heaven)
• and to wield the life force energy (vril).

The ruler of this Underworld has many names -- in Egypt he was Hades, Lord of Death, or Amen (the source of the "amen" ending of Christian prayers). To the Chaldeans he was the Black Sun or Hidden Sun. He was known to deposit his semen in rocks, where it solidified into precious gems, and was credited with the ability to reveal buried treasure.

BAAL: THE LORD

When the sun arose on the dawn of its turn at the wheel of mothership earth, Judeo-Christian tradition sought to erase the old-time, nature-centered religions and populated Hell with the biblical *baalim*. *Baal* means "the Lord." Every ancient god from Aphrodite to Zeus was a baal, including Yahweh or Jehovah, the head of the Elohim himself!

Some of the other *baalim* revered by the Hebrews were:
• *Sin*, the moon god of Sinai;
• *Horus*, the Egyptian Golden Calf whose image was made by Moses' brother Aaron and later "smashed" by Moses;

• *Nehushtan*, the "fiery flying serpent" of lightning, made by Moses (2 Kings 18:4, Numbers 21:9), and

• *Melchizedek*, the ultra-mysterious priest-king of Salem who initiated Abraham into the ancient mysteries, is credited with forming the Order of Melchizedek, a priesthood of which Jesus was a member (Psalm 110), and may have been the true founder of the Essenes.

In Egypt, the headquarters for the Baal was just north of Cairo in a city called *Heliopolis* (City of the Sun), the biblical *On* or *An*.12 The priests of Heliopolis were responsible for the care of sacred texts. Their activities reached extensively throughout the earth.

Are the Biblical priests of Heliopolis the Shining Ones of An? This is a distinct possibility. The Celtics tell us the Baal or *Bel* were one and the same as the Tuatha de' Danann, the former Atlantean scientists and magicians who became the dwellers of the inner earth.

In Nordic tradition Baal reincarnated as the Aryan god Odin (or phonetically O-Dan), who is known as the poster boy for the journey to the Underworld and for downloading the esoteric knowledge of the runes.13

Odin, or *Wot-An*, hung, self-impaled, from a tree for nine days (in Hindu tradition Odin/Wot-An is known as *Godan*, or God-An.) This Nordic savior crucified himself not to liberate or save humanity, as did Jesus (who was called the Son of God and whose Grandmother's name was *Anne*).

Instead, his goal was to gain the secret knowledge of the runes, and the word of power which gives one the "wise blood" of the gods and the ability to wield the life force energy.

THE RETURN OF THE FIRST CHRISTI-AN

In his Second Coming, Jesus returns with this very word of power etched upon his thigh: "he has on his vesture and on his thigh a name written, KING OF KINGS, AND LORD OF LORDS" (Revelation 19:16).

After he slays a dragon, Jesus sets up a New Jerusalem (literally a "New City of Peace") and busts open the doors to heaven, perhaps using the word of power to do so.

It is interesting to note the evolutionary development of the New Jerusalem.

• Originally, it was *Salem* (Peace), its priest-king was the baal god Melchizedek, who initiated Abraham.

• Then it became *Ur-Salem* or *Jerusalem*, its priest-king was David, the grandson of Abraham.

• Next it is to be the *New Ur-Salem* or *New Jerusalem*, with David's descendent Jesus as its priest-king. (Does anyone else see USA in New Jerusalem?)

We'll talk more about the New Jerusalem concept and its role in the Holy War of WW II momentarily. For now, it is key to notice the competition between savior figures that is at the heart of the Holy War of WW II and New Age politics.

It is common practice for upstart religions and political groups to label the gods and saviors of their predecessors or enemies as demons or devils.

The early Christian politicos, most of whom were Roman (ironically the persecutors of Jesus), did this with gusto, performing wholesale re-writes of ancient history and demonizing the nature-centered pagan gods to fit the ideology and political agenda of the Roman new world order.

Depending upon one's perspective, this is either a triumph or a tragedy of incalculable proportions. In pre-Roman times the savior figures (including Jesus) sought and shared their esoteric knowledge. Often, after acquiring this knowledge they led revolts against the existing world order. As a wielder of powerful cosmic knowledge, perhaps even terma, Jesus was certainly a political enemy of Rome.

In a remarkable turn of events, beginning in the 4th century AD Rome began to wield Jesus as a political force, conquering, converting and integrating (to put it politely) in his name and centralizing his knowledge and power in one location: Rome.

The Church launched a ruthless campaign to destroy the temple literature containing the secret science of competing religions, and even, as in the case of the Cathars in 1,200 AD, of Jesus himself. In addition, they took control of ancient sacred religious sites, constructing Christian churches on the pads of former pagan and Egyptian temples.

As a provider of secret knowledge, and the teacher of the means to download the superknowledge of the ancients, Baal became a pet name for the Christian devil, the archenemy of Rome. Christian political censors assigned this name to any person or group whose competing knowledge the Church wished to demonize.

For example, as Bruce Rux points out in *Architects of the Underworld*,[14] after their banishment to the interior world, the Tuatha de' Danann were transformed into devils by the Catholic Church. Their stature was considerably shrunk in size, too. This is evidenced by the term henceforth applied to them, *fairy folk*. The Tuatha de' Danann were described as tall, blond and fair-skinned. By simply adding a "y" suffix to their name, a demonic or diminutive image was created. The Church is understandably reluctant to admit this (just as the Japanese are sheepish about discussing their ancestors the Ainus -- the Children of Diana -- who were fair, tall and blond and came from the sky, left for the skies, and said they will return from the skies.)15

Was this campaign geared toward erasing knowledge of the existence of the dwellers of the inner earth and therefore of the survivors of Atlantis?

If so, it was effective in most parts of the world, save for northern Europe where as Odin, Baal, Bel, or Balder and the former Atlanteans retained their popularity.

Like Jesus, Baal/Odin's disciples anticipated his Second Coming, which would take place at Ragnorok, or doomsday,

MICHAEL

The demonization of Baal or Odin is unfortunate. It is also a little bizarre given that in art Odin is frequently depicted not as an anti-Christ or a devil, but as slaying his enemies with a spear just as Jesus' partner, the archangel Michael, in Christian art "slays the dragon" with his favorite weapon, his "sword".

Michael's sword is linked mythologically to the Spear of Destiny, the spear used to pierce the side of Jesus by the Roman soldier Longinus. The Sword of Destiny and Spear of Destiny are traced to the original four treasures the Tuatha De'Danann gave to the Celtic people.

While living in Vienna as young man, Hitler, a drug addict and artist, was seized by the occult. He was especially attracted by the legend of the Spear of Longinus and the Holy Grail.16 In *Mein Kampf*, Hitler tells of standing before the spear at the Habsburg Treasure House in Vienna and going into a trance, whereupon a "Superman" hovered over and possessed him. Hitler believed he was to use this power to wipe out the dragon -- which he interpreted as the inferior races.

In Matthew (10:34) Jesus tells of his mission: "Think not that I am come to send peace on earth: I came not to send peace, but a sword."

In Revelation (19:15) the Second Coming of Jesus is described. Here we learn Jesus has turned the tables on his former persecutors and has reclaimed this sword: "And out of his mouth goeth a sharp sword, that with it he could smite the nations: and he shall rule them with a rod of iron."

Jesus' acquisition of this sword (the Sword of Destiny?) and the rod of power (the Spear or Staff of Destiny?) marks a turn in the long-standing battle of antagonisms between man and God, one battle of which we can now appreciate was WW II. Long ago, as the Hebrew storysmiths documented in the book of Genesis, a conflict arose with a jealous god whom they called Yahweh or Jehovah.

ONE FOOT IN ATLANTIS

Fearing the spiritual potential of Adam, and the early human race, Yahweh expelled Adam and Eve from the Garden of Eden (Atlantis). He placed "at the east of the garden of Eden Cherubims and *a revolving Flaming Sword*, which turned every way, to keep the way of the tree of life" (Genesis 3:24) -- the entranceway to this place, the land of immortality. He forbade anyone to tamper with this Sword, and he took away the teachings that enable us to re-enter the Garden.

How do we explain the psychotic behavior of Yahweh -- on the one hand a god of love, on the other a ruthless slave master who quickly dispenses with his prized creation? Is it possible that "Yahweh," described in book of Genesis in the plural form as Elohim, is more than one god?

Could "Yahweh," as some including the gnostics believe, be more than one being in competition with one another? In fact, is it possible Yahweh is not *the* God at all, but just another Baal?

Indeed, at the heart of the Nazi ideology and other occult theology is the idea that Yahweh, is, in fact, at least two extraterrestrial or Atlantean god-*men* in conflict over control of the destiny of the human race. One god seeks to uplift humanity to the level of the gods (or beyond). The other seeks to keep humanity perpetually enslaved as sex objects and spiritual pawns.

Ever since Eden, humanity has sought the compassionate Yahweh and the rest of the Elohim's place of eternity, the land of immortality. And, ever since, Christians have waited for the gate opener with the (s)word, the powerful Word of Power or "open sesame," to arrive. This is anticipated to happen at Armageddon, the time of the Second Coming.

From time to time, throughout history, spiritual super-heroes have challenged the dictatorial faction of the Elohim. They have sought and pulled this all-important sword from the stone of its keeping. The Archangel Michael, for example, shared this (s)word from Moses, the Hebrew lawgiver, who used its power to part the Red Sea and to perform other magical feats.

Moses, as we have seen, inherited it from a baal, whom Rome claimed was a devil, but who may in fact be a good guy. However, according to Celtic tradition, Moses' generous acquaintance, a baal priest named Nehushtan or Nahash, may have been a former Atlantean.

This makes sense. Nahash is the name of the trouble-making serpent of the book of Genesis who got man kicked out of Eden/Atlantis. His name means "he who knows copper," and "he who knows secrets." What copper? What secrets?

Interestingly, *Odin* is sometimes depicted Moses-like as a gray-bearded wise old man leaning on a copper staff or column with a serpent entwined around it.

This is precisely the image we find in the inspirational dream of Carl Jung, who saw "*a thick copper column* whose top, branching into a network of tiny capillaries, *drew from the air an ineffable spiritual substance.*" Are the stories of Odin and Jung describing the staff of Moses?

Does the synchronicity between Jung's description of the copper column emitting life force or vril energy and the ancient myth of the serpent seems to suggest that the Baal archetype had reappeared in the guise of a psychoanalyst to unlock the spiritual Mysteries of the ages?

With Odin the secret revealer possibly whispering in the ear of the world's most famous psychoanalyst, could it be the return to Eden/Atlantis was imminent?

Could it be the gates to heaven would soon open?

Notes:

1. Richard Noll, *The Ayran Christ: The Secret Life of Carl Jung*, (Random House, New York, 1997) p. 111

2. ibid.

3. Dusty Sklar, *The Nazis and the Occult* (New York, Dorset Press, 1977) p. 106

4. John Matthews, *The World Atlas of Divination* (Boston, Bulfinch Press, 1992) p. 34.

5. ibid.

6. ibid.

7. Johanna Drucker, *The Alphabetic Labyrinth* (New York, Thames & Hudson, 1995) p. 116

8. Barbara G. Walker *The Woman's Encyclopedia of Myths and Secrets* (New York, HarperCollins, 1983) p. 871.

9. Victoria LePage *Shambhala* (Wheaton, Ill., Quest Books, 1996) p. 44-45.

10. ibid. p. 870

11. ibid. p. 985.

12. Zecharia Sitchin *The Stairway to Heaven* (New York, Avon Books, 1980) p. 36.

13. H.R. Ellis Davidson *Gods and Myths of Northern Europe* (London, Penguin Books, 1964) p. 141.

14. Bruce Rux *Architects of the Underworld* (Berkeley, Ca., Frog, Ltd., 1996) p. 348.

15. ibid. p. 346.

16. Trevor Ravesncroft *The Spear of Destiny* ((York Beach, Maine, Samuel Weiser, 1973).

CHAPTER SEVEN

THE THULE SOCIETY
AND THE BLOOD OF THE GODS

Identifying the Nordic legends of Odin (who shares many attributes with Michael, Moses and Jesus), along with the legends of the sword, Spear and the Holy Grail, shows us where the Nazis went overboard in their worship of the Aryan blood.

In myth, Odin's nemesis is the wild boar. In French, the wild boar is *le sanglier*. The chase for the the wild boar, *la chasse sanglier*, is a code for the chase for the Holy Grail (the sacred container of the blood of Jesus after the crucifixion) since *san graal*, or holy grail, could also be *sang raal* or holy blood.[1]

The Holy Grail is simultaneously perceived as an object and a heightened spiritual state, which grants passage to the underworld. In this way, the Grail legend is a perfect match with the story of Odin's search for the word of power, the open sesame, which grants passage to paradise, and a god-like blood.

Despite the ancient promise that *all* humans have a bit of the divine within, and Jesus' affirmation of this concept in his "I said, ye are Gods" statement (John 10:34), in Germany the idea that the German blood is *the* ancient pure blood line became the new conventional wisdom.

Even children's comic books presented larger than life German heroes with expanded psychic powers defending the "collective soul" of the German people against subhumans.[2] The German youth were brainwashed to believe in a spiritual force which only the Aryans can tap and which will give them special powers.

The innocent Volkish, back to nature movement, gave way as a cult of race based on the supremacy of the Aryans

54

and the vilification of the Jews gained popular appeal. This took a turn for the worse when living conditions became intolerable in Germany after their defeat in WW I. Food and fuel were scarce. German pride was wounded.

Parnoid German philosophers blamed the Jews for the bastardization of the "racially pure" Aryans -- and for their economic and social fall. *The Protocols of the Elders of Zion*, a fanatical, largely discredited publication which claims the downfall of Germany was caused by world Jewry, was released in Germany and won wide acceptance. (It is still circulated worldwide today.)

Racism turns violent. The inner Nazi was lurking in the dark corners of the German soul and was about to be released.

Against this backdrop, another German club called the Thule Society began to thrive.

THE THULE SOCIETY

The Thule Society was a turn-of-the-century neo-pagan German literary society comprised of well-to-do spiritual adepts, judges, lawyers, doctors, university professors, leading industrialists, surgeons, and scientists.

This misguided crew sought to find freedom for Germans in blood-centered mysticism.[3] Its chatfests spawned the Nazi party and provided a launch pad for Hitler-the-house-painter to become Hitler-the-diabolical-mass-murderer.

The basic tenet of the Thule Society is that there once was a land in the far north (or south) called Hyperboria or "the White (or Pure) Island" (or mountain) and its capital city and mecca for learning, *Atlantis, Thule* or *Tula*.[4]

Hyperboria traces its lineage to Greece. According to the Greeks, Apollo, the Greek sun god, came from Hyperboria. The *Mahabarata*, the holy book of India, and the Vishnu Purana (2000 B.C.?) the oldest of the Hindu *puranas* or books of legend, also devote considerable attention to *Atala* (the letters T-L-A indicating Tula), the "White Island," describing it as "an island of great splendor."

Was this land, as the ancients believed, the Garden of Eden of our race?

According to HPB,[5] Thule was believed to be the magic center of a vanished civilization of gods. She said it had been destroyed by flood.

Some of these god beings survived the flood, found sanctuary in India, and later emerged moaning and groaning as daylight broke on the morning of the post-Atlantean civilization as the Aryans or Indo-Europeans -- the Germans.

The Thulists asked the question; did traces of this lost paradise survive the cataclysm of Atlantis? For many, the answer was a resounding yes.

Evidence of this civilization was plainly evident to those with open minds and spiritual vision in myths, and in megalithic monuments, pyramids, statues, and ancient observatories and temples. Runes are another artifact which prove their existence to believers.

While Thulists are most closely associated with Germany, Thule legends and Thulists cross all the boundaries of the world: Tibet, East India, Greece, Arabia, America and Mexico. Allah, the God of Islam, was originally called *Al-lat* or Tula.6 In America, the *Anasazi* ancestors of the Hopi and the Delaware Indians possess legends of Tula.7 For the Anasazi (notice the Ana prefix), Tula was the anticipated kingdom of heaven on earth.

In Germany, the inner circle of the Thule Society saw themselves as Masters of the Universe-wannabes. Why? They claimed to be in contact with the Nordic gods of Thule. By being in contact with these beings the Thulists believed they had one foot in Atlantis, one foot in heaven.

Thule members who were destined to play key roles in the Nazi party were Alfred Rosenberg, Rudolf Hess and Dietrich Eckhart, a mad man who promoted Hitler as the long-awaited Messiah.

Rosenburg, whose *Mythus* was second only to Hitler's *Mein Kampf* on the non-fiction best seller list in Nazi Germany, claimed the Aryan race originated in Atlantis. He believed that Atlantis was pre-maturely destroyed because the Gods condemned Atlantean genetics experiments which mated animals with women to create a hybrid half animal-half human slave race. When Atlantis faced a cosmic catastrophe, said Rosenburg, initiates fled to safe havens in Asia and the Middle East.

Other beliefs of the Thule Society include:
• the hollow-earth theory,
• the belief that the earth was a spherical bubble, with humanity on the inside, not the outside,
• and the Swiss Cheese theory of the universe, the idea that there are holes in space.8

In its highest form, Thule or Tula adherents sought to transform humanity into a higher state. Tula, they believed, is the source of original matter and life force energy. The Thulists were attempting to connect with it.

Among other names, this energy is called *vril*, *Prana* (in Hindu and yoga thinking), life-force or *orgone* energy, a name derived from the words *organism* and *orgasm* and given by Dr. Wilhelm Reich,9 a disciple of Freud to the universal preatomic energy. (Reich's books concerning the power of the orgasm were later burned by the F.B.I. after his death in 1957.)

The Thule society developed into two factions, with Rudolph Steiner,10 who became Hitler's occult archrival, trying to take it in this positive direction. Drunk with lust for power, Hitler and his cronies took it in the opposite direction. The Nazi's armed gangs broke up meetings of Steiner and his followers by force, threatened them with death, drove them out of Germany and, in 1924, burned the Rudolph Steiner center in Switzerland to the ground. Lost were Steiner's archives. Without his works Steiner was unable to continue. He died a grief-stricken man years later.

THE GALACTIC CORE

The members of the Thule Society were in search of the secrets of the past. From the shadows of time, they adopted a dualistic cosmology. Dualists believe in the ancient Hermetic law "as above, so below," which is attributed to the Egyptian teacher Thoth (whom the Greeks called Hermes).

Dualistic cosmology lifts our eyes to the heavens, suggesting earthly forms are copies of heavenly originals. From the heavens come the patterns and energies which rule human events, say the dualists. It has been the dream of dualists throughout history to transform earth into heaven on earth.

The original earthly Thule, said the dualistic Greeks, was named after the heavenly original, which existed in Hyperboria, the Greek name for heaven. Thule or Tula is the name for the *Central Sun, Spiritual Sun* or *the Galactic Core,* at the center of our galaxy. From this still and distant shore, says virtually every creation myth, our souls came fluttering to their destinies on earth.

The word *galaxy* originated from the Greek *gala,* "mother's milk." In numerous traditions the Four Rivers of Paradise (Eden, Thule or Tula) were characterized as four streams of milk from the four teats of the white, horned, milk-giving Moon cow.11

It is important to pay attention to this description, for Egypt revered Tula's representatives as *Hathors,* the heavenly cows, and depicted them as goddesses wearing two horns. Figures such as Isis and Alexander the Great were later depicted wearing the horns of Tula on their head. Michelangelo's sculpture of Moses (who received his priestly training at Heliopolis, the City of An) depicts the great lawgiver with horns. Could it be Michelangelo did so to connect Moses with the Shining Ones of Tula?

Where, exactly, is Tula in the night sky?

Once we locate the bright Dog Star Sirius, and the three belt stars of the constellation Orion, we are well on our way to the galactic Tula. Gazing slightly to the right of Orion, the next point of light over from these stars is the constellation *Ophiuchus*, the Serpent Holder. Ophiuchus is the nearest constellation to the galactic core.

Until recently a massive cloud of dust literally obscured our access to and ability to see "downtown" Tula directly. However, through the magic of powerful radio telescopes, which extended our senses, astronomers have been able to determine that the galactic core region is like none other in the entire Galactic system.

Tula has a large reservoir of gas -- enough to make 100 million stars![12] These suns are capable of creating planets, which blossom into habitats for souls.

Astronomers discovered the millions of stars making up Tula's bright star cluster are clumped together extraordinarily tightly. Many of them are blue.

This astonishing detail may correspond with the Hopi prophecy given in 1914 (coinciding with WW I) and 1940 (the time of WW II) that a "blue star" would soon be discovered. According to Hopi prophecy, the discovery of the "blue star" would bring peace.[13]

The Hopi (whose name means the "peaceful ones") believe they were a Chosen People saved from the world previous to this one before it was destroyed by flood.

To insure their survival the Hopi were led "underground". When they emerged into this world their guardian spirit *Massau* (Messiah?)[14] appeared and gave the Hopi a sacred teaching concerning the proper way of life.

Everywhere he went, this pale-skinned, blue eyed, blond-headed prophet performed miracles, healed the sick, taught the principles of peace and encouraged vegetarianism. When he departed, he gave the Hopi a prophecy of his return as Pahana, the "true white brother".

It is believed the "blue star" prophecy corresponds with the prophecy of the return of Pahana.[15]

The Hopi prophecy says there will be two heralds to the return of the "true white brother" who will witness for him. One messenger (the Hopi term refers to populations of people) will carry a swastika and the other an enclosed sun cross (the symbol of Tula), which many interpret to be Germany and Japan.

In this regard it is interesting to read Revelation 11:3:

"And I shall give my power unto my *two witnesses*, and they shall prophecy..."

Could it be the two traditions are speaking of the same events? Are the Hopi, the children of the Ana-sazi who left the Hopi a prophecy promising the rebuilding of Tula, somehow related to the early Christians? Is it possible a messiah visited them as well leaving matching prophecies? (For further discussion of these questions please see my book *The Peacemaker and the Key of Life*.)

THE LORDS OF TULA

Periodically, say the Mayans, "Lords of Time" emerge from the celestial Tula. The Buddhists call these figures *tulkus* (literally "shining ones of Tula"). Tulkus are esteemed as super compassionate beings who have escaped the cycle of earthly incarnation and have returned to earth to lead others to paradise.

German writer and researcher Holger Kersten[16] traced Jesus' journey through Asia to *Taxila* (obviously a Tula word), a northern Indian Buddhist university town where Buddhists believe Jesus was recognized as a tulku.

These navigators, or mapmakers, say the Mayans, came to earth to build earthly Tulas, temples, which are spiritual centers for new civilizations.[17]

These Tulas are "houses of the messiah" and learning centers whereby entire civilizations become enlightened and then literally vanish into higher realms of existence. Is it possible Jesus was a Shining One who came to earth to teach us to return to our heavenly home?

THE MONGOLIAN CONNECTION

Strangely (or perhaps not) this Mayan Lords of Time myth also accompanied tales of bearded white men who became the gods of the Maya, Toltecs and Aztecs of Central and South America and who took up earthly residence in Mongolia(!).

Myths of these bearded white gods from Mongolia proliferate in the tales of antiquity.[18] One such book postulates a large immigration of Mongolians into Mexico in antiquity. They were thought to have come from a kingdom in Mongolia located near Lake Baikal and the river Tula.

After a long sea journey, these Mongolians founded a new Tollan or Tula named after places in their homeland. These Mongolians identified themselves as *Nahuatlaks*, and said they had come from Aztlan or Atlantis, although they called it by its most sacred name *Tollan, Tonalan,* or *Tula*.

This is extraordinary because the Mayan word "Maya" means "not many." Could it also mean "the chosen few"?

Another interesting connection is revealed by the fact that Maya (Maia) was the mother of Hermes, Thoth, Atlas, Quetzalcoatl, and Buddha. Maya is one of the seven stars of the Pleiades, which were also called the Atlantides by the Greeks.

The meaning of the word Maya itself would appear to be quite consistent with the possibility that the Maya's remote ancestors may have been a small group of survivors of the Atlantean cataclysm, as Edgar Cayce has hinted.

The Mayans called Tula the "white (pure) place" or "place of herons."[19] Assuredly, this was in reference to the heron being the bird of resurrection and ascension which is sacred to the Hebrews and Christians as the phoenix, the symbol of the returning Christ or Messiah.

In Egyptian mythology the Savior archetype takes the form of the heron.[20] At the beginning of each New Age it lands on top of the pyramid and delivers a teaching designed to transform the earthling from homo sapiens to homo angelis.

Coincidentally (or not), the Egyptian hieroglyph for the heron is identical to the Christian fish symbol for Jesus. Does this suggest, once again, that Jesus was acting out the role of the heron or Shining One from Tula?

Further, the Egyptian symbol for the savior -- the heron atop the pyramid -- is matched by the Mayan depiction of Quetzalcoatl, the Mayan god of Peace, who came to earth to build a temple called Tula.

Quetzalcoatl, who had Caucasian features, is shown standing atop a pyramid. He is frequently depicted with wings, and is known as the "feathered serpent."

The Egyptian and Mayan depictions appear to be symbolically equivalent, their meaning the same -- a Shining One from Tula once appeared who delivered knowledge designed to uplift the human race.

Will this happen again in our time?

Notes:

1. Lionel and Patricia Fanthorpe *The Secrets of Rennes-le-Chateau* (York Beach, Maine, Samuel Weiser, 1992) p. 4
2. Dusty Sklar *The Nazis and the Occult* (New York, Dorset Press, 1977)
3. ibid.
4. Jocelyn Godwin *Arktos: The Polar Myth* (Grand Rapids, MI, Phanes Press, 1993)
5. Helena P. Blavatsky *The Secret Doctrine*

6. Barbara G. Walker *The Woman's Encyclopedia of Myths and Secrets* (New York, HarperCollins, 1983) p. 22.
7. R. Cedric Leonard *Quest For Atlantis* (New York, Manor Books, 1979)
8. ibid
9. W. Edward Mann *Orgone, Reich and Eros* (New York, Simon & Schuster, 1973).
10. ibid
11. ibid.
12. Nigel Henbest & Heather Couper *The Guide to tthe Galaxy* (New York, Cambridge, 1994)
13. Moira Timms *Beyond Prophecies and Predictions* (New York, Ballantine Books, 1980) p. 159
14. ibid.
15. L. Taylor Hansen *He Walked the Americas* (Amherst, WI., Amherst Press, 1963).
16. Elmer Gruber & Holger Kersten *The Original Jesus* (Rockport, MA., Element, 1995).
17. Jose Arguelles *The Mayan Factor: The Path Beyond Technology* (Santa Fe, Bear & Co., 1987)
18. ibid.
19. Zecharia Sitchin *When Time Began* (New York, Avon Books, 1993)
20. Veronica Ions *Egyptian Mythology* (New York, Peter Bedrick Books, 1968)

CHAPTER EIGHT

ATLANTIS, THE BLOOD OF THE GODS AND F.D.R.

If, as legends suggest, the original earthly Tula was indeed in Mongolia, it becomes clearer and clearer why F.D.R. authorized the search for Jesus in Mongolia. This is where the ancients said the Shining Ones of Tula lived.

Important connections between F.D.R. and Mongolia are found in the story of Osiris, the Egyptian savior and "g o d" of the Freemasons,[1] whose logo -- the Eye or god-being atop the pyramid -- F.D.R. ordered stamped on the one dollar bill.

The Greek historian Herodotus learned from the Egyptians that in *ancient Egyptian history*(!) a group of souls descended to earth from the constellation of Orion and began to reincarnate in successive bodies. They called themselves the *Ousir*, a name which the later Egyptians called *Osiris*.

Plutarch said the name Osiris comes from *Os*, meaning many and *Iri*, meaning eye, *i.e.* the "many eyed." It is important to note that Odin was the King of the *Aesir* and was called the Great Eye.[2] This connects him with the *Ousir* or *Osiris* of Egypt, which is the root for Arthur, the King of Camelot who pulled the sword Excalibur from the stone and guarded the Holy Grail.

Just as Christians believe the *Christos* (literally "healing moon-man")[3] lived in an actual man called Jesus, and the Founding Fathers believed this figure would make his Second Coming in America, there is unanimous agreement among Eyptologists: the Osiris lived in a man in Egypt in antiquity. Osiris is described as a blond haired, blue eyed man who is more often depicted with his face painted green. (Is this why Quetzalcoatl was buried wearing a green jade mask?)

The Egyptians said that Osiris was Un-nefer, the "Good One" or Savior, and that he could give eternal life. Prayers to him began with "O Amen, O Amen, who art in heaven." Some researchers compare this with the first line of Jesus' Lord's Prayer, and present it as one proof of the theory that Jesus was revitalizing an Egyptian (or older) priesthood and teaching.4

In the Egyptian myth, the Osiris and his wife Isis came to earth from Sirius to aid in the development of mankind. Together, they travelled throughout the world teaching and uplifting the fledgling human race through the teaching of agriculture, music and other arts.5

THE BLESSED ONES

Nicholas Roerich, who persuaded F.D.R. to place Osiris' logo on the back of the one dollar bill, tracked the origins of Hindu-Buddhist mythology, believes this wisdom tradition emanates from a group of beings called the *Blessed Ones* who came to earth from the constellation Orion. These beings, the Ousir, lived in the *nine-storied* Mount Meru, which is located in Mongolia.

Meru's Buddhist name, "Sumeru,"6 obviously rings of Sumer or Sumeria, the home of the ur-religion. A great scholarly debate exists as to whether or not the original home of these gods was located in Sumeria in Northern Africa, Sumeru in Asia, or even another place altogether.

The Thule Society's mission was to prepare Germany and Europe for the return of the Messiah, whom they believed would emerge from the Habsburg Dynasty.7 Occult authors claim the Habsburgs (formerly the Merovingians) were the bloodline of Jesus and the family of the Holy Grail or Holy Blood.8

The word *meru* displays the root *mer*, which represents the original waters or matter, and is a reference to Maya, illusion. Interestingly, the researchers who trace the alleged bloodline of Jesus to the Merovingians of France believe this bloodline to be descendents of those who landed on Meru, which is the source of their name Merovingians.

Hitler rejected the Habsburg connection. He immediately disbanded the Thule Society after he come to power, having no need for a literary society which claimed to possess the teachings which could elevate ordinary men to the level of "supermen".

Hitler, the messiah wannabe, had his sights set on a mass movement led by a few select, homo Nazis, banning the use of astrology and occult practices by ordinary Germans, even though the Third Reich continued to use them.

SHAMBHALA/TULA

In myths and legends the Mongolian Shambhala and Atlantis or Tula myths share many fascinating links. Dr. Jose Arguelles, who researched Mayan mythology for more than twenty years, equates Shambhala with Thule or Tula. According to French mythologist Rene Guenon, author of *Fundamental Symbols*,9 Shambhala is associated with the astrological sign of Libra, symbolized by the scales or "balance." In Sanskrit, "tula" means balance. In the Hindu tradition, the *Azara*, yet another word closely related to Osiris, are the name for Tula's guardians. No matter where we go: Egypt, Asia, India, or even America, we find Tula associated with balance, or, the joining of earth with Heaven, and with beings who came from the constellation Orion or its neighboring star Sirius. Do these glaring similarities indicate common cultural contact with these beings?

In his *Dawn Behind the Dawn*,10 Geoffrey Ashe tells us of an Altaic (or Mongolian) myth of a sky god who sat on a mountain in the middle of the sky and connected (or reconnected) the earth to this mountain. "Altai" means "golden." As we can see, the first three letters of this word are the T-L-A significator letters of Tula. The word "altai" itself (phonetically all-tie) calls to mind the word altar. Combining these elements reveals the picture of a god who came to Altai or Tula to reconnect or re-tie earth with heaven, using gold as an interface.

Gold is known to be more than plentiful in the Altaic region of Mongolia. Fascinatingly, notes Ashe, the Mongol Earth Mother *Etugen* lived in this area in a paradise called *Altan Delekei*, the "Golden World." This Tula complex was located atop Mount Meru. As we know, in legend Meru is constantly associated with beings which came from Orion.

THE GOLD OF THE GODS

Gold is also constantly mentioned in Tula legends. Fascinatingly, in his book *The Keys of Enoch: The Book of Knowledge*,11 author Dr. James J. Hurtak displays a map of a dozen former "regions of Altai" or "Tula" complexes. The Great Pyramid of Giza, Mongolia, Atlantis, and Southern France are all shown. These locations form what the goddess religions referred to as "the Necklace of Diana."

One link in this chain of sacred sites is a little known area of Nova Scotia known as Oak Island.

For more than 200 years, the mysterious labyrinth of shafts and tunnels under Oak Island, which is close to the mouth of the Gold River which flows across Nova Scotia and empties into the Atlantic Ocean, has been the subject of an intense search by treasure seekers. Millions of dollars have been spent in trying to recover what is believed to be billions of dollars in Templar gold and treasure hidden here. As a young man of twenty-seven F.D.R. owned shares in a mining company attempting to pull the Templar gold from its ingenious repository on Oak Island.[12]

F.D.R. AND THE OAK ISLAND MYSTERY

As a boy, Roosevelt spent his summers on Campobello, an island off the coast of Maine, near Oak Island. Did he hear of the legends of Oak Island from the locals who wielded impressive stories about Captain William Kidd, pirates and the bullion of the Templars?

While we cannot say for sure, it is a fact that in 1909, at the age of 27, F.D.R. bought shares in a treasure search group who sought to recover the treasure of Oak Island. F.D.R. visited Oak Island several times during the summer of 1909.

Though it is probable F.D.R.'s group was unsuccessful in recovering the Oak Island gold -- no one to this date, even those using the most advanced engineering techniques, has been successful in doing so -- there must have been something there which held his attention. F.D.R.'s personal papers include letters regarding Oak Island that date as late as 1939, when F.D.R. was serving his second term as President of the United States.[13]

One wonders; was gold the true treasure of Oak Island that attracted a man of F.D.R.'s intellectual stature? Could there have been something more buried at Oak Island?

The fact that the Knights Templar may be involved in this mystery does not do anything but expand the possibilities for what may have been buried at Oak Island in addition to the gold.

The Templars are believed to have recovered the secrets of the Temple of Solomon which included billions of dollars in gold (at today's values) and the holy relics of the Hebrew people including the Ark of the Covenant.[14]

Equally, or even more importantly, included in this treasure was the language system embedded within Solomon's Temple, the Language of the Birds. According to the Cathars, who interacted heavily with the Templars, the secrets of Jesus are encoded using this language.[15] As we have noted, the Koran states this language of the angels was the true source of King Solomon's immense wealth and wisdom.

The Templars were reportedly the wealthiest order in the years between their founding in 1119 AD and their sudden overthrow on November 2, 1308. Since Hitler, and now it appears F.D.R., spent considerable energy seeking the secrets of the Knights Templar, it is worthwhile to take a momentary interlude to pull in the Templar piece to this puzzle.

THE KNIGHTS TEMPLAR: GUARDIANS OF THE GRAIL

History records that in 1118 nine French knights, pure, holy and believing in God, appeared to the king of Jerusalem Baldwin II. The nine knights presented their plan to form themselves into a company of knights whose purpose was to protect the pilgrims journeying to the Holy Land from robbers and murderers and to police the public highways. The king graciously accepted their proposal. Generously, he gave them a house to live in on the site of the original Temple of Solomon atop Mount Moriah in the city of Jerusalem. History tells us this is the source of their name, Knights of the Temple or Templars. Next, these "warrior monks" took on their famous white mantle decorated with a red cross and made known their wish to be considered "Soldiers of Christ".

Solomon's Temple was literally a House of God. The Holy of Holies, or inner sanctuary, in Solomon's Temple was the womb of the goddess Ashtoreth (or Inanna), who was openly worshipped by the Israelites until the 6th century B.C. She was the beloved of El, or Yahweh, and together they were the "Divine Couple."16

When the nine knights set about excavating the Temple of Solomon they uncovered one of the greatest secrets known to man. Deep beneath Solomon's Temple were the legendary stables of Solomon, which had remained sealed for more than one thousand years. This stable was described as being so massive it could hold more than 2,000 horses. Furthermore, they were believed to contain the Ark of the Covenant.

That's not all. In 1953 the Qumran *Copper Scroll*, which once belonged to the Essenes, was found in a cave near the Dead Sea. This Scroll told of an enormous Temple treasure -- estimated at 138 tons of gold and silver which had been buried by the Jewish priesthood in 64 locations before the Romans destroyed the Temple in 70 A.D.17

Twenty-four of Solomon's gold caches were underneath the Temple. Among the most provacative legends concerning Temple is the legend that Solomon was an alchemist and that he manufactured by alchemical means the vast quantities of gold used in his temple. Perhaps this technique is among the secrets the Templars discovered.

The knights became instantly wealthy, as well as loved, feared and dreaded. The whole of France and Europe clamored to be associated with the Templars. Overnight they became the single most powerful group in the world. No power could touch them, save, perhaps, the Pope in Rome. Their conflict with Rome, as we will see, would prove to be the Templars downfall.

In resonance with the members of the elite Essene Community in which Jesus lived, the Knights Templar were taught to keep pure hearts because that was the requirement for entering the Kingdom of Heaven.

Did this belief come from Egypt, as has been speculated? Was it derived from the Egyptian "Opening of the heart ceremony" in which the heart was weighed against the feather of Truth (Maat) before entrance into the inner earth world, the Tuat (which may be the source of the name Tuatha de' Danann)?

Before Jesus, Moses was the only Biblical figure known to have had intimate knowledge of the Egyptian secrets (Moses learned them at Heliopolis or An). Is this knowledge also stored in the Hall of Records underneath the Sphinx? Is this why the Sphinx is called the book of Revelation? (Or is it because the Sphinx is comprised of the same four creatures -- the lion, bull, man and eagle -- as the four beasts of the apocalypse?)

Some believe the enormous wealth of the Templar Order was built by the contributions of individual members of Europe's most powerful familes who were required to take the three vows of chastity, obedience and non-possession of personal property.

Like Jesus, who implored his followers to cut themselves off from their families (Matthew 10:35-37), the Templars demanded strict obedience to their Order. Even the founder of the Templars, Grand Master Hugues de Payens, took these vows. Sons of nobility throughout Europe rushed to do the same to take the title of Templar ambassador or political consultant.

With the enormous funds pouring into their coffers the Templars invented the first check and the first international banking network. They were not only power brokers, but also financiers of virtually every throne in Europe. They were also keepers of another remarkable treasure.

Recently released scholarly research[18] reveals the knights discovered something more valuable than gold underneath the ancient top of Moriah: the secret scrolls of Jesus. These scrolls, which the Cathars claimed were written in the Language of the Birds, are believed to contain Jesus' most personal teachings.

New Testament scholars agree that Jesus, and his closest companions including Mary Magdalen, shared in a teaching not revealed to the common folk. These mysterious "lost" teachings have been sought for centuries.

Primarily they are presumed to fall into two categories: One is a process for resurrection. The second is a means to establish a social order, a Kingdom of Heaven on earth, based on spiritual principles.

In this context, were Jesus' teachings used to transform ordinary people into beings capable of perceiving or manifesting the higher vibrational world of the Kingdom of Heaven, the new reality that would commence at the "End Times"?

Interesingly, at this time, said the Scrolls, the star called *Merika* will shine.19

Notes:

1. Christopher Knight & Robert Lomas *The Hiram Key* (Rockport, Ma., Element, 1996)
2. Zecharia Sitchin *The Twelfth Planet* (New York, Avon Books, 1976)
3. Barbara G. Walker *The Woman's Encyclopedia of Myths and Secrets* (New York, HarperCollins, 1983)
4. ibid.
5. Murry Hope *The Sirius Connection* (Rockport, Ma., Element, 1996)
6. Victoria LePage *Shambhala* (Wheaton, Ill., Quest Books, 1996)
7. Michael Howard *The Occult Conspiracy* (Rochester, VT, Destiny Books, 1989).
8. Michael Baigent, Richard Leigh and Henry Lincoln *Holy Blood, Holy Grail* (London, Crowns, 1982)
9. Rene Guenon *Fundamental Symbols: The Universal Language of Sacred Science* (Cambridge, Quinta Essentia, 1995)
10. Geoffey Ashe *Dawn Behind the Dawn* (New York, Henry Holt, 1992)
11. Dr. James J. Hurtak *The Keys of Enoch: The Book of Knowledge* (Los Gatos, The Academy for Future Science, 1977)
12. William S. Crooker *Oak Island Gold* (Halifax, NS, Nimbus Publishing, Ltd., 1993)
13. ibid.
14. Lois Charpentier *The Mysteries of Chartres Cathedral* (London, Rilko Boos, 1966)
15. Margaret Starbird *The Woman With the Alabaster Jar* (Santa Fe, Bear & Co., 1993)
16. Deanna Emerson *The Mars/Earth Enigma* (Lakeville, MN., Galde Press, 1996)
17. Grant Jeffrey *Armageddon: Appointment with Destiny* (New York, Bantam Books, 1991)
18. Ibid.
19. Ibid.

CHAPTER NINE

THE SOLDIERS OF CHRIST IN AMERICA

When the Templars were persecuted by the Church in 1308, the massive Templar fleet vanished into the night. Researchers trace their path to Scotland and then to Nova Scotia or New Scotland in the New World or the New Atlantis.1

Another interesting Oak Island secret concerns the Druids (literally "men of the oak trees"), the keepers of the wisdom for communicating with the Tuatha de' Danann, the dwellers of the inner earth.

The Druids are named after the Celtic word for "oak," or *duir*. In Welsh, which is closely related to old Celtic, *derw* is "oak," *drws* is "door" and *dwr* is "water".2

Mythologically, the Druids are believed to have come from Hyperboria, the heavenly Tula (could it be otherwise?)!

Do these linguistic and mythological connections suggest Oak Island is a water door to the inner world of the Tuatha de' Danann? Or, since "water" is the mystical term for "wisdom," does it suggest this area was a repository for the secrets of the ancients (which once may have belonged to Jesus), perhaps concerning doorways to other worlds?

Suppose for the sake of argument that a brilliant young man discovered this secret cache. If F.D.R. could demonstrate his personal control over the enigmatic contents of the Oak Island repository, or even more fantastically demonstrate his knowledge of the exact nature of its secrets, would that not have increased his political stature considerably?

This question is not intended to diminish F.D.R. in any way. In fact, it is the view of the author that if answered in the affirmative it would demonstrate his shrewdness and further reinforce the notion that F.D.R. was a great man of destiny.

The Oak Island connection to our story becomes even more intriguing. In 1803 three original Oak Island excavators found a stone with strange runic inscriptions.

One modern investigator who has looked into the Oak Island stone is Harvard professor Dr. Barry Fell. He claims the inscription is a religious writing written in a Libyan-Arabic dialect.3 Fell has also discovered similar stones in Iowa with Egyptian hieroglyphs dating to 700 B.C.4

Is it possible, as claimed by Oak Island theorists, that early Egyptian settlers, or descendents of Egyptians, established friendly relationships with the local Amerindian tribes, the Micmac, Manitou, and Montauk? Intriguingly, the word *montauk* has a Tibetan meaning: "bright light."5

Further, Native American shamans are also known to have spirit helpers who are referred to as the "Manatu" or "Manitou." The root "Mon" or "Man" is Moon. "Tu" is "Tula."

According to Dr. Hurtak's glossary in the *Keys of Enoch*, "Tak" is the Tibetan word for Orion.

Interestingly, *Muyaw*, the Hopi word for moon is the Tibetan word for sun. *Tiawa*, the Hopi word for moon is the Tibetan word for sun.

Once again, the linguistic connections are interesting. But do they really mean anything?

JEFFERSON WAS HERE

F.D.R. was not the only U.S. president with an interest in the occult history of this region and the religious beliefs of the Indians of the northeast corridor of North America. Thomas Jefferson's activities in this area may even be more explosive than F.D.R.'s.

Dr. H. Spencer Lewis, a turn of the twentieth century author whose works on Atlantis are now classics in the field, claims to have found among Jefferson's personal notebooks "some strange-looking characters"6 previous biographers had taken to be code Jefferson had invented. These inscriptions bear striking resemblance to the runes. Jefferson's interest in secret languages is well known among historians, who call him the Father of American Cryptography.

In *The Peacemaker and the Key of Life*7 I detail the influence of Deganawidah the Iroquois Peacemaker on the Founding Fathers. Deganawidah, who lived in this area of North America, was the founder of the Iroquois Confederacy, the first federal form of government on earth.

Among the participants in this confederacy were the Delaware, who have what is thought to be a myth of a glorious land called "the Talega country," where in the beginning "all kept peace with each other." If we carefully reread the word "talega" do we not notice the letters T-L-A, a tip-off to its origins in Atlantis or Tula? In fact, the Delaware *Hymn to the Flood* tells of the destruction of their lost homeland.8 "Much water is rushing, much go to the hills, much penetrate, much destroying. Meanwhile at *Tula*, at that island, Nana-Bush becomes the ancestor of beings and men . . . the beings and men all go forth from the Flood, creeping in shallow water or swimming afloat, asking which is the way to the turtle-back (island), Tula-Pin." Does this legend suggest the Delaware and their Iroquois brothers may have been descendents of Atlanteans? If so, does this corroborate the belief that America was founded as a New Atlantis?

Upon further investigation, Deganawidah's legend reveals even more astounding details. In summary, it is as follows: In the year 1000 A.D., relations among the tribes in the northeastern corridor of America are stuck in a barbaric hell.9 With his companion and interpreter, Hiawatha, (not the same as Longfellow's fictional character) the Peacemaker emerges from this time of crisis and brings five fiercely antagonistic tribes together under a set of divinely inspired principles known as the Great Tree of Peace.

Deganawidah's political concepts were way ahead of his time. Stories about him were widely circulated among the early colonists, traders and especially the missionary priests. His ideas migrated to Europe, influencing not only Francis Bacon but also Thomas More and his highly esteemed vision of a perfect society expressed in *Utopia*. John Locke and other great minds of the French Enlightenment including Voltaire, Rousseau and Montesquieu were also deeply influenced by the Peacemaker. Benjamin Franklin, a man who, like Moses, used a "key" (or staff) to harness the power of "lightning," published his writings.

It is a corruption of history to say that the white man imported the ideas of democracy to America. They were exported to Europe first and then brought back.

Historian Gregory Schaaf, Ph.D, author of *Wampum Belts and Peace Trees: George Morgan, Native Americans and Revolutionary Diplomacy*,10 conducted fourteen years of research on the authenticity of this piece of history.

Schaaf tells the story of the discovery of the Morgan papers, which chronicled the career of an Indian agent named George Morgan (1741-1810).

His papers are comprised of his personal diary and contained previously unknown and unpublished letters written by George Washington, Thomas Jefferson and John Hancock, which prove that the very structure of the U.S. Government was explicitly modeled after the Iroquois Confederacy.

George Morgan was a wealthy Philadelphia merchant with a wife and five children. On April 10, 1776, John Hancock summoned the thirty-two year old patriot before the newly formed Continental Congress. The about-to-be-born country, the United States of America, was preparing to declare war on the British. They had an enormous problem. The American Indians held the balance of power to determine the outcome of the Revolutionary War. They had to be convinced to stay neutral in the conflict.

George Morgan was the man chosen by the founding fathers to perform this crucial mission of peace.

Morgan was widely respected by the Indians with whom he shared a vision of a future in which people of all races, creeds, and colors could live to together with respect for natural law.

But Morgan's love for his wife and family was equally strong. Bounties were placed on the heads of men like him, revolutionary traitors to the British crown. His mission among the Indians would be a very dangerous one.

On April 17, 1776, Agent Morgan and his companion Chief White Eyes rode out of Philadelphia on their mission of peace.

While the tale of their adventure is both fascinating and suspenseful, I won't push the reader's patience. As Schaaf concludes, there is only one reason why the American Indians chose to remain neutral in the Revolutionary War. George Morgan's brilliant diplomacy, founded on the shared spiritual foundation of the Great Tree of Peace, is that reason.

For his efforts, the Lenape Indians, members of the Iroquois Confederacy, conferred on Morgan the title, Brother Tamanend, after the Peacemaker - one of the greatest honors a white man ever received from an Indian nation.

They believed George Morgan to be the third incarnation of Deganawidah the Peacemaker! The second incarnation of Deganawidah, the Indians believed, founded the state of Pennsylvania along with William Penn. With all of this in mind, should it surprise us that the Delaware and Iroquois Indians are thought to be the descendents of Atlanteans?

Schaaf's superb work culminated in his 1990 testimony before the U.S. Senate Committee on Indian Affairs. As a result of his convincing evidence and testimony, Congress passed a resolution that was signed by President George Bush.

In the resolution, for the first time in history, the U.S. government officially recognized that the basic principles of the U.S. Constitution actually came from the American Indian people and that the very structure of U.S. government was "explicitly modeled after the Iroquois Confederacy" as designed by the Peacemaker.

The United Nations is also based on the principles of the Peacemaker's Great Tree of Peace (which is modeled after the Tree of Life, which grew in Eden/Atlantis).

F.D.R. was the first to use the words "United Nations" in the Declaration of the United Nations in January, 1942, when twenty-six nations gathered together to fight the Axis powers of Germany, Italy and Japan.

In June, 1945, while WW II wound to a close, a conference on International Organizations met in San Francisco with the purpose of securing peace after WW II. They scoured the planet searching for a model by which to design their body. What did they settle upon? The Iroquois Confederacy.

If Thomas Jefferson had indeed stumbled upon and deciphered the language of the gods, we must pose the question. Where, exactly, did Thomas Jefferson's muse, who drove him to write the Declaration of Independence, come from? Could it have been the same as the voice of the Constitution?

THE WISSAHICKON

We have already mentioned the Founding Father's mystic ties with the Freemasons. One additional story catches our attention in this regard. This story is documented in a Rosicrucian document entitled, "The Fulfillment of the Prophecy, The Consecration of Washington, the Deliver, The Wissahickon." The Wissahickon is a creek near Philadelphia.

This story first catches our attention as the name *Issa*, the Muslim name for Jesus, is evident in the name *Wissahickon*. Also present is *On*, the biblical name for Heliopolis, the repository of ancient teachings.

The text of the document provides some fascinating commentary concerning the Constitution of America.

"Wissahickon," says the document "is much more than a word, or the name of a stream, however beautiful. To the true American *it is synonymous with a pure Mystic religion*, with the freedom of all religious sects, for it was here that the many sectarians established themselves; with the founding of the American Republic, *because here was conceived the constitution*, and here was held the first American Rosicrucian Supreme Council, here was Washington, one of its Acolytes consecrated, and here formed the Grand Temple of the Rosy

Cross. Wissahickon the beautiful and to many of us, sacred as the Ganges is to the Hindu."11

Can there be any doubt that the Founding Fathers understood the importance of certain sacred places as terma: sacred places where the god-beings communicated important knowledge to man?

As we have seen, rivers and creeks were a favorite of the Asian god beings. Can there also be any doubt that Jefferson's understanding of the language of the gods would have been instrumental in these open air meetings?

We shall pick up this thread again in a later chapter.

Notes:

1. Andrew Sinclair *The Sword and the Grail* (New York, Crown, 1992)
2. Lionel and Patricia Fanthorpe *The Secrets of Rennes-le-Chateau* (York Beach, Maine, Samuel Weiser, 1992)
3. Ibid.
4. Dr. Barry Fell *America B.C.* (New York, Pocket Books, 1976)
5. Peter Moon *Black Sun* (New York, Sky Books, 1997)
6. Robert Hieronimus, Ph.D. *America's Secret Destiny* (Rochester, Vermont, Destiny Books, 1989)
7. William Henry *The Peacemaker and the Key of Life* (Anchorage, AK, Earthpulse Press, 1997)
8. R. Cedric Leonard *Quest For Atlantis* (New York, Manor Books, 1979)
9. Steve McFadden *Ancient Voices Current Affairs* (Santa Fe, Bear & Co. 1992)
10. Gregory Schaaf *Wampum Belts and Peacetrees: George Morgan, Native Americans and Revolutionary Diplomacy* (Golden, CO., Fulcrum Publishing, 1990)
11. Ibid.

CHAPTER TEN

THE ISRAELITES
AND THE TEMPLE OF SOLOMON

So far, I have posed a heart-racing question. Were Moses, Jesus, Thomas Jefferson, and Franklin D. Roosevelt weavers of a mystic golden thread which, once pulled, reveals they each had one foot in Atlantis? Did they become weavers after they learned to communicate with the survivors of Atlantis, the An, or the Shining Ones of Tula?

Did Hitler and his cronies seek to communicate with these same beings, and weave this same mystic thread into a Nazi net? Once Hitler grasped this thread, why did he become hell bent on eliminating the Israelites, and all non-Germans?

Since our goal is to understand the occult reasons behind Hitler's desire to eliminate this spiritual group, it will be worth a few moments of our time to explore the Israelites and their remarkable occult history and legends further.

In the process, we will discover more eye-opening occult Secrets at the heart of the Holy War of WW II and New Age Politics.

GOT WISDOM?

One of mythology's most intriguing stories is found in the biblical description of the Israelite's sacred headquarters, Solomon's Temple. King Solomon built his temple after the Lord had "given him wisdom."

This wisdom, we have learned, was the Language of the Birds or angels, the original language spoken by Adam and Eve in the Garden of Eden (Atlantis). It gave Solomon "abundance of all things" and enabled him to fly like an angel.

Solomon is famous for travelling to Ophir ("Op" means abundance, "phir" means fire), normally a three year voyage from his court, on his "magic flying" vehicle to mint the tons of gold required for his Temple.

The ancient gold mine of Ophir has been located at the entrance to the Amazon jungle, in Peru. A map "facilitating the explanation of Holy Scriptures" published in 1571 places Ophir in the Rocky Mountain region of the United States.1 (Of course, as we have mentioned, Solomon may have made this gold by alchemical means, opening up the possibility that something else of value was "mined" at Ophir.)

Inside Solomon's Temple was the Holy of Holies, a room in the shape of a perfect cube devoted to the Goddess. Only the High Priest could enter this cube -- and then only on one day of the year. In it sat the prized Ark of the Covenant, a spectacular technology which we will explore momentarily.

In the Book of Kings, we learn that outside the Holy of Holies of Solomon's Temple are two pillars and a Sea of Brass (I Kings 7:21-23).

The two sacred pillars, named Jachin and Boaz, were a remarkable 40 feet high (about as tall as a five story building). Some say these pillars are copies of Egyptian originals,2 which united upper Egypt and lower Egypt: or, according to Egyptian dualistic thinking, heavenly Egypt and earthly Egypt.

When united, say myths, the two pillars upheld a great archway to eternity.

In the middle of the archway was peace.

It must be emphasized that the "peace" or unity these pillars create does not refer to the absence of conflict between warring factions. Peace refers to cosmic Peace: the unity of heaven and earth.

The book of Revelation forecasts the recovery of these pillars in the New Age along with a Thousand Years of Peace.

One of these pillars will be installed on one side of a river that flows through the New Jerusalem, (the New Atlantis?) and its twin will be installed on the other side of the river.3 Since the "river" in question is actually the Milky Way galaxy, does this mean that one pillar will be on earth, while clear across the galaxy will stand the other pillar? Are the two pillars connected?

Beyond the two pillars of peace standing at its front, Solomon's Temple is famous for its Sea of Brass. This is a strange description.

What is a Sea of Brass?

Its explanation is even stranger than that of the pillars. However, it holds the key to unlocking the Secrets we are seeking.

THE SEA OF BRASS

Numerous scholars have observed that the Holy of Holies of ancient temples, including the Temple of Solomon, were living memorials to the Great Mother, in this case the Goddess Inanna, and that these temples were designed and constructed as models of Her female body and physiologic processes.4 The entrance to these temples and the Holy of Holies were replicas of the birth canal and womb. In turn, the entire earth, herself (as well as other planets), was seen as the Goddess/temple.

Let us suppose Solomon's "temple" *is* the female human body and the earth. With this in mind, let us consider that, in Hebrew, brass is *nekhashat*. In Aramaic, it is *nehash*, which is similar to *nahash*, the Hebrew word for serpent. The Hebrew word for soul is *neshamah*. These words are linguistically and phonetically similar. In the Language of the Birds, they are interchangeable.

This raises a provacative question. Are the ancient Hebrew storysmiths asking us to connect the Hebrew term for brass with the words for *soul, serpent,* and *electricity*?

If so, are we now in a position to ask if one Secret the Hebrew initiates are telling us through their multi-leveled word play is that outside the Holy of Holies -- the womb of the temple/female body/earth -- there is a sea of electricity, serpents and souls?

That the ancients would believe there is a sea of electricity surrounding the earth makes a lot of sense. Lightning strikes the earth thousands of times a minute.

But what about serpents? Is there a sea of serpents outside the earth? This makes no sense. What of the third word, souls? Is there really a Sea of Souls surrounding the earth? Is this what is meant by the occult expression that a soul is "earthbound"?

According to the ancients, there is indeed a Sea of Souls surrounding the earth. Further, these souls are serpent shaped. The individual souls are part of one giant serpent-shaped soul that long ago surrounded the earth.

This Sea of Souls, soul atmosphere or *soulsphere*, then separated itself into tiny pieces and inhabited the energy field surrounding first the female body of the earth, and then the energy field (or aura) of the human body.

In mythology, this soulsphere is called the *ourobouros*, the world-serpent (or worldsoul), the serpent with its tail in its mouth. Sometimes it is shown with a dove in the center, sitting atop a concealed Tree of Life.

While the idea of a soulsphere may sound outrageous, is it possible this notion may be *the* pre-eminent occult Secret in the minds of not just the ancient Hebrew storysmiths, but also the leaders of WW II?

Does the soulsphere idea relate to Carl Jung's collective unconscious?

Is there any evidence that at any of the WW II political bosses took this idea seriously?

In fact, there may be. In his *History of the Island Nation*, Winston Churchill describes the sequential evolutionary phases of the mutating English *folksoul*.

Is he referring to a separate English group soul?

Just as Hitler believed the German *volk* or group soul was real (and reincarnating), are we to infer that Winston Churchill believed in a similar, but separate British soul? Churchill chronicles this folksoul's beginning, middle and its latest fulfillment: the creation of the British Empire. Churchill even outlined this group soul's next evolutionary task. Destroy the vile German group soul then unfurling itself in Nazi Germany.5

While Hitler believed he was the Messiah of the German volk soul, Churchill believed the spirit of the English folksoul spoke through him. Also, bits of this folksoul had migrated to America.

F.D.R. recognized that these bits of soul, like a body, need to be sheltered, clothed, fed and they must be nourished. (Remember, myths say the nourishment the soul seeks is the blood, the word of power, and the use of vril, the serpent or life force energy, which the Indians said could be found on Turtle Island.)

Were these occult beliefs in separate soulspheres a contributing factor in WW II? Exoterically, WW II had the appearance of being a race war: the Germans versus all the inferior non-German creatures. Esoterically, did the leaders of the Axis and Allied powers understand the spiritual dynamics of the soul groups inhabiting the bodies of the soldiers and peoples involved?

As we'll see, there is remarkable evidence to suspect that these soul groups had been battling throughout history for control of a prized collection of power tools which legends going all the way back to the Garden of Eden claim enable the souls to exit the earth. WW II was merely the latest episode in an ongoing Holy War between man and a group of gods over control of these devices.

Does understanding the belief in the existence of these soul groups and their aims lifts us to the "top of the mountain," the occult level from which the political bosses of WW II were operating?

It may. Occult history and mythology is much more fun, anyway, and wonderful opportunities for mind expansion arise, when we're sitting at the philosophical level from which the stories were written.

Go ahead. Sit down and relax. The view is breathtaking. The air is clean. Makes you feel light as a feather. Let us let the wind take us on an esoteric ride to the land of one of these soulspheres: Atlantis.

THE ALIEN BOOK OF GENESIS

As we lift off, let us remember that this theory proposes the Founding Fathers of America (the New Atlantis), and the ghouls of Nazi Germany (who were seeking to build a New Atlantis) spoke a different mythological language than you and I. They also read different history books. One of these books is the *Enuma Elisha.*

The *Enuma Elisha* is named after its first few words "when on high." This is one of the books that came out of the earth at the turn of the 20th century and gave the Germans hope that they might connect with their ancient Aryan ancestors.

I call this book the "Alien (or Aryan) Book of Genesis" because of the heightened, indeed extraterrestrial, perspective from which it is written. Its remarkable text uncovers direct answers to fundamental questions that have always perplexed humankind: Who are we? Where are we? How did we get here? What are we doing here? Where do we go when our work is done? How do we leave?

The Alien Book of Genesis is essential (and disturbing) reading for every thinking person. It provides essential background material for understanding the rivalry between the soul groups which is at the heart of the Holy War of WW II. Each of the leaders of WW II had one foot in Atlantis, and by extension, one foot in the tantalizing story recorded in the *Enuma Elisha.*

According to the Alien Book of Genesis, the colonization of souls into our remote solar system began while the solar system as we know it was still in formation. This was a time before the earth was created. In this book we learn the great watery abyss of the cosmos was teeming with both devils and gods, with both types of souls seeking homes.

Into this strange and wonderful document of the ancient peoples is woven the record which testifies to the migration of soulspheres, the history of the people of An, and the terrible, stomach-turning sinking of a planet in the cosmic ocean.

It all sounds like science fiction, however, we are assured it is not.

Further, it tells of a conflict between soul groups or soulspheres over control of the remains of the sunken planet, earth. For centuries this ancient creation tale lay buried like a time capsule (or time bomb) beneath the sands of Iraq awaiting just the right pivotal moment in history to be remembered, reinterpreted and understood anew. Could it be today is that day?

AN: THE PLANETARY HOME OF THE GODS OF ATLANTIS

The Alien Book of Genesis tells of a massive twelfth planet in our solar system which the Sumerians called *Nibiru* or *An*, the creator or home of the An or An-nun-aki, the gods of Atlantis. An is believed to make a staggering 3,600 year orbit of the Sun in an elliptical orbit far from Pluto. It is called the "Planet of the Crossing," and is symbolized by an enclosed cross.6

An-nun-aki is plural of An, as the biblical *Elohim* is the plural of *El.* or Shining Ones. Are they the same beings? (If so, as is widely believed, this suggests a mythological link between the history of the Israelites and the history of Atlantis.)

In *The Twelfth Planet*, Sumerian scholar Zecharia Sitchin, who interepreted the *Enuma Elisha*, writes: "The Sumerians had no doubt that the Twelfth Planet (An) was a verdant planet of life; indeed, they called it *NAN.TIL.LA.KU*, ''the god who maintains life'''.

An, says Sitchin, was also known as the;
• "bestower of cultivation,"
• "creator of grain and herbs who causes vegetation to sprout,"
• "who opened wells, apportioning waters (souls?) of abundance,"
• and the "irrigator of heaven and earth."7

Due to the emphasis on the agricultural connection in Sumerian lore, may we think of An, or the beings who live there, as "the gardeners" of our solar system?

The answer to this question may be shocking.

Central to Nazi cosmology was the belief in a group of extraterrestrial beings who came from outside the solar system and founded the first *Thule, Tula* or *Atlantis* on earth. The Nazis tell us this was the Garden of Eden, its primary god-being a gardener.

At the exact same time (1935), F.D.R. stamped Osiris's logo on the back of the one dollar bill. Osiris is thought to be a god-being who, along with his beautiful wife, came to earth from Sirius, settled in Mongolia and Egypt and taught the art of agriculture to the people of earth.

Osiris also is a gardener.

His lush, verdant paradise is periodically re-tooled in human history. One of its names is Tula.

In the Sumerian story of "NAN.TIL.LA.KU," a name
which contains the T-L-A significator letters of Tula, have we
discovered the heavenly Atlantis and the common occult
inspiration to the Nazis and F.D.R.?

THE HEART OF THE OCEAN

The planet An, said the Sumerians, originates from "the
heart of the Deep," the cosmic ocean. The mathematically
determined center or heart of our Milky Way galaxy is in the
southern portion of the constellation *Ophiuchus*, a missing or
hidden thirteenth constellation in our zodiac also known as
Dinah or Diana, the "light of An."8

Ophiuchus is called the Serpent (soul?) Holder. It is also
the Greek name for an Egyptian healer and serpent holder
named Imhotep ("he comes in peace") who, according to
ancient Egyptian documents, was believed to have been the
reincarnated Thoth (called Hermes by the Greeks).9

This connection links the Serpent Holder with Thoth, the
son of Osiris, whom the early Christian Gnostics believe was
the personification of the world serpent soul.

According to the Gnostic Gospels, Jesus told Mary that
the serpent that surrounded the world was the Egyptian *Tuat*
(Thoth) and the *ouroboros*, the giant soul which was shattered
into tiny pieces and inhabited individual human bodies.

From this can we conclude that Thoth is another name for
what the mystics call the "god within," one of the two souls
which inhabits the human body? Further, does this
connection imply that the Tuatha de' Danann were among
the early children of this soulsphere?

If the constellation Ophiuchus is where the Shining Ones
of Tula lived, and this is also where the soulsphere originated,
does this allow us to unveil yet another profound secret of the
Israelites?

That is, when the Biblical book of Kings tells us Moses
"held the serpent" *Ne-hush-t-an*, is it secretly linking him
with the varied myths of Ophiuchus and Thoth, two previous
Serpent Holders? Like his co-serpent-holders -- Thoth,
Hermes, and Imhotep -- does Moses emerge as a Shining One
of Tula?

We are not the first to question Moses' connection with
these three early Peacemakers. In the tile work at Sienna
Cathedral in Italy Moses is portrayed with the inscription:
"Hermes Mercury Trismegistus, Contemporary Moses."10

This is because up until the Middle Ages there was great
scholarly debate as to how it was that Thoth (the Greek
Hermes) and Moses could share so many traits. Thoth and
Moses led their people during a time of crises, both received
Divine law directly from God, and both were Peacemakers. A

middle ground was established in the debate. The scholars simply stated that Hermes, Mercury and Thoth are the same as Moses.

Does this explosive mythological evidence suggest Moses is the Jewish link to Tula or Thule? Further, does it link Atlantis, Thule or Tula with the Promised Land of the Israelites?

If so, does this help to explain the competition between the Nazis and the Jews and why Hitler was so rabidly anti-Semetic?

Israelite mythology, like the mythology of virtually every culture on earth, tells of a chosen group of souls who are awaiting a Messiah who will reconnect them with a Promised Land.

This Messiah, whom the Christians call Jesus, is said to be born of a virgin. Incredibly, the Hebrew word for virgin is *bethula*, or "house or vessel of Tula." Her child, the Messiah, is called a *tulku* by the Buddhists, a Shining One of Tula.

What if Moses and Jesus were both Shining Ones of Tula?

How would that change our understanding of Hebrew and Christian religion?

Would bringing these religions in mythological alignment with Buddhism and Islam weaken or more fully empower these religions?

THE HEAVENLY TULA: *THE* PROMISED LAND AND THE SOURCE OF THE RIVERS OF SOULS

It is interesting to note that the Messiah's message is the same wherever this figure appears, we are all one.

Is this message based upon a common belief held by nearly all the mythologies of the ancient world (and still believed by many today) that all the "waters" or "souls" on earth originated from the same pure place, the center of our Milky Way galaxy?

Doesn't this center, the birthplace of all the tribes, belong to everyone?

The Milky Way is a spiral-shaped galaxy. Earth resides on the Orion arm of the Milky Way. 11 We are literally on the fringes of the galaxy. When we look at the Milky Way in the night sky, we are looking along the edge of a spinning wheel, like looking into the silvery hub of a spinning bicycle wheel.

At the center of the galaxy, say the legends, sitting upon his Sacred Rock, the King of Tula observes as souls, once released from their holding tank, fan out along four rivers.

The idea of a four-fold spring of souls emerging from a common center is found in the Garden of Eden story in Genesis 2:10:

82

And a river (of souls?) *went out from Eden* (the center of the galaxy?) *to water the garden* (earth?); *and from thence it was parted...into four heads.* (author's amplification in parenthesis)

In Genesis (2:14), the river of souls is called *Hiddekel,* which is a copy of the Akkadian name of the Milky Way, *Hiddagal,* or "River of the Divine Lady."12 The Nordic *Edda* confirms the four streams of souls came from a central fountain -- in the home of the gods. The Hindu texts describe a *fourfold headspring of all waters* (souls?) at "the center of heaven."

The Sun-cross, also known as the Cross of Light or the enclosed Sun cross, depicts the four life streams fanning out from Tula. The Sun-cross appears prominently in many religious traditions.

Like the six pointed Seal of Solomon (the star of Israel or Jewish star) it is one of a family of symbols, which represents balance and harmony between opposing forces: negative and positive, male and female, man and god. It serves as the symbol of the *original* Holy Land, from which our souls are said to have originated. Humans appear to be programmed to return to this home.

As we have seen, the word *galaxy* originated from the Greek *gala,* "mother's milk." In numerous traditions the Four Rivers of Paradise were characterized as four streams of milk from the four teats of the white, horned, milk-giving Moon cow.

Egypt revered Tula's reprentatives as *Hathors,* the heavenly cows. There were seven Hathors, corresponding with the seven stars of the Pleiades. The Egyptians and Sumerians depicted them as goddesses wearing two horns. Were Moses and Alexander the Great their disciples? Is this why they were later shown wearing the horns of Tula?

In Nordic mythology, *Niflheimr* was the home of the nurturing energies of the cow Audumbla, from whose *teats flowed the galaxy.*13 Could this be the source of the Biblical *Nefilim*? Generally *nephilim* is translated as "giants," but more accurately, says Sitchin, it is interpreted as "those who came from heaven to earth," or "shining ones," whom myths say came from this region of space.

WHITE HOLE

Did you know that in 1997 NASA pointed a gamma ray observatory directly at this region of space?14 Soon thereafter, the space agency reported the existence of a massive river of exotic particles spewing from the galactic core. Physicists speculate this is coming from a white hole, a "cosmic gusher" of matter and energy, which inhabits this region.

University of Arizona astronomers, using a new high-speed, infrared camera mounted on a Kitt Peak telescope, have also looked at this area. They believe they have discovered a black hole inhabiting the area *near* the center of our Milky Way galaxy.15 Theoretically, physicists view black holes as time machines which may open gateways to parallel dimensions.

Unfortunately, for those thinking about hopping through these gateways, these celestial bodies, due to their small size and staggering gravitational forces, draw in all surrounding materials on a one-way course toward their centers.

Therefore, venturing toward a black hole is dangerous business. Not even light escapes its grasp -- hence, the name *black hole.*

If for every action there is an equal and opposite reaction and our premise is that humans are programmed to go back "home," could this be the reason that physicists were driven to discover white holes leading to Tula?

ANGELS THIS WAY

In physics circles it is said that, whatever a black hole can devour, a white hole can spit out. These white holes precisely conform to the image the ancients held of the center of our galaxy.

White holes are the subject of intense scientific research in America and Europe and have led scientists to ponder the mysteries of interstellar passageways called *wormholes.*

In the past few years, the scientifically-rooted concept of worm holes, star gates, have become popular topics of such television shows as *Star Trek: The Next Generation* and *Sliders* and movies such as *2001: A Space Odyssey, Stargate* and *Contact.*

Interestingly, the Shining Ones left star maps for the ancients on their ancient tablets. To many observers, these maps prove the Shining Ones came from outside our solar system.

The Sumerians, for example, knew of ten planets (twelve including the Sun and moon) at a time when scholars say they were still learning to say their own names. No names are given for the planets depicted on the tablets. However, they accurately describe the appearance of the seven satellites of Saturn, the phases of Venus, and the four moons of Jupiter, none of which can be seen without a telescope.16

Also, the Sumerians made a habit of adding one ray to each star symbol for each planet *in*, from the outside of our solar system.

Take Saturn, for example. It is the furthest planet from earth, but closest when approaching our solar system from

ONE FOOT IN ATLANTIS

another place. It has four rays, Jupiter five, Mars six, etc. To
the children of An, earth is the seventh planet, or "the seventh
heaven."
Does this accurate astronomical knowledge, as well as
other advanced knowledge on other tablets, reveal that the
Sumerians spent a great deal of time in cosmic kindergarten
learning the universal basics from the Shining Ones?
One of these tablets, the Alien Book of Genesis, describes
the Sumerian cosmology as taught by the gods. In it we find
the story of a celestial confrontation between An and another
planet called *Tiamat*. In the next chapter we will take a brief
look at this story. The reason for this examination is that it
will provide the mythological foundation we need for
evaluating more of the occult beliefs of the leaders of WW II.

Notes:

1. David Hatcher Childress *Lost Cites of Atlantis, Ancient
Europe and the Mediterranean* (Stelle, Ill., Adventures
Unlimited Press, 1996)
2. Christopher Knight & Robert Lomas *The Hiram Key*
(Rockport, Ma., Element, 1996)
3. Ibid.
4. Deanna Emerson *The Mars/Earth Enigma* (Lakeville,
MN., Galde Press, 1996)
5. Trevor Ravenscroft & T. Wallace Murphy *The Mark of the
Beast* (Secaucus, NJ, Citadel Press, 1992) p. 25
6. Zecharia Sitchin *The Twelfth Planet* (New York, Avon
Books, 1976) p. 254
7. Ibid. 255
8. Ibid. p.286
9. Robert K.G. Temple *The Sirius Mystery* (Rochester, VT,
Destiny Books, 1976) p. 76
10. Antoine Favre *The Eternal Hermes* (Grand Rapids, MI,
Phanes Press, 1995) p.148
11. Nigel Henbest & Heather Couper *The Guide to the
Galaxy* (New York, Cambridge, 1994) p. 121
12. Barbara G. Walker *The Woman's Encyclopedia of Myths
and Secrets* (New York, HarperCollins, 1983) p. 657
13. Johanna Drucker, *The Alphabetic Labyrinth* (New York,
Thames & Hudson, 1995) p. 116
14. *Time* May 12, 1997, p.77
15. Ibid. p. 240
16. D.S. Allan & J.B. Delair *Cataclysm* (Santa Fe, Bear &
Co., 1997) p. 218

CHAPTER ELEVEN

THE BATTLE WITH TIAMAT

The Alien Book of Genesis, the original upon which the story in the Hebrew book of Genesis is based, tells us that before the earth was created, An split a planet called Tiamat in half during a celestial confrontation.

The importance of Tiamat to our story cannot be overemphasized. Tiamat was a planet that was once one of the Pleiades, a star cluster that was also called the *Atlantides* or *Atlantis*.

In the story of Tiamat we learn of:
• a planet and a group of souls that sank in the night,
• of which there were survivors,
• who engaged in a long march to regroup,
• and reclaim a collection of power tools to assist in rebuilding their civilization
• so that the souls might return home.

Could it be, the story of Tiamat, the former Pleiadean homeworld, is the Atlantis story in the stars?

THE PLEIADES

The Pleiades are in the constellation Taurus the Bull. They were believed by the earliest peoples to be composed of six visible stars, plus a hidden seventh. We now know there are actually hundreds of stars packed into this cluster which may explain why the ancients also called it the "Beehive."

Beehive you say? In the thirteenth-century, while the Knights Templar were constructing Chartres Cathedral in France, occultist Michael Scot was proclaiming that honey falls from the air into flowers, and then is collected by bees. To us, this sounds poetic. However, Scot was writing in the

Language of the Birds, which the Templars may have recovered from Solmon's Temple and built into Chartres. In this language the bee is an ancient symbol for the human soul, and honey is the food which feeds the souls. Many occult groups, including the Merovingians and the Rosicrucians, incorporated the symbol of the bee, especially the bee hovering around the rose, as the symbol of the human soul. The beehive is a related symbol. The hive represents not only the bee's industrious nature, but also the "collective soul."

One further connection between the bee and the Pleiades is most illuminating. The Latin for bee is APIS. This word is also the Latin name for the sacred bull, which was worshipped in ancient Egypt. The bee and the bull made the journey together in the Greek and Roman mystery religions where the two creatures are found side by side on depictions of the goddess Diana, "the light of An."

In the Language of the Birds, the bull and the bee refer to the duality of human nature: one part earthly, one part heavenly.

Since the earliest times, people have connected the constellation of Taurus the Bull with the flood in Noah's day and the Pleiades with the ark of Noah and the souls that were saved in it. The root of the name *Pleiades* means "to play" or "to sail."[1]

In myth, the Pleiades are known as the nymphs who loved to play. Beltane, or Baal's day, is the first day of May. This is when the Pleiades appear in the night sky, when the nymphs come out to play.

The bright-reddish star in the eye of Taurus the Bull is lined up with the belt of *Orion*, which was associated with Osiris, whose logo F.D.R. stamped on the back of the one dollar bill, and with beings who connect earth with heaven. Orion, or Arian (Aryan) -- the Light of An, was one of the suitors of the Pleiades. He is the mighty hunter with a huge club raised in his right hand. In his left hand he holds the skin of a lion which he has killed.

In occult symbolism the lion is a symbol for Atlantis and its destruction during the Age of Leo.[2]

THE PLANETARY HOLOCAUST

The Pleiades are said to have spurned Orion's initial flirtations. To protect them, the gods turned the Pleiades into doves. The name Oannes or "dove" has been applied to prophets with a connection to the Pleiades. Perhaps, however, this initial passion turned obsessive, then deadly. For as the Sumerians recorded, it was An who was responsible for the destruction of Tiamat.

Tiamat is described as physically resembling Jupiter and Saturn, her mass 90 times the size of earth.3 From the ancient myths of the destruction of Tiamat we learn of a soul line that was the victim of a planetary holocaust (the ancestors of the Egyptians who called Maat the Mother of all things). As a result of her disfunctional relationship with Orion or An, "the watery dragon," or "the monster" Tiamat was shattered.4

An trapped Tiamat in its net, shot a flaming arrow into her open mouth, and smashed her skull.5 Then, An split Tiamat in half. One half of Tiamat's body became the asteroid belt circling the Sun between Mars and Jupiter.6 The other half of the dragon became earth.7

Mythologically speaking, Tiamat, the dragon, was slain by An, the dragon slayer.

Is Tiamat the prototype for all future "dragon slaying" myths including those of Yahweh, Michael and Jesus?

In the book of Genesis we learn a similar story. There arose a Great Dragon or Sea Monster called *Tehom*. Tehom, in the plural, becomes Tehomot (Tiamat),8 which God, in his fiery chariot, rode the waves and attacked, flinging at her great volleys of hail, lightning and thunderbolts. He killed her ally Leviathon, also called the serpent monster Rahab or Nahash, with a thrust of his sword -- *the Sword of Destiny*.

The Bible makes vague reference to this War in Heaven. The Alien Book of Genesis fills in the details of one of its battles. In these details we find the conflict which became the crux of the Holy War of WW II and New Age politics.

THE BATTLE WITH TIAMAT AND THE EXPLODED PLANET HYPOTHESIS

The battle began, says Sitchin in *The 12th Planet*, as he reinterprets the stories on the Sumerian tablets, when the enormous gravitational forces of the approach of An deeply affected Tiamat.

Under these forces, Tiamat began to bulge and convulse. An unleashed "streams" which disturbed Tiamat. These "streams" appear to be a spiritual weapon as they had the result of carrying the gods away, nullifying their protection.

Tiamat is thought to have been home to a technologically advanced civilization. If this is so, it would make it easy for us to interpret what happened next. An "diluted Tiamat's vitals" and "pinched her eyes."

What do these terms mean?

Could her "vitals" refer to Tiamat's atmosphere or life support system?

Could the "eyes" describe her inhabitant's orbiting satellites, telescopes or "eyes," which enabled her to peer into the cosmos? Without her eyes Tiamat was blind. She "paced about distraught."

The next event is stomach wrenching. As An approached Tiamat, pieces of this living planet were blown away, either from the massive gravitational forces of An or some powerful weaponry. Mayhem undoubtedly ensued as earthquakes and volcanos tore at Tiamat's harmonious structure, crumbled her tectonic plates, and ripped away her flesh.

RETALIATION

The result was an awesome retaliation. From within Tiamat emerged *eleven* "growling, raging" "monsters" who "marched at the side of Tiamat." These life-like objects had names like the Viper, the Dragon, the Female Monster, the Great Lion, the Mad Dog, the Scorpion Man, the Howling Storm, the Flying Dragon, the Bison, and the Fish Man.

New Age Armageddon watchers and poltical types will want to take serious note. These eleven monsters are identical to the eleven horns written of in the book of Daniel.[9] These horns have been wildly misinterpreted as harbingers of a future End Time. Were they actually participants in an *ancient* apocalypse: the sinking of Tiamat?

It was long ago, but not so far away, that these enormous monsters, some even being described as the size of planets, set themselves in battle formation. Tiamat, who herself assumed the shape of a monstrous dragon, crowned the monsters with "halos". With this act Tiamat declared war.

Or, did Tiamat surrender? In the Greek version of this tale, we learn the battle lost, Tiamat exploded herself. It may have been evident to the inhabitants of Tiamat that the total destruction of the planet was inevitable.

However it occurred, like the civilization of Atlantis on earth, Tiamat the unsinkable sank into the cold waters of the night.

But not before releasing ten large lifeboats, and one smaller one.

THE SUPPRESSED SECRET OF REVELATION

What if it were possible the eleven "monsters" released from Tiamat were, in fact, not only warships, but also enormous safety boats or evacuation vehicles?

What if, as some researchers into the exploded planet hypothesis believe, the Moon and Mars are examples of these vehicles?

Might we expect to see the survivors, the souls, in these vehicles attempt to find a safe place to rebuild their civilization?

Might they have also tried to rescue their brethren after the sinking of their homeland? Would those who lived on Mars or the Moon attempt to make contact with the other ships?

Perhaps we have stumbled upon *the* suppressed Secret of the book of Revelation and New Age politics whose central fear is an *impending* apocalyptic battle in the Middle East. As Tiamat's destruction is virtually identical to the book of Revelation's description of Satan as "a huge dragon, flaming red ... whose tail swept a third of the stars from the sky and hurled them down to the earth" (Revelation 12:3-4), is it possible Revelation is telling the story of a *past* event?

Perhaps the most well-known (and least understood) image from the Christian prophecies is this Beast who will rule during the time of the Christian tribulation. Frequently it is associated with Babylon. What is *Babylon*?

In Psalm 89:10-11 the seat of Babylon is called *Rahab*: "Thou hast *broken Rahab to pieces*, as one that is slain; thou hast scattered thine enemies with thy strong arm. The heavens are thine, the earth also is thine..."

"By his wisdom he cut Rahab to pieces. By his breath the skies became fair; his hand pierced the gliding serpent" (Job 26:12-13).

In the book of Revelation (17:1-5), we learn of Mystery Babylon the Great:
• a great whore that sitteth upon many waters,
• who has a golden cup in her hand (*the Cup of Destiny?*)
• with seven heads and ten horns,
• with whom the kings of earth fornicate.

From these accounts are we to deduce that Tiamat, or one of her satellites, was also known as Rahab, the seat of Babylon?

Is this confirmed in the Sumerian stories (from which the Old Testament stories are derived), where the beast of the Daniel narrative parallels the Sumerian story of the destruction of Tiamat, the great and terrible watery dragon of chaos. In the backstory provided by the Sumerians, Tiamat was a great beast who was attacked by a predatory planet (An/Marduk/Michael).

Tiamat's story may be further alluded to in the Bible in Baal's strange encounter with Mot (or Tiamat?).10 In Canaanite (and Nordic) mythology, Baal was part of a group of Gods. The creator was El or An. El's brother and son was Dagon or Enki, both of whom were depicted as half-man, half-fish. Baal was Enki's son in the Sumerian version of the story where Baal was called Marduk.

I realize following these names is like playing the game "follow the bouncing ball." However, it is imperative that we locate the original versions of this story and understand the mythological meaning of the names of its heroes.

The original version of Baal or Marduk's encounter had been recorded in the Sumerian texts and found its way into the Babylonian creation myth, the *Enuma Elisha*. There we discover that Mot is Tiamat and Marduk is another planet, actually An, home to the An-nun-aki and the other *An* people we have been discussing as the founders of Atlantis. When he rose to power, Marduk carelessly edited the history books, substituting his name for the original gods. In Egypt, we learn that early Egyptians believed they came from Maat (phonetically "mot") and lived by Maat or "truth." The Hebrews called this planet *Mer*, her inhabitants are the mythological *mer-man* -- half-man, half-fish.

LADY LIBERTY

Despite the glaring mythological connections between Bayblon and Tiamat, Babylon has remained a mystery for Biblical scholars and New Age prophecy watchers. She is most often equated with the ten-nation confederation of the revived Roman Empire. Mystery Babylon is supposed to use those ten "Roma" nations as a means to rise to power

This is interesting considering Winston Churchill traced the mutating British folksoul from Greece, and Rome to America. Does this make America Babylon, and the revived Roman Empire of prophecy?

Mystery Babylon, we are told, is a whore who will guide the governments of the world during the End Time. In her hand she holds a golden cup. Is this the *Cup of Destiny* or Holy Grail, one of the four treasures of An, and one of the primary occult images of WW II and of New Age politics?

Interestingly, a Frenchman, Auguste Bartholdi, sculpted a statue of Mystery Babylon's exact description: the Statue of Liberty. It was placed in New York harbor. She wears a Roman toga. In her hand she holds a stone book. Her official name is "Liberty Enlightening the World."

There are some unusual occult facts concerning Lady Liberty. First, she wears the seven-rayed crown of the Pleiades. Is this by coincidence or by design? Interestingly, two other famous women wore seven-rayed crowns.

The Egyptians depicted Seshet, the wife of Thoth, the founding father of Egypt, with the same seven-rayed crown.

Mary Magdelen, whom the Church Fathers called a whore, but whom Jesus, who founded a new nation of Christians, called his chief disciple, was cured from possession by seven demons. Could Jesus' "cure" have been a fantastic tale of the Pleiades?

Is this the connection with the seven-rayed crown?

One of the most fascinating occult visions of Lady Liberty was that attributed to George Washington, which the founding father of America allegedly had while at Valley Forge in 1777. Things looked dire for Washington and his army, whom he sometimes called "Christian soldiers." They were starving and cold. Washington was known to spend enormous amounts of time alone, in prayer. One night, while in his tent, a beautiful woman appeared to him (thought to be the Goddess of Liberty) and revealed to him three visions of the future of the United States. Each vision dealt with a challenge to the growth of America.

At the end of the third vision the Goddess of Liberty is said to have said to Washingon, "Son of the Republic, what you have seen is thus interpreted: Three great perils will come upon the Republic. The most fearful is the third, but the whole world united shall not prevail against her. Let every child of the Republic learn to live for God, his land, and the union."11

The three challenges have been interpreted as the American Revolution, the Civil War, and a future crisis in America.

Notes:

1. Dr. E.C. Krupp *Beyond the Blue Horizon* (New York, Oxford University Press, 1991) p. 250
2. George Hunt Williamson *Secret Places of the Lion* (Rochester, VT, Destiny Books, 1958)
3. D.S. Allan & J.B. Delair *Cataclysm* (Santa Fe, Bear & Co., 1997) p. 220
4. Zecharia Sitchin *The Twelfth Planet* (New York, Avon Books, 1976) 5. Ibid.
6. Ibid.
7. Ibid.
8. Robert Graves & Raphael Patai *Hebrew Myths* (New York, Anchor Books, 1964) p. 31
9. Daniel 7:8
10. John Gray, *Near Eastern Mythology*, p. 28
11. Robert Hieronimus, Ph.D. *America's Secret Destiny* (Rochester, Vermont, Destiny Books, 1989)

CHAPTER TWELVE

TIAMAT: THE MOMENT OF TRUTH

A hundred years ago few knew the story of the destruction of Tiamat. In the 1840's the Germans, seeking to prove their Aryan nation theory and that their god-kings were blond Atlanteans from the Atlantic shores of Europe, found this story while digging in the sands of Iran and Iraq. Libraries and museums throughout the world are now in the possession of over 500,000 artifacts, drawings and historical texts.

What if it were proven these artifacts reveal the Sumerian stories, including the recollection of the horrifying planetary holocaust on Tiamat, were actual events?

Suppose these stories present a rather startling, spine tingling, version of the beginnings of humankind and our future? Today, would we not face a moment of truth?

What might the impact be on New Age politics if millions of Muslims, Jews and Christians were to suddenly understand the story of Tiamat and discover that the End Time prophecies they have grown to love and fear are actually the *history* of events from the distant past? What if it was discovered all the souls on earth truly did come from the same pure place?

From this brief introduction to the story of Tiamat we can see the value of tracing Biblical stories (and especially prophecies) to their origins. Otherwise do we not run the risk of becoming victims of the children's game of telephone in which we inherit garbled messages that lose more (or gain more) of their original meaning with each generation?

As we further explore the Alien Book of Genesis in the pages to come, it may be interesting to do so with a question in mind. That is this; What might the impact be on your world view, or on New Age politics, if we were to discover that, in occult terms, the Holy War of WW II had its roots in the celestial war between the dragon Tiamat and An (Orion or Aryan)?

Certainly, if we have factions at war, we have leaders. How would it change our world view if we were to learn that these stories not only introduced the leader of one of these warring factions by name, Enki, but they also told his remarkable story?

Further what if this story details his role as the missing link in the evolution of humanity?

ENKI: THE MISSING LINK

Some 450,000 years ago, says the historical accounts of the Sumerians, a group of extraterrestrials called *An-nun-aki* – "those from heaven to earth came," splashed down in the Persian Gulf and established a colony called E.RI.DU ("Home in Faraway Built")1 on its shores in present day Iraq.

They were led by EN.KI ("Lord Earth" or "Lord of the Waters")2 and came to earth (called *Ki* by the Sumerians, *Ta-Meri* by the Egyptians) on a rescue mission.

Today, few people are as advanced in their assessment of the Sumerian writings as Oriental and Sumerian scholar Zecharia Sitchin. Using the Old Testament as a reference point, and a bottomless fascination with the strange world of the Shining Ones that drove him into history books ever since he was a child, Sitchin devoted over thirty years to researching and synthesizing the archaeology and history of this era in human history.

While others read the Sumerian tablets metaphorically, the clever, open-eyed scholar Sitchin perceived them as a kind of ancient *New York Times*, believing they recounted factual events. From this he concluded that earth was visited long ago by beings from An and that a person called Enki was the active presence or *Word* alluded to in Genesis as the creator of mankind. Further, he was one of the Shining Ones.

According to Sitchin, Enki and the gods came to earth to mine gold (viewed dualistically, gold is the occult symbol for soul). When the gods tired of their work, they revolted.

As a solution, Enki genetically altered early man to become slave workers.

Later, he implanted highly evolved souls in these beings, and put humanity on the path to its present evolutionary stage.

We want to pay attention to this story, for some believe this soulsphere reincarnated during WW II.

ENKI'S WORLD

Before examining the researches of Mr. Sitchin and Enki's world, it is important to note that the ramifications of the disclosure of his research were both immediate and overwhelming to New Age politics.

In 1981, just five years after the publication of his first book, *The Twelfth Planet*, astronomers from NASA (among whose founding members were prominent former German scientists) and the US Marine Observatory in Washington D.C. were actively searching for this mysterious planet An (and presumably her alleged inhabitants).

Simultaneously, geneticists backed by billions of dollars in public research money began decoding the Book of Life, our DNA, possibly in search of Enki's, the genetic artist's, "signature". (In 1997, the first alarm bells rang in the world press when it was announced that geneticists possessed the technology to clone a human being.)

In 1982, the space telescope IRAS (infrared astronomical station) saw what had not been seen for perhaps two thousand years. On December 30, 1983 the world press reported that the advanced space telescope:

"Discovered a celestial body in the direction of the constellation Orion, which possibly is as big as the gigantic Jupiter and perhaps so close to the earth that it could belong to our solar system.... When IRAS researchers saw the mysterious celestial body and calculated that it was possibly eighty billion kilometers away from earth, they speculated that it is moving towards earth."[3]

In 1987, NASA confirmed what the ancient Sumerians knew: *"an eccentric tenth planet orbits the Sun."* (It is the twelfth planet if you count the Sun and moon.)

Sitchin's research reveals the An civilization is a galactic civilization a few hundred years in advance of our own New Age science, and possibly even our science fiction. 450,000 years ago An could literally reach out into the stars to purloin whatever resources they required and busily colonized other worlds including Mars, which Sitchin believes was a "midway station" between earth and An.[4]

THE MYSTERY OF MARS

Mars you say? When most WW II generation Americans think of Mars they think of the infamous 1938 Orson Welles radio broadcast, *War of the Worlds*. The program began as a Halloween joke, but wound up scaring the nation half to death, leaving listeners believing the Martians had landed in New Jersey and were devastating the land with death rays.

As the millennium turns, Mars is one of the mysteries of New Age politics. The cosmic rumor mill surrounding the possibility of life on Mars (or some say the conspiracy to cover it up) was stirred in 1976 (America's Bicentennial). NASA's Viking Orbiters sent back images of what looked like huge artificial constructions including the now famous "Face on Mars" from the Cydonia Region of Mars. The discovery of the Face on Mars led many to wonder: if there's a face, is there life on Mars too?

This arresting possibility was ridiculed by many until 1988, when two Russian space probes, Phobos 1 and 2, both headed for Mars, encountered strange fates. During its descent to the surface of Mars Phobos 1 "suddenly and inexplicably" disappeared.

Likewise, Phobos 2 reached Mars, entered its orbit, and actually began beaming pictures of the Red Planet's surface to earth. Within two days Phobos 2 experienced a "sudden interruption of the radio connection." Suddenly, it went into a spin, seemingly "hit by something" as the Russians said. A moment later the probe went inexplicably dead. In 1990, the last two Phobos 2 photos were released. Both pictures showed an elongated object moving toward the probe.

Did missiles (or their equivalent) from the surface of Mars destroy the Russian probes? Or was it pure chance, the equivalent of a cosmic lightning strike? On August 21, 1993, history (or another timely cosmic lightning strike) repeated itself when the American Mars Observer mysteriously went silent during its Martian mission.

During this same time period (1988-1993) mysterious crop circles or pictograms began showing up in the barley fields of England. One of the pictograms has been interpreted as lettering from a mixture of Phoenician, Hebrew and Iberian language. This remarkable inscription is thought to read as "Ptah/Enki, the Creator, wise and kind".5

What if these events are directly connected? Do they play a part in the larger New Age political picture that is presently developing?

DOWN WITH THE EVIL EMPIRE: UP WITH STAR WARS

Even more startling than the confirmation of ancient knowledge was the reaction to this information by New Age political leaders. The entire political philosophy of President Ronald Reagan, for example, changed overnight. Reagan, who previously taunted the Soviet Union as "the Evil Empire", and pressed the button on a five hundred billion dollar plus apocalyptic escalation of the Arms Race with Russia, suddenly and dramatically changed his mind. Why?

Then, Reagan appeared on national television one night. He proposed his trademark "Star Wars" defense system in space. His vision was so simple even a child could illustrate it with crayon drawings (an example of which was featured in a television propaganda campaign aimed at making Star Wars seem like a friendly idea).

Reagan left us spellbound with a beautiful vision. When Soviet ICBM missiles, loaded with their nuclear payloads, were launched at U.S. cities, said Reagan, the "Star Wars" system, parked in near earth orbit, would shoot super-high powered lasers at the missiles, knocking them out of the air.

Millions of Americans, who had ponied up hundreds of billions of dollars to build up their military complex at the cost of their society, nearly choked when Reagan stated that once the gazillion dollar Star Wars system was in place, they would give it to the Russians. Our former enemy would copy the technology, settling the nuclear bet once and for all.

Is this grim New Age reality? Or is this New Age politics at its best: one part high-concept science fiction story and one part inexplicable about faces.

MIRROR WORLD

With Reagan's announcement of Star Wars it was as if we had suddenly switched into a brand new parallel or mirror world America in which everything seemed to be reversed. The freezing tensions of the Cold War instantly thawed as if zapped by a laser.

The triumph of Reagan's warm and fuzzy America over Russia was seen as a triumph of Christianity over cold-hearted Russian atheism. The new America reflected this victory. Reagan, the smiling cowboy in the white hat, became political allies with Russian leader Mikhail Gorbachev, a man who, because of a birthmark on his forehead, many fundamentalist Christians (including several in the White House) were certain was the biblical anti-Christ.

Why the about face? What force flipped the switch? Could it be the same inspiration behind Star Wars? Could news of a potential discovery of An and the possibility that it or Mars is inhabited by a superior, technologically advanced (though psychologically flawed) civilization, have been the baptismal wisdom for Reagan's dramatic New Age conversion? Did Ronald Reagan read the Alien Book of Genesis?

THE GREAT COMMUNICATOR'S GREAT MESSAGE

For those who were unaware of the flood of discoveries and bizarre occurrences in space, Reagan's statements at the Summit talks with Gorbachev soon after the revelation of the existence of An might sound like the meanderings of a space case. To those "in the know" however, they may be the greatest message the Great Communicator ever delivered.

Said Reagan:
"How easy his task and mine might be in these meetings that we held if suddenly there were a threat from some other species from another planet outside in the Universe. We would forget all the little local differences that we have between our countries, and we would find out once and for all that we really are human beings here on this earth together."

The Presidential Guru Reagan would repeat this New Age message:
- at a Summit in Geneva in 1985,
- in his address before the United Nations in 1987,
- at the Summit at Washington DC in 1987,
- in 1988 at the National Strategic Forum,
- and again in 1988 at the Moscow Summit.

All of this Presidential talk about space aliens, and the noticeable silence on the matter from future Presidents (all the while propaganda campaigns and efforts to obtain up close information about Mars are stepped-up) leads one to wonder: is An on its way to earth?

Are we about to experience a new Atlantean moment?

Why now? Is this what is meant by the "time of the Messiah", or the "dawning of the Heavenly Kingdom on earth"? Is this the Apocalypse, which many associate with the millennium, the appearance of Mystery Babylon and celestial "signs" in the sky?

MARS AND *TITANIC*

Since Reagan's New Age Revolution, America has made enormous advances in its Martian research project. On Independence Day 1997, for example, the Mars Pathfinder finally landed on Mars and began beaming home new maps of the Martian surface. After spending billions of dollars studying how to colonize the Red Planet, NASA now stands on the brink of moving the first fragments of humankind to Mars.

However, is it possible this may be like moving a colony of people to the *Titanic*?

Many scientists now believe that there was once life on Mars -- and some even believe Mars is An, and was left devastated after the collision with Tiamat.

Does this scenario make Mars (or An) a second cosmic Atlantis or *Titanic*, left lifeless after sideswiping an iceberg, the cold-hearted dragon Tiamat?

Having not one but *two* Atlantis's at the same time would really put a twist in things, but it may be what really happened.

In a paper in *Scientific American*, William Hartman, a senior scientist at the Planetary Science Institute in Tuscon, Arizona also speaks of the possibility of a "large interplanetary body" entering our solar system, being torn apart by gravitational forces, and unleashing a catastrophic destruction of life on Mars.

I've already commented on the effects of the possibility of life on Mars on New Age politics. Does Mars also play any role in human mythology and in the occult history of WW II? Yes, indeed.

According to HPB's interpretation of Aryan mythology, the seven Pleiades were the nurses of Mars, the god of war, who commands the armies of heaven.6 What if this army is the fleet of warships which evacuated Tiamat? What if it were the seven heads of the beast? Wouldn't this align Mars with the archangel Michael (aka Marduk), who commands the army of heaven and who killed the dragon of Tiamat?

In *The Secret Doctrine*, HPB also tells us that the Sanskrit word for Mars, *Karttikeya*, is derived from *Krittika*, the Sanskrit word for the Pleiades.7

Rome (or Roma, which was later revived as Britain and America), for another example, is named after Romulus, whose father was Mars. The seven hills upon which Rome was founded correspond with the seven stars of the Pleiades. In Roman mythology, Mars was an agricultural god (like Osiris) before he became the god of war.8 This suggests Mars may have indeed been a living, green planet at one time, as scientists suspect.

But then, a cataclysmic change occurred. *Mars Gradivus* "to grow" became *Mars Gradivus* "to march": soil became spoil.9 That Mars was once a living planet is reinforced in the name Mars, from the root *mar*, "to shine."10 Like Marduk (who is also Baal, the Lord), Romulus was originally the Sun and the son of the union of Juno, the queen of heaven, with a mystic "flower," or tender of flowers, a gardener.

Interested researchers will find astonishing reading in astronomer Richard Hoagland's controversial analysis of alleged building activities on Mars, including the alleged pyramid complex in the Cydonia Region of the Red Planet. In his *Monuments on Mars*,11 Hoagland assembles a variety of well-researched viewpoints of astronomers and scientists to prove this region on Mars was arranged according to precise laws of harmonic geometry.

What message, if any is contained in the observation, made by Hoagland and his associates, that identical laws and plans were followed for the construction of similar ancient complexes on earth, for example, Avebury, England and the Great Pyramid?

Much of the recent controversy around the possibility of extraterrestrial life has focused on the issue of the impossible distances between stars and planets. What would happen to that debate if it turns out the survivors of Tiamat are living in enormous pod-like craft within our own solar system?

One thing is certain. The truth is out there.

KINGU AND THE STONES OF DESTINY

What if the realization that Tiamat's total destruction was imminent provoked not only a mass evacuation of the planet, but also explains why Tiamat made her satellite, Kingu, the captain in this battle?

Could it be that in an attempt to salvage the knowledge and enlightenment of their civilization, the rulers of Tiamat moved the Tablets of Destiny or *Stones of Destiny* to Kingu, empowering him?

According to Sitchin, An (or Mars) had designs on (and even took control of) these Stones. Some interpreters suggest An's destruction of Tiamat was done out of jealousy, as in the myth of the Mother Eve's sons Cain and Abel. Tiamat had embarrassed An and chosen rulership by another -- Kingu.

Significantly, Kingu is identified with our own desolate Moon and the Moon God, whom the Chaldeans called Sin, from which Moses' Mount Sinai derives its name. Since the Egyptian word for law and truth is Maat, as in Tiamat, does this suggest the Tablets of the Law given to Moses on Sinai may, in reality, be the Stones of Destiny of Tiamat?

Throughout ancient times, and even as we shall see in modern history, the Stones of Destiny given to Kingu have been highly contested and widely sought after items. They are one of the four Atlantean power tools, which also include the Sword of Destiny, the Cup of Destiny and the Spear of Destiny.

From the Alien Book of Genesis, the *Enuma Elisha*, we learn the prequel to Genesis and the other four books of the Old Testament which recall a primordial Star War over the possession of the Stones of Destiny (of Tiamat).

As we'll soon see, numerous earthly battles, including WW II, have also been fought over control of all four of these extraterrestrial treasures or power tools. Is it possible these power tools correspond with the souls and their allegiance?

In the next chapter we shall examine this question.

Notes:

1. Zecharia Sitchin *The Twelfth Planet* (New York, Avon Books, 1976) p. 288
2. Ibid. p. 102
3. Michael Hesemann *The Cosmic Connection* (Bath, UK, Gateway Books, 1996) p. 102
4. Zecharia Sitchin *Genesis Revisted* (New York, Avon Books, 1990) p. 232.
5. Ibid. p. 130
6. Helena P. Blavatsky *The Secret Doctrine* (New York, The Theosophical Publishing Company, 1888) II, p. 549
7. Ibid. II, p. 549
8. Stuart Gordon *The Encyclopedia of Myths and Legends* (London, Headline, 1993) p. 442
9. Ibid. p. 442
10. Ibid. p. 442
11. Richard C. Hoagland *The Monuments on Mars* (Berkely, North Atlantic Books, 1987)

CHAPTER THIRTEEN

THE SOULS OF THE DAMNED

While researching the ancient myths of Tiamat, a startling question began to emerge: given that the ancients appeared to be discussing the existence of soulspheres, was it possible that during the cataclysm on Tiamat that a soulsphere (or possibly multiple soulspheres) collapsed?

When one half of the planet was blown into the solar system, the one later to become earth, was it possible that there were souls trapped in the newly created earth's bowels (that part of the Goddess Tiamat's body that remained)? Did these souls need to be rescued?

The basis for these questions is the Israelite legend of the Temple of Solomon, Sumerian and Egyptian legends, as well as the Mandaen literature, which refers to the serpent-shaped souls of the damned who inhabit the Sheol.1

The *Mandaens* (Man D'ans or Man of Dan) were the Gnostic followers of John the Baptist, who worshipped a savior known as the King of Light or *Manda d'Hayye* ("the Knowledge of Life"). A few of their descendents still live in Iraq. These mystics wrote of the Fifth Earth, *Arqa* (which reminds us of the ark of Noah), which contains Gehenna (where the wicked are confined) and its seven layers.2

The highest of these is *Sheol*, which John's followers embroidered with striking features, saying it is the belly of the Great Fish, the Underworld, the Pit.3

We call this "Pit" the earth.

The Mandaens believed a messiah would appear who would construct a resurrection machine to fish these souls out of the Pit and return them home.4 The idea that Jesus would "crown" Mary Magdalen with a story about the destruction of a home world in the seven stars of the Pleiades does not sound so far-fetched any more in light of what John's followers believed, does it?

We have already encountered this Savior or "Fisher of Souls" several times under other guises:

- In Sumeria he was called Enki or Ea ("Lord Earth" or "Lord of the Sacred Eye, Lord of the Underworld").
- In Egypt he was Osiris, whose logo F.D.R. placed on the back of the one dollar bill and which symbolizes the divine destiny of America.
- In Babylon, he was called Hani-Oannes, who was half-man, half-fish.

One Chaldean priest who wrote a history of his people, Berossus (c. 300 B.C.), tells of no less than six appearances of Oannes in the ancient world. Oannes rose from the sea, from the "heart of the ocean" (coincidentally the name of the prized jewel in the 1997 movie *Titanic*, and also a description of Tula). He continuously reincarnated during successive periods to rescue souls from the Great Fish: the Underworld, earth. It was he who created the human body as a resurrection machine to lift the embedded souls out of the Pit of earth.

A SERPENT NEEDS A TREE

Ancient teachings reveal that a serpent (or soul) cannot stand erect of its own accord. By analogy, a serpent needs a tree to wind its way up toward the world of spirit. Thus, the human spine represents a tree on which the spiritual life force or soul can ascend. And thus comes the association with the serpent and the Tree of Life.

Unless it has a vehicle in which it can ascend, a serpent is doomed to isolation in the lower worlds. Likewise, a body without spiritual animation is a meaningless heap of chemical compounds.

According to Sitchin's research,5 Enki's additional symbol was the serpent, presumably for its ability to climb the Tree of Life, but also for its ablity to shed its skin and, therefore, to achieve a sort of immortality by successively reincarnating.

As Enki was a biospiritual genetic engineer, the serpent symbol would have been appropriate for his profession in ancient times, just as it is appropriate today for use by the American Medical Association.

In fact, Enki may be the "first healer" on earth.

It is worthwhile to note that one of Enki's earthly hobbies was sailing. This detail is fascinating given its association with the Pleiades, which means "to sail". Sitchin makes it sound like this has to do with sailing a boat on a lake.

Fascinatingly, however, the imagery of a *soul* traversing the watery regions of the underworld by boat or ark runs throughout Egyptian mythology. *Spiritus* or soul primarily means breath or wind.6 Hieroglyphically, the sail signifies air, wind or breath and often is found in the hieroglyphs for the gods.7

Is this why the soul is symbolized by an object such as the sail, which catches the wind of God?

The boat is another powerful image of the soul. Remember, the Egyptians believed the divine beings sailed on the waters of the Great River of the Milky Way. In order to join them, does our soul need a boat?

According to Sitchin's research, Enki was assisted by his chief nurse, the goddess Ninharsag, called "lady of life," in a series of genetic experiments which resulted in the alteration of *home sapien* to *homo erectus*.8 Is the present forms of humanity a resurrection machine capable of manifesting this boat or ark?

At Eridu, their Edenic research lab, the two scientists, and lovers, conducted extensive genetic research.9 The Bible calls the serpent who tempted Eve *Nahash*, a Hebrew word meaning "serpent," but literally, says Sitchin, it means "He Who Solves Secrets."10 A related word means soul. Is this the source of the connection between serpent and soul?

THE FISH MAN AND THE BIRTH OF NAZI

Interestingly, Ninharsag saw her role as that of healing Enki, the Serpent or Soul. In this way she shares with Isis the archetypal story of the goddess who heals her mate. In the story of Isis and Osiris, the king was cut into pieces and floated down the "river." Thoth assisted Isis in the search for and reassembly of these pieces.

Let us suppose the story of the dismemberment and reassembly of Osiris is a cleverly concealed account of a soulsphere that was constructed in one part of the galaxy, and then floated down the river of the Milky Way, and reconstructed on earth. Could it be Ninharsag's "healing" of Enki and Isis' resurrection of Osiris are recollections of similar stories?

In order to heal Enki the goddess Ninharsag created eight children (prototype humans), one who was named *Nazi*. This is believed to be the first use of this word in mythology.

In the Egyptian version of the story, Osiris was cut into fourteen pieces (the soulsphere dismantled) by his brother Set and needed to be healed (made "holy" or "whole"). Isis (Ninharsag) reassembled (or resurrected) him after she found his body embedded in a column or tree at Byblos (later Babel or Babylon).

This column is his djed pillar, the Egyptian Tree of Life. It is the model for the later Tower or Column of Babel. Statues of Enki/Dagon show him depicted as a merman (*mer* means sea) half-man, half-fish, or as a serpent-man.11 As the god of the Dogon tribe of Africa he was known as Oannes -- the Dove. Statues found of him depict Oannes as a muscular, bearded man wearing a fish skin and holding a basket in one hand and an object which looks like the Key of Life in the other. His fish-skin is removable at will, suggesting it is similar to a diver's wet suit. A statue of an identically clad god-man was found in the vicinity of the Yucatan in Mexico in temples dedicated to the god Quetzalcoatl ("He Whose Home is Water").12

The Dogon claim Oannes came from Sirius to aid mankind, primarily by teaching the art of agriculture or gardening.13 This links him with the Egyptian savior Osiris, with Mars, and with the three belt stars of Orion, which point to Sirius.

It is also possible he is the Fish Man, one of the vehicles, which emerged from the destruction of Tiamat, and sought safety in the vicinity of Sirius at the time of the cataclysm.

Astronomer Carl Sagan hotly contested the primitive Dogon's controversial testimony, stating they knew that Sirius had a companion star, invisible to the naked eye, small, extremely dense and heavy, which circles Sirius A in a fifty-year orbit.

They also said there was a third Sirian star the called the "*emme ya*". Sirius B was not discovered by western science until 1862 and not photographed until 1970. The Dogon said Oannes came to earth in an "ark". The symbol for his name, a fish, is drawn so that it simultaneously evokes the image of a bearded man and a rocket, his ark.

Like Osiris, whom the Egyptians said came from Sirius and taught agriculture, and the Dogon fish god, the Philistine god Dagon was also a god who taught the art of growing vegetation, a gardener.14

While he is considered a vegetation-bearing good guy in most ancient traditions, his publicity coordinator apparently dropped the ball with the editors of the Bible. Christianity cast him along with Hades as the ruler of Hell.

The trashing of Oannes or Dagon by Christianity is bizarre (or an example of ancient power politics, just as the trashing of the Dogon's advanced star knowledge by Sagan is an example of egotistical New Age politics). It's bizarre because John the Baptist was also called *Johannes* ("the Dove"), after Oannes, the Fish Man.15

Should we trash John too?

Further, as the King Fisher or Fisher King of the Holy Grail myths, Jesus' primary symbol is the fish.16 Jesus is also associated with the Phoenix bird,17 making him symbolically the fish-bird-man. Also, Jesus' symbol, the vesica piscis or fish, is a copy of the ancient Egyptian hieroglyph for the heron, the bird of light.

Do these mythological connections implicate Jesus in this Sirius-based plan for the development of humanity?

THE SECRET OF THE PILLARS

The intrigue increases. The Mandaens were an offshoot of the Essenes,18 the priesthood which raised Jesus and out of which Jesus preached. Their Dead Sea Scrolls (discovered in 1947 and instantly covered up by many mainstream Judeo-Christian scholars) are believed to be full of sensitive details about the Essenes and their life at Qumran.

In the Scrolls we find a tittillating reference to "*the secret of the pillars.*" Are these the very same pillars which created the arch of peace at Solomon's Temple?

According to Scroll scholar John Allegro,19 the nature of this secret is embedded in the word Qumran. The verbal root of "Qumran," he says, is "vault, arch or doorway".20 The Essenes who lived in Qumran associated themselves with this doorway.

Could this doorway be a (star) gateway leading to (or from) other worlds, perhaps Sirius or Tula? Was this doorway kept secret because it leads to immortality?

The good news in the Scrolls about the doorway and the pillars possibly linking earth and heaven should have made global headlines. But it didn't. We could be in the process of opening this doorway in preparation for the return of Jesus and a mass ascension. But we're not.

Instead, New Age politics came into play. The Scrolls were slammed, the faithful encouraged by carpet-bagging evangelists to avoid them like the plague, and the originals tucked away from prying hands under glass in Jerusalem.

One additional reason for the sensitivity with which the Scrolls have been treated may be that the people who wrote these documents anticipated the arrival of not one, but two, messiahs working together.21 This blows the lone savior theory of modern Christianity out of the water.

Another concern over the Scrolls may be over their revelation of the secret identity of "the other savior" who is believed to be the founder of the Essenes, the mysterious Teacher of Righteousness, or Melchizedek.22

As it happens, another name for this hidden god-man is none other than Oannes, Osiris or Enki. In the Essene scheme of things is it possible that Jesus emerges as a "co-savior" rather than as *the* Savior as in the Roman editor's version of these events? Did F.D.R. understand this in 1935 when he placed this god-being's logo on the back of the one dollar bill? If he is not *the* Savior, what role did Jesus play exactly?

MELCHIZEDEK

The Melchizedek Scroll, a rare Dead Sea Scroll, offers an amazing identification of Melchizedek with the promised Messiah or Fish Man. Some of the amazing phrases used to identify Melchizedek include: the Messiah, the Anointed One who proclaims Salvation, the Prince, the Judge, the Avenger, the Messenger of God and Michael the Great Prince.[23] Many of these names are associated with Jesus. According to the Gnostics, the key difference was that Melchizedek was the savior for angels, Jesus came to save humans.

In *The Bloodline of the Holy Grail*, Laurence Gardner offers an intriguing explanation for the origins of the name Melchizedek. He claims the name is actually Michael-Zadok. The line of Zadok were priest kings descended from the Archangel Michael.

If this is so, it seems Oannes appeared before and after the flood to lead humanity.

As the Michael, he both slayed the dragon Tiamat, and as Melchizedek was a biospiritual engineer, sent to rescue her survivors.

This may not be as strange as it sounds. Suppose Enki were a real scientist. What we are asked to believe in the myths of Atlantis is that this civilization was destroyed when its scientists (or a scientist) botched genetics and the power of light. Suppose Enki lived on Tiamat (he is considered her "spouse" in the Babylonian version of the story) and he was partly responsible for blowing up the planet.

Would it not make sense that he, like Michael, would be both the dragon slayer and the redeemer sent to clean up his mess?

THE FISH MAN IS THE GREEN MAN

In Egypt, Osiris was the name of the god being who came from the stars to bring new life to earth and clean up the mess of Tiamat. In India he is the god of love, Kama, who also is considered to be the god of growth.[24] Both Osiris and Kama were shown with green faces, setting them apart as ascended beings known as the Green Man or the Gardener.

The Greeks recorded that the Green Man is the immortal ruler of Hyperboria,[25] the Greek name for heaven. At the center of Hyperboria is a mecca for learning called Tula. Does this mean the Green Man or Gardener is the King of

Tula? (This also fits with the story of Enki, who is believed to have originally come from An/Tula and "married" Tiamat.) The Green Man or Gardener is a powerful mythic image known to every civilization. He is depicted with vegetatation symbolizing the vril, Life Force or Word of God spewing from his mouth. He is known by many names throughout the world: Adonis (Greek, Roman), "the Lord," and Dionysus are a few of his names. 26

Unbeknownst to many, it is quite possible this figure was present on Easter morning along with Jesus.

JESUS AND THE GREEN MAN

On Easter morning, in the Book of John, Jesus appeared to Mary Magdalen along with a mysterious figure that she called "the Gardener." Evangelists and scholars alike assume this Gardener is Jesus. What if it is not Jesus? Have you ever since a depiction of Jesus with his face painted green?

If he is not Jesus, can we identify the Gardener? Yes. In the Islamic tradition, a highly revered mythological figure is depicted wearing a shimmering green robe, and is called the "Guardian of the Source of the Waters of Immortality." He is called *Al Khidr*, the Green Man or the Evergreen One. The Islamic people believed Al Khidr was Elijah!27 Didn't Jesus say John the Baptist was the reincarnated Elijah?28 John, through his name Johannes, is also connected with the Fish Man, Oannes, linking him further with the Gardener.

If John is the Green Man, why didn't the Gospels simply say so? Or, when they said the Gardener was there, did they expect us to understand what they were talking about?

If it were an intentional omission, why would the editors of the New Testament story of Jesus omit a crucial detail such as this? Are there any other significant details about John the Baptist, which have been omitted? Is so, why?

It is vital that we attempt to piece together Jesus' story. If John the Baptist is the King of Tula, this may also make him the king of Mongolia (the site of the original earthly Tula), the personage whom F.D.R. was seeking and honoring by placing the All-Seeing Eye on the back of the one dollar bill. This logo, which we have called the symbol of Osiris, the Green Man or Gardener, is also John's logo.

It is crucial that we question the identity of the Green Man or Gardener for another reason. When the Russians invaded Berlin in 1945 they found six Tibetan monks lying dead in a ritual suicide circle. In the center was a monk wearing green gloves. It is said this "Monk with the Green Gloves" was in constant contact with Hitler. He was called the "Guardian of the Key" to the Nazi paradise at the center of the earth.29

THE GREEN MEN AND THE NAZIS

The sinister academic Dr. Karl Haushofer is said to have introduced the Monk with the Green Gloves to Hitler. This fiendish mind is credited with inventing the idea of "Geo-Politics"30 -- the idea that a nation or soul group can control the world if it can control the destiny of its own people.

The Nazis instantly incorporated the doctrine of Geopolitics into their religion. In Haushofer's opinion, after he conquered Europe and Central Asia, his homeland, Aryan man could rule the world.

Haushofer is believed to have been a member of the inner circle of the Thule Society and a secretive Japanese society, the Green Dragon Society.31 It is through him and his Eastern contacts that Hitler was said to have contacted two separate orders of black magicians. These secretive orders: the Order of Shambhallah and the Order of Agarthi allegedly operated in underground cities in Central Asia.

Beginning in 1926, Hitler is said to have sent Nazi expeditions to Tibet every year until 1942. During these expeditions Hitler's agents are supposed to have met with representatives of both orders. Only one -- the order of Agharthi -- would do business with Hitler. The Order of Shambhalla claimed Hitler was not materialistic enough. Besides, they were already working with "certain lodges" in Britain and America.

Was this "certain lodge" Nicholas Roerich and his gang?

Was meeting with either of these two secret Orders a contributing factor in explaining how Roerich could persuade F.D.R. to send agents to Mongolia seeking Jesus (or possibly John the Baptist, the Green Man or Gardener)?

Ferdinand Ossendowski and Nicholas Roerich both claimed Agharti was founded 60,000 years ago by a holy man and his tribe,32 the Green Men,33 who evacuated the surface of the earth through tunnel systems they created. These tunnels are alleged to be interconnected with other points on the planet, including North and South America -- Turtle Island, upon whose back they later re-established civilization.

According to occult sources, the Order of Agarthi were specialists in setting-up dictatorial regimes.34 These magicians sent a contingency of their membership to Germany to assist Hitler.

The Nazis are reported to have called them "The Society of the Green Men." Himmler featured their teachings in his *Ahnenerbe*, the SS "Department of Ancestral Heritage," which was formed to trace the origins and lifestyles of the ultimate Aryan man.35

The results were less than spectacular.

Notes:

1. G.R.S. Mead *The Gnostic John the Baptizer: Selections from the Mandaean John-Book* (Kila, MT, Kessinger Publishing) p. 13
2. Robert Graves & Raphael Patai *Hebrew Myths* (New York, Anchor Books, 1964) p. 35
3. Ibid. p. 35
4. Terrence McKenna
5. Zecharia Sitchin *Genesis Revisted* (New York, Avon Books, 1990) p. 202
6. *Webster's Dictionary* (New York, Publisher's International Press, 1979) II, p. 1751
7. E.A. Wallis Budge *The Gods of the Egyptians* (New York, Dover Publications, 1969)
8. Zecharia Sitchin *The Twelfth Planet* (New York, Avon Books, 1976) p. 105
9. Ibid. p. 348
10. Zecharia Sitchin *Genesis Revisited* (New York, Avon Books, 1990) p. 202
11. Robert K.G. Temple *The Sirius Mystery* (Rochester, VT, Destiny Books, 1976)
12. Maurice M. Cotterel *The Supergods* (London, Thorsons, 1997) p. 71
13. Ibid.
14. Reader's Digest *Who's Who in the Bible* (Pleasantville, NY, Reader's Digest, 1994) p. 67
15. Ibid. p. 18
16. Laurence Gardner*Bloodline of the Holy Grail* (Rockport, MA., Element, 1996) p. 130
17. J.C. Cooper *Symbolic and Mythological Animals* (London, Aquarian Press, 1992) p. 182
18. Hugh Schonfield *The Passover Plot* (Rockport, MA., Element, 1965) p. 208
19. John M. Allegro *The Dead Sea Scrolls and the Christian Myth* (Great Britain, Prometheus Books, 1984).
20. Ibid.
21. Christopher Knight & Robert Lomas *The Hiram Key* (Rockport, Ma., Element, 1996) p. 209
22.Ibid. p. 53
22. Grant R. Jeffrey *Messiah* (New York, Bantam, 1991) p. 341
24. Janet and Stewart Farrar *The Witches' God* (Custer, WA., Phoenix Publishing, 1989) p. 192
25. William Anderson *Green Man: The Archetype of our Oneness with the Earth* (London, Harpercollins, 1990)

26. Ibid.
27. Stuart Gordon *The Encyclopedia of Myths and Legends* (London, Headline, 1993) p. 397
28. Matthew 11:13-15, 17:10-13, Mark 9:11-13
29. Peter Moon *The Black Sun* (New York, Sky Books, 1997) p. 213
30. Dusty Sklar *The Nazis and the Occult* (New York, Dorset Press, 1977) p. 62-69
31. Walter Kafton-Minkel *Subterranean Worlds* (Port Townsend, WA., Loompanics, 1989) p. 225
32. Alec Maclellan *The Lost World of Agharti* (London, Souvenier Press, 1982) p. 216
33. Ibid. p. 168-172
34. Trevor Ravesncroft *The Spear of Destiny* (York Beach, ME., Samuel Weiser, 1991)
35. Ibid. p. 225

CHAPTER FOURTEEN

DISTURBING THE UNIVERSE

The legends of the Green Man, his connection with Tula and John the Baptist, and Hitler and F.D.R.'s possible search for this god-being in Asia compel us to look deeper at the stories of Enki, the original Green Man or Gardener, found in the Alien Book of Genesis.

In these stories, the Gardener emerges as biospiritual genetic engineer who cultivated human DNA in order to create a resurrection machine -- a flow-er or flower of souls -- designed to rescue the stranded souls from the holocaust on Tiamat. The Gardener's first creation, these stories inform us, was a robotic type of human called a *lulu*.[1] This was his prototype resurrection machine. (The singular for Enki is used. However, it should be made clear we are likely talking about a group of gods called Enki.)

Early accounts, especially those of Berossus, the Chaldean chronciler, reveal that these master geneticists used earth as a no-holds-barred laboratory interbreeding species from across the animal kingdom in ways that leave modern geneticists foaming at the mouth. Berossus' account corresponds with the Hebrew recollection of *Tebhel*, the Sixth Earth, which arose after Arqa. The seventh earth is called *Hel*.[2]

Berossus lists some of the reported results as being the exotic creatures of myth: centaurs, minotaurs, medusas, griffons, sphinxes, goat-hoofed humans, etc.[3] Other creatures were fantastic, some had the head and body of an ox, but were endowed with human speech. Others were grotesque, having twin heads, four ears and four eyes, twin noses and mouths, four hands and four legs, yet only one trunk. When seated they look like two people; but when they walk, like one. Numerous identical Chaldean, Egyptian and Sumerian reliefs depict these monstrous research subjects being hunted down and exterminated.

The lulu, the first robotic humanoids, were separate from Enki and the other the creator beings. At termination, their souls were programmed to reincarnate (or is it reincarcerate?) on earth. At death, the Shining Ones returned to earth only if they chose, as tulkus.4

Reinforcing the rescue argument is the fact that in the Buddhist tradition these tulkus have vowed not to enter Nirvana or heaven themselves until every other human soul has gone before them. This suggests another distinguishing factor: an advanced moral system.

From the ancient accounts we learn the Shining Ones of Tula excelled the lulu in other ways. They:
- utilized the power of *vril* or life-force energy,
- possessed a precise soul science,
- spoke the Language of the Birds or angels,
- activated their Third or Spiritual Eyes
- reproduced through in vitro fertilization, and
- had a higher vibrational blood running through their veins.

According to Sumerian myth, Enki decided to make a new model of mankind in "the god's image."5 In so doing, he went too far. He ended up disturbing the universe. For in order to create these new beings he imported genetic material to earth. Not just any genetic material either. Enki is accused of bringing genetic material from Tiamat to earth.

Where did he get this material?

Shortly before the destruction of Tiamat she released a satellite, Kingu, our Moon.6 It is from the blood or genetic material of Kingu that the Sumerians claim Enki created this new model human on earth.7 The Chaldeans later changed the name of Kingu to "Sin."8

The enormity of this single name change on human history is beyond comprehension.

When the Christian interpreters came along they repeated the story that we were born in sin. They were entirely accurate in their statement. However, they omitted the fact that Sin referred to the Moon, the source of our genetic material!

Generation after generation of Christians were taught the erroneous idea that we are born ugly and shameful. Adding salt to this cancerous wound is the fact that the word *christos*, the Greek word for the Messiah sent to lead us to the Promised Land, was a term from the goddess religions which originally literally meant "healing moon man."9

If this is so, we must ask, how did we lose so much understanding of our origins?

THE TREE OF LIFE

Accelerating the evolution of homo erectus and leading them to the Tree of Life appears to have been the second part of Enki's rescue plan. According to my interpretation of Egyptian and Sumerian myths concerning this event, this next step called for Enki to bring a second sphere of souls or soulsphere to the newly created earth.

Let us suppose this soulsphere really is a collective Christ soul as myths suggest. Would not awareness of the existence of this soul group inhabiting the earth (not to mention our bodies) be the dread of every earthly regime bent on enslaving humanity? Is this why only a select few initiates appear to have been aware of its existence?

Incredibly, once we begin to look for it, we discover Sumerian and Egyptian creation myths, are filled with the details of how Enki, the Gardener, transferred this soulsphere through the galaxy to the awaiting Tree of Life in the Hall of Osiris underneath the earth.10 In the Egyptian depiction of this device found at Abydos, Egypt, we find a forty foot tall golden pillar, an antenna-looking device. Is it possible this device is one of the two pillars found at the entrance to Solomon's Temple that were used to open gateways to higher realms?

Once the soulsphere arrived on earth, say the myths, the Tree of Life's component power tool, the Key of Life, was used as the conductive force to guide the souls into specific human bodies.11 Enki is depicted by the Sumerians with the Key of Life in hand performing his genetics operations. According to Hebrew legend, the Key of Life was made from a branch that grew on the Tree of Life in the Garden of Eden12 (Atlantis). Can the Key be envisioned as the remote control for operating the Tree of Life?

THE ACT OF LOVE

At first, Enki had to guide the Christ souls into human bodies. Then, he taught the human beings to make love. The souls, free-floating in the energy field of the earth, were attracted by the sexual energy created by lovemaking and attached themselves to the human body. The "Christ soul" would then chase and battle the stranded female soul of Tiamat up the Tree of Life within, the spinal cord.

By this plan, the opposing forces of the two soul currents would cause an expansion and contraction effect, lifting the souls through the spinal cord system. Mystics claim their destination is the mysterious pineal gland near the center of the human brain. "Pineal" is phonetically close to "Penial," the place where in the Bible Jacob said he had seen the doorway to heaven and the face of God. From here the

combined souls could exit the earth through the doorway --
actually a Rainbow Bridge -- and return home. Rescue
complete.

It appears the Key of Life is part genetic and spiritual,
and also part sexual. This sexual aspect of the Key of Life is
called *Tantra*, a magic sex act whereby the Divine Presence or
Holy Spirit is channeled through the interplay between male
and female energies of a couple. Sex magic is considered the
Left Hand path of Tantra.13

Was it used by the Nazis in the hope of creating the
Master Race?

SEX MAGIC AND HOMO NAZI

The SS considered themselves the first stage in a
superhuman mutation,14 *homo Nazi*. One of the occult secrets
omitted from the Nuremberg Trials was the Nazi interest in
occult sex acts designed to bring specific souls to earth.

Himmler motivated SS members by a belief in a coming
utopian society, similar to the Christian New Jerusalem15 -- a
Thousand Years of Peace. They renounced personal identity
for their place in this society.16 In SS training ordinary men
were turned into robotic killing machines, who believed they
were living in the last days. Their "divine mission" was to
fight the Jew, whom they were brainwashed into believing was
Satan in disguise.

At Wewelsburg Castle, the SS Chapel, Himmler made a
12,000 volume occult library available to SS members.17 In
training classes SS members studied material on the Holy
Grail, knighthood, alchemy, and Gnostic history. Sex training
was also part of the curriculum.

Himmler urged elite SS members and older, vigorous
Hitler Youth males to mate with blond females as a duty to
the state to produce Aryan offspring.18 He provided lists of
ancient Nordic cemetaries for fornication. Himmler gave the
impression that when conception took place in these select
cemeteries, babies inherited the spirit of ancient Nordic
heroes.19 Does this suggest Himmler had awareness of the
notion of free-floating souls within a soulsphere?

Suppose certain SS were also taught to combine this
awareness with the art of Tantric sex.

The object of Tantra is to produce a specific spiritual
vibration. Orgasm, as through Tantra, can liberate the soul,
awakening the Divine power within.20 In theory, an awakened
couple's orgasm will attract a Magical Child (or Christ soul)
who leads the human race to the Light. This is one of the
innermost Secrets of the Key of Life.

As in the story of Jesus, a single Christ soul has the ability
to wreak havoc on the existing world order. A battalion of

occult-trained Christ souls, theoretically, could upset the entire apple cart of New Age politics.

Tantra emphasizes the notion that the Key of Life is an inner spiritual process. This idea of awakening latent spiritual power, especially through intercourse, was "too much" for certain early religious authorities to discuss publicly. Mention of this was deliberately removed during the Middle Ages. This assisted the Church in its struggle against contenders to its power. In all mystical traditions it was recognized that it was the female, not the male, who held the keys to awakening the inner spiritual power.21

SEX-POLITICS AND DR. REICH

Hitler was a master of sexual propaganda. He promised the subjugation of woman to man, the enforcement of her economic dependence, and was highly against both birth control and abortion.22

Hitler's propaganda techniques were loaded with sexual imagery. Sex and magic is the basis for all goddess religions, including those of India, Egypt, Greece and pre-Christian Rome. Is this the reason it was fundamental in Nazism?

One who kept a close eye on Hitler's perverted sexual propaganda was Dr. Wilhelm Reich, a genius whose books containing his sex-laced theories concerning the universal "orgone energy" were later burned by the FBI.

Reich claimed to have understood Hitler's techniques of "sex-politics," as he called it.23 A protege of Sigmund Freud, Reich was a practicing psychoanalyst, and master of sexual symbolism. In 1927, Reich published *The Function of the Orgasm*, which proposed that civilization is based on the repression of sexual energy or love energy which creates a barrier to true happiness.

As Reich conceived it, *orgone* or *orgasmic* energy is:24
• present in the atmosphere,
• is related to the Sun,
• is present in all parts of the galaxy like the "ether," and can be drawn in by all organisms.
Further,
• all matter is created from orgone or orgasmic energy,
• it is *the* Life Energy (vril),
• separate streams of orgone energy may be attracted to each other and then superimposed. The superimposition function is held to be the fundamental form of the creative process.

Reich claimed to have isolated vril force or orgone energy in the form of *bions* (vesicles of bio-energy: vril). One form of bions was orgone energy. Reich believed Hitler was using negative sexual energy in his politics. The only political answer to this was positive sex-politics. Reich was personally committed to defeating the Reich by his own brand of sex-politics.25 Claiming only Jesus had anticipated his ideas on sex-politics, Reich set about a crusade teaching the importance of orgasm in uniting body and soul.26

THE SWASTIKA

To combat Hitler, Reich studied the design and history of the swastika cross.27 He concluded that the swastika was the representation of two intertwined bodies (or could it be two intertwined serpents or souls as shown in the caduceus?).

Those whose only understanding of the swastika as the Nazi logo may be surprised to learn that it is one of the oldest symbols on earth. Swastikas appear on Stone Age carvings on mammoth ivory dated from 10,000 B.C., about the time of the sinking of Atlantis.28

Swastikas are among the oldest of Indian symbols. In the 1930's, the Nazis adopted the swastika because they believed it was a "pure Aryan" sign. Sanskrit *svastika* means "so be it" or "amen"29 Among Buddhists, it symbolizes the "key to paradise."30 In Japan, home of the Nordic Japanese, according to Himmler, the "Buddha of Immeasurable Light" wore a left-handed swastika on his breast. In Japan it was an ideogram for "infinity."31

There are two types of swastikas: the left pointing, counter-clockwise or Moon Swastika, and the right-pointing, clockwise version called the Sun Swastika.32 The left pointing was associated with the Left-Hand Path of the Goddess, the right-pointing with the Right-Hand Path of the God. Hindus said the Right-Hand or lunar swastika stood for Kali-Maya, the bride of the Lord of Hosts, symbolized by the Left-Hand.

Maya, the mother of the Buddha, was also a name for one of the seven stars of the Pleiades. Tibetan Buddhists said the right-handed swastika was the Savior, the left-handed swastika meant the magic of Mother Maya.33 Do these connections point us to Enki and his bride, Tiamat, as the source of the swastika?

Notes:

1. Zecharia Sitchin *The Twelfth Planet* (New York, Avon Books, 1976) p. 348
2. Robert Graves & Raphael Patai *Hebrew Myths* (New York, Anchor Books, 1964) p. 35
3. Ibid. p. 346
4. Jocelyn Godwin *Arktos: The Polar Myth* (Grand Rapids, MI, Phanes Press, 1993) p. 71
5. Genesis 5

6. Ibid. p. 220
7. Barbara G. Walker *The Woman's Encyclopedia of Myths and Secrets* (New York, HarperCollins, 1983) p. 508
8. Ibid. p. 940
9. Ibid. p. 464
10. E.A. Wallis Budge *The Gods of the Egyptians Vol. I* (New York, Dover Publications, 1969)
11. Ibid. p. 352
12. Zecharia Sitchin *The Stairway to Heaven* (New York, Avon Books, 1980) p. 108
13. Andre Van Lysebeth *Tantra: The Cult of the Feminine* (York Beach, ME, Samuel Weiser, 1995)
14. Dusty Sklar Dusty Sklar *The Nazis and the Occult* (New York, Dorset Press, 1977) p. 89
15. Ibid. p. 95
16. Ibid. p. 95
17. Ibid. p. 100
18. Ibid. p. 113
19. Ibid. p. 114
20. Dr. John Mumford *Ecstacy Through Tantra* (St. Paul, MN, Llewellyn Publications, 1994)
21. Ibid. p. 17
22. Myron Sharaf *Fury On Earth: A Biography of Wilhelm Reich* (New York, St. Martin's, 1983) p. 165
23. Ibid. p. 166
24. W. Edward Mann *Orgone, Reich and Eros: Wilhelm Reich's Theory of Life Energy* (New York, Simon & Schuster, 1973)
25. Ibid. p. 166
26. Stuart Gordon *The Paranormal: An Illustrated Encyclopedia* (London, Headline, 1992) p. 573
27. Ibid. p. 166
28. Barbara G. Walker *The Woman's Encyclopedia of Myths and Secrets* (New York, HarperCollins, 1983) p. 964
29. Ibid.
30. Ibid.
31. Ibid.
32. Ibid.
33. Ibid.

CHAPTER FIFTEEN

BIG BRAINS

Modern science now believes homo erectus evolved from the apes about six million years ago. This creature spent most of the next six million years spiritually asleep. Then, suddenly, as if by the wave of a magic wand, about 200,000 years ago, homo sapiens abruptly replaced homo erectus.[1]

The separating factor was a 50 percent increase in brain size,[2] including the addition of a spectacular neo-cortex or new brain, language ability, a sleeker anatomy and a head which is proportionately much too big and heavy for this sleeker body. This big new brain required a lot of armor to protect it.

This remarkable increase in hardware also represented a spiritual awakening and a capacity to "run" far more complex software. To this day we do not approach anything near the top levels of our mental capability.

The timing of these events correspond with the Sumerian chronology and the time when the Sumerians claim Enki, the Gardener, performed the genetic alteration which activated more of our brain's potential.

Does the increase in brain size have anything to do with lifting the stranded souls out of the Pit of earth?

Could it be that it was a hardware upgrade for running more complex spiritual software?

THE RAINBOW: E.T. FON HOME

At the apex of the Key of Life mystery in the Tibetan tradition, and all occult traditions, is the creation of the *antekeranna* -- the Rainbow Bridge of consciousness between earth and Tula. Was the size of the human brain increased in order to hold spiritual software for creating this bridge of consciousness?

I often wonder if this Rainbow Bridge is truly just an immaterial or spiritual bridge. Here is why. The boat-shaped Ark, or crescent Moon, which the goddess Diana wore was believed to represent the container of the seeds of life. The Celts called Diana's container, cup or vase *Ker-Anna* (which is contained in the Tibetan word *ante-ker-anna*).

The Sumerians were taught that the Moon was one of the satellites of Tiamat from which the Gardener claimed the DNA or seeds of life. Does this imply the Rainbow Bridge we are seeking goes to the Moon? If so, is the Key of Life a teaching designed to lift us off the earth and travel to the Moon?

In the story of Noah the rainbow is symbol that God would never again destroy the world by flood. As evidence of his "covenant" or contract God set his rainbow in the sky. To the Nordic ancestors of the Nazis, this same rainbow is the bridge Bifrost, joining the human world with the land of the gods,[3] the Nefilim, who live in Thule or Tula. In the Hebrew and Christian tradition, Moses and Jesus later renewed God's contract with humanity. Did this renewal have something to do with the Rainbow Bridge to Tula?

The Rainbow Bridge also appears in the mythology of Africa and India. Among the Hopi the rainbow is the symbol of the serpent.[4] In China, the rainbow is the sky-dragon joining earth and heaven.[5] Virtually everywhere it is found the rainbow is a universal symbol for deliverance.

For example, Pythagoras ("I am the Python"), whose theories were exploited by the Nazi and American scientists in the development of weapons systems, spent time in India with Buddha. When he returned to Italy he taught the means to escape earth life in one lifetime: by finding the rainbow bridge which led first to the Moon and then to the Pleiades, which the ancients considered the stargate to Tula.

In the creation myth preserved by the Fon (or Bon) tribe of Africa[6] we find a myth directly connecting the soulsphere brought to earth by Enki, the serpent, with the rainbow. The Fon see the earth as floating on water (the cosmic ocean). The Rainbow Snake *Da* or *Dan*, who is the son of a combined male-female God *Mawu-Lisa*, who created the first being. (Phonetically Mawu-Lisa is Ma El Isa. *Ma* means Mother; *El* is the Shining One, *Is* is Isis. This man-woman, or androgyne, was recreated by Leonardo da Vinci in the *Mona Lisa*. Fascinatingly, Da Vinci was believed to be the grandmaster of the Priory of Sion, a secret religious organization which worshipped John the Baptist and sought to put a descendent of Jesus on the throne of Europe.)

To stop the world from sinking, Mawu asked the serpent to support the earth, tail in mouth. The Rainbow Snake took the job. It is said he holds the earth in his coils, 3,500 above, 3,500 below. He arches in the rainbow and flashes in the lightning.

The number 3,500 is highly symbolic. 3 plus 5 equals 8, which is the number of infinity, Tula, Thoth and Jesus. Pictographically, the "8" illustrates the entwined serpents, and the path of the souls between earth and the Central Sun. *Nahash* is the Hebrew word for serpent, soul is *neshamah*. The word for number 8 is *shemonah*. Obviously, as evidenced by their word plays, the Hebrews knew of the connection between the serpent, the soul and the 8.

The Biblical *Book of Jubilees* supports the Rainbow Serpent myth stating a group of "angels" of the Lord came down to earth to "instruct the children of men, and that they should do judgment and uprightness on the earth" (Jubilees 4:15). Numerous other traditions record an identical story. By helping the soul walk upright in the human body, Enki, whose personal symbol is the entwined serpents or figure 8, gave it a vehicle in which to ascend.

THE PATH OF 8

Do the two twisting serpents of the caduceus represent the two lovers, the two different soulspheres, and the two souls within each of us? Does this explain why the 8, the swastika and the Key of Life symbols have been said to conceal one of the most important of all gnostic teachings?

Numerous ancient mystical traditions record the spiritual evolution of the human soul occurs through the unfolding of the two opposing energies of yin and yang, light and dark, matter and spirit represented by the entwined serpents (which may represent entwined souls).

According to Egyptian legend, it was the Peacemaker Thoth, by separating the two opposing forces with his golden wand or rod of transformation (symbolically the spinal cord), who introduced the third equilibrating or balancing force, symbolized by the dove.

This third, balancing force is the teaching of the Holy Spirit which enables the descent of a Shining One of Tula as well as the *ascent* to Tula of the combined Shining One and earthbound soul.

This is why the Key of Life in all its forms, but especially a staff with entwined serpents topped by a dove, is the symbol for the teachings which lead to Tula.

In the Greek myth, Thoth was transformed into Hermes the guardian of roads, pathways and gates, including those of consciousness.

121

Sacred to him, and presumably to the priesthood of the Peacemakers, was THE PATH or THE WAY. The Way was not only the "signature" of Jesus ("I am the Way..." John 14:6), but also was the original name of Christianity. This referred to Jesus' teaching of "the path between opposites." Jesus, whose spiritual number is 8, sought to help humanity transcend the polarities of light and dark into a higher dimension symbolized by the dove of the Holy Spirit. As we have noted, in the sacred tradition the name of the dove of peace is *Ionah* or *Ionas* and John the Baptist, the reincarnated Elijah, was called *Ioannes*.

THE RETURN OF THE DOVE
According to Biblical prophecy, at the time of the Second Coming, the New Jerusalem or New Atlantis will be built. Within this fifteen hundred square mile city the Tree of Life will be reconstructed.7 Upon this sacred Tree of Peace, the dove of the Holy Spirit will reappear.

Virtually every earthly political and religious regime has sought to control these power tools, including the Tree of Life. Legends and scripture suggest these tools can open gateways to higher dimensions or allow material objects to cross the rainbow bridge and toggle between dimensions.

Do regimes seek to control these power tools for the obvious reason that when one is able to change channels in this way does he becomes a master of the universe beyond the control of a earthly politics?

According to Jewish mythology, ever since Eden, these power tools have been kept in the "Cave of Treasure" at the Gate of Paradise.8 However, the terma tradition hints that it is possible to download the plans for the creation of these power tools directly from God. Possibly one such big brain found himself in the employ of the United States military during WW II. We'll explore his amazing story in the next chapter.

Notes:

1. Zecharia Sitchin *The Twelfth Planet* (New York, Avon Books, 1976) p. 410
2. Alan Alford interview in *Atlantis Rising,* Number 13, p. 27
3. Stuart Gordon *The Encyclopedia of Myths and Legends* (London, Headline, 1993) p. 575
4. Ibid.
5. Ibid.
6. Ibid.
7. Revelation 22:2
8. Robert Graves & Raphael Patai *Hebrew Myths* (New York, Anchor Books, 1964) p. 105

CHAPTER SIXTEEN

PROJECT RAINBOW AND
THE PHILADELPHIA EXPERIMENT

And to the angel of the church of Philadelphia write;

These things saith he that is holy, he that is true, **he that hath**
the key *of David, that openeth, and no man shutteth; and*
shutteth, and no man openeth; (Revelation 3:7)

In John the Revelator's vision in the book of Revelation,
the city of Philadelphia, from which the city of America's
birthplace in Pennsylvania received its name, was associated
with the ultimate evolutionary stage -- full divinity.
Philadelphia was the city of deliverance.
The first part of the book of Revelation begins with John's
Seven Letters to the Seven Churches of Asia (including
Philadelphia). It has been observed by occultists that these
letters outline the spiritual evolution of human life on earth.1
They correspond with the seven chakras of the human body
attached to the spinal cord or inner Tree of Life and the seven
points on the caduceus. At the top of the caduceus is the
dove, the symbol of the Holy Spirit.
During the Babylonian remembrance of the destruction
of Tiamat, a live dove would be split in half. Is this why the
dove of deliverance is the crucial metaphor of the book of
Revelation and the goings on at Philadelphia?
The Greek word "philadelphus" means "one who loves
his brother." The ancient city of Philadelphia was known as
the gateway to the East.
For Jesus, who dictated the letters to John, "Philadelphia"
symbolized elusive the gateway to the Christian ideal of a city
of good will, balance and love. Her Christ-like citizens live

123

humble and peaceful lives in satori, or enlightenment, the ultimate altered state of consciousness.

After achieving this, John refers to the Second Coming as the next step:

...behold I have set before thee an open door, and no man can shut it....

The open door, as popular a theme in the Bible as it is in Atlantis research, is the opening that appears once Christ-consciousness enters. It the physical Eastern Gate through which Jesus comes and goes.

Could it be that America, specifically Philadelphia, Pa., is the "door" through which Christ-consciousness is to enter the earth in the Age of Aquarius?

• Is this what happened beside the Wissahickon River during the time of the writing of the U.S. Constitution?

• Is this why the Founding Fathers connected themselves with the Israelites?

• Is this why F.D.R. was so interested in the Oak Island "water door" mystery and sent agents to Mongolia looking for the reincarnated Jesus?

It is with these thoughts and questions in mind that we look at an alleged Naval research project begun in the early 1930's into the manipulation of "force fields" or the unified electromagnetic quantum field. Its purpose was to learn how to shift not souls, but airplanes, tanks and warships, between dimensions.

However, once the technique of dimension shifting is mastered, anything can be moved around the universe. Snap. Like that.

It is fascinating to view this naval research with its occult implications in mind. Especially since the acients attributed dimension shifting capabilities to the Tree of Life device and also made clear that it had the ability to channel a Christ soul to earth.

THE PHILADELPHIA EXPERIMENT

In 1933, the Institute for Advanced Study was formed at Princeton University2 to study the nature of relativity and invisibility. (Nothing is ever invisible. It is simply "hidden" in a neighboring dimension.) The founders of the Institute included big brains Albert Einstein and mathematician John Von Neumann.

In the 1930's there had been a massive brain drain out of Europe in response to Hitler's escalating madness. Many Jewish scientists, including a few *doktors* flooded to the U.S. to Princeton and Chicago.3 These "second rate" universities, as they used to call them, were now their blessed homes. One of the projects these displaced Israelites worked on was the

Philadelphia Experiment,4 which is widely hailed by many as a street myth, but which has enough of a kernel of truth to make it worth briefly discussing.

In 1934, the Navy is said to have taken over the project from the big brains at the University of Chicago. It transferred it to Princeton University, classified it as ultra top-secret, and gave it a peculiar name: *Project Rainbow*.5 In 1936, the project was given the green light by F.D.R. Nikola Tesla, a Yugoslavian-born genius and friend of F.D.R. was put in charge. With war imminent, say researchers, the project received whatever funding it required to build offensive weapons systems.

Tesla (whose name smacks of Tula) was not just any genius. He was *the* big brain, and metaphysician and occultist of his time who, after working for Thomas Edison, went out on his own, eventually coming up with a plan to bring light to everyone in the world -- for free.

Tesla claimed he could make 3-D models of his inventions in his head, set them to work, forget about them, and test them for weeks before he built them in "real life".

While conducting his experiments in Colorado Springs around 1900, Tesla publicly claimed that extraterrestrial intelligences had contacted him when *Mars* was near earth. This also happened in 1926 when he had constructed radio towers atop the gilded roof of his home, the Waldorf Astoria hotel in Manhattan.

Under Tesla's direction Project Rainbow attempted to make a warship invisible. Von Neumann and Einstein provided theoretical input. In 1941, Tesla's theory is claimed to have been successfully tested on an unmanned ship at the Brooklyn Naval Yard.

In October 1943 (six months after Tesla's death), a full-scale experiment involving humans was conducted at the Philadelphia Naval Yard on the destroyer USS *Eldridge*.

Allegedly, the *Eldridge* disappeared from the sight of onshore observers, materialized out of thin air in the harbor at Norfolk, Virginia, and then reappeared a few minutes later at Philadelphia.6

If this experiment indeed happened as described, the US Navy would have been on its way to mastering the art of teleportation and invisibility. However, this first piece of work was a disaster.

Many of the crew, exposed to the energy field, reportedly went insane, fell sick and died, burst into flames, ended up embedded in steel walls, or disappeared from the face of the earth completely.

The Philadelphia Experiment was abandoned.

TESLA'S DREAM

While invisibility and teleportation holds excitement, it is the golden thread of Tesla's dream to provide unlimited supplies of free electric power to all persons on earth through his technology that draws our attention. In following his thread we slam into the iceberg of New Age politics.

It was Tesla who invented the basic concepts for Reagan's Star Wars defense system. The technology Reagan described had already undergone fifty years of secretive development by the time the Great Communicator promoted it.

Tesla planned to light the world by broadcasting electrical power across vast distances the same way as does radio. In Reagan's vision, the same beams which Tesla envisioned could bring new life to millions who do not have electricity (the same three billion plus people on earth who do not have access to a toilet and are two-and-a-half days walk from the nearest telephone) could also be directed at the speed of light to destroy an enemy ICBM.

Advancing Tesla's technology requires application of the elusive Unified Field Theory of physics, the understanding of which was Einstein's unfulfilled life dream. Tesla believed he could play this field like a harp, broadcasting power by producing vibrations in the atmosphere that were perfectly in phase with the natural vibrations that exist in thunderstorms.

Then, anyone, anywhere with a receiver could simply tap into broadcasts and acquire electricity just as they receive radio or television broadcasts. Through his technology Tesla believed he could transform the world. All it would take is a little help from the Planetary Grid.

THE PLANETARY GRID

In his discourse *Phaeado*, Plato -- who reintroduced the story of Atlantis to the modern mind -- makes the astonishing observation that "the earth itself looks from above, if you could see it, like those twelve-patched leather balls." Did Plato have some means of travelling into earth's orbit to make such an observation? Or, did someone who had seen the earth from this vantage point give him the information?

A twelve-patched leather ball describes a *dodecahedron*. To the mathematicians of ancient Greece, "heaven" beyond was symbolized by the fifth Platonic volume the twelve-faced dodecahedron.

This twelve-fold pattern was modeled after the constellations they saw in the night sky. By mirroring the activity of the heavens on earth, the ancients believed that the constellations revealed a path or stairway to heaven.

Remember Thoth's (or Hermes') dualistic edict, "As above. So below"? This helps to explain why "twelveness"

ONE FOOT IN ATLANTIS

appears throughout history in the myths of the twelve tribes, twelve-gated cities, twelve disciples, twelve signs of the zodiac. Is this also why clocks, calendars, and measures are all based on twelve? Did the concept of "twelveness" also lead modern geneticists to theorize that there are twelve chemical steps, like twelve notes of the chromatic scale, in every spiraling turn of the human DNA helix, manifesting our genetic makeup? (In each story, look for a missing, or hidden, thirteenth seat, tribe, apostle, helix strand, gate or sign -- representing Ophiuchus, or Diana, the light of An.)

The dodecahedron with twelve five-sided faces was used as a teaching tool to instruct the initiate to know him or herself as an energy system like the earth. The study of the Planetary Grid was considered an integral part of a person's education because, like Tesla's work, it unifies all the sciences of the Key of Life, including physics, astronomy, chemistry, biology, mathematics and geometry, genetics, meteorology, astrology, geology, and anthropology.

In the western mystical tradition, the concept of the Planetary Grid was first introduced by Thoth, who, as we have seen, was one of the original Peacemakers and keepers of the Key of Life. According to the wisdom traditions of the Mayan, Egyptians and others, the Peacemakers are a universal brotherhood who travel the universe carrying teachings for aligning worlds with the Central Spiritual Sun, or Tula. Peace is created when earth and Tula are aligned.

These Shining Ones of Tula erect various Tulas (temples) as resonators and conductors of spiritual (Tula, vril) energy. Implicit in this statement is the notion that a Tula on earth is connected to Tulas on other worlds (the 450 billion plus galaxies revealed by the Hubble Space Telescope). Hence, there is a Grid of Tulas on earth and a larger interstellar Grid of Tulas in the cosmos.

These Shining Ones are the very same group F.D.R and Hitler were attempting to contact in Mongolia and Tibet. However, we know that the network of Tulas throughout the earth includes:
• the Great Pyramid of Giza and Heliopolis ("the City of the Sun")
• the massive 1,000 foot high pyramids in the jungles of southern China, 90 degrees opposite of Giza.
• Easter Island, 180 degrees opposite the Great Pyramid.
• the City of the Sun at prehistoric Cuzco, Peru.
• Teotihuacan in Mexico.
• the vortices of the Four Corners area of the USA.
• the Mississippi valley of the southeastern USA.
• Oak Island, Nova Scotia,
• Rennes-le-Chateau, France.

127

The activation of this Planetary Grid is called the "quickening" of the earth, an increase in the vibratory levels of humanity and earth which is thought to trigger higher intelligence and increased linkage between minds. Occultists claim it was under the guidance of the Shining Ones of Tula that this was accomplished, and will be again, soon. When this occurs, will the locations listed above, and/or others, become active Tula complexes once again?

TESLA'S TREE OF LIFE: JUNG'S COPPER COIL

The place Tesla selected to attempt his modern Planetary Grid experiment was Colorado Springs, Co. Interestingly, after WW II President Dwight Eisenhower came here to establish the North American Aerospace Defense Command (NORAD) facility deep inside the granite of the Cheyenne Mountain. Conspiracy theorists claim NORAD was once a fully functioning extraterrestrial command center and that it was re-established by the U.S. Tesla came here because he needed the extraordinarily powerful lightning that comes to earth at Cheyenne Mountain. (In the Language of the Birds, Cheyenne is Chi-Ann. "Chi" is "life force" or "vril")

At the foothills of the Cheyenne Mountain, Tesla erected a gigantic Tree of Life-like device known as the Tesla Coil, a device that produces arcs of electricity by rapidly changing its resistance. In *Prodigal Genius: The Life of Nikola Tesla*,[7] John J. O'Neill describes Tesla's apparatus as a square, barnlike structure one hundred feet long on each side. Its sides and roof sloped twenty-five feet into the sky. From the middle of the roof rose a wooden pyramid.

The top of this tower was nearly eighty feet above the rugged Colorado landscape. Like a rough-hewn cathedral, extensions of the sloping roof beams projected outward to the ground to serve as flying buttresses to stabilize the tower. Through the center of the tower extended a mast nearly two hundred feet high. At the top of this tower was mounted a *copper ball* about three feet in diameter. In the adjacent building were many forms of Tesla's famous coils, or current transformers.[8]

Does this description, a towering coil with a copper ball atop it emitting lightning, sound familiar? Does it not precisely match the description of the apparatus Carl Jung had seen in the dream in which he saw a medieval castle with a tower? Hidden in the tower Jung saw was the source of his power, *a thick copper column* whose top, branching into a network of tiny capillaries, *drew from the air an ineffable spiritual substance.*

As I mentioned, Jung's substance may be *vril* or Life Force, an energy which the fictional Ana scientists of *The*

Coming Race learned to draw from the atmosphere (like Reich's orgone energy) and which instantly bumped the Ana race a few rungs up the evolutionary ladder. This mysterious cosmic energy dramatically enhanced psychic powers and was wielded by the inhabitants of the inner earth. It could also produce a laser-like death ray. Was Tesla working with this same energy?

It should be stated that at these preliminary stages the goal of Tesla's Colorado Springs experiments was not to test his technology, but merely to learn how the Planetary Grid would respond to his theory.

Tesla biographer John O'Neill describes an excellent picture of Tesla's problem.9 Tesla wanted to know if the Planetary Grid was charged and if it could be set into electrical vibration.

If the earth is visualized as a bath tub, an uncharged earth would be like an empty tub. The charged earth would be like a full tub into which Tesla would move his hand back and forth. By doing so, he would mix the water and cause waves.

Think of the earth as an enormous balloon full of fluid, with the Planetary Grid overlaid on the balloon. In the center of the balloon is a small plunger-type technology, which can be moved up and down. Now we can visualize where Tesla believed he was sticking his hand.

If he could make the plunger move he could mix the water and create waves that would travel to the edge of the balloon and reflect back to the center, from which they would return to the edge. Free energy would result on the layer of the Planetary Grid.

Here, it is interesting to note that in the Babylonian creation myth Enki (Sweet Water) mixed with Tiamat (Salt Water) and created the gods, Mummu (the Waves), and Lakhmu and Lakamu (gigantic twin serpents.).

It was this "mixing of the water" that led to the destruction of Tiamat.

Perhaps in mixing the waves, the soulspheres, Tiamat had botched its genetics. Or, perhaps the waves had to do with light (which has a wave and particle duality), the other alleged culprit in the demise of Atlantis.

Moses performed an insightful miracle with his staff of miracles. "Near the field Helyon in the Promised Land is the river Marah, whose *bitter waters Moses made sweet with a stroke from his staff* and the children of Israel drank thereof" (Exodus 15:23-25).

Moses' staff was called Nahushtan which means "he who knows copper." Could this staff be the same as or similar to the copper column described by Jung?

BLUE AS THE BLUE STARS OF TULA

On the long-anticipated evening of his experiment Nikola Tesla tapped into the electrical supply system of the city of Colorado Springs. Properly attired in a black derby hat and cutaway coat, Tesla gave his assistant the signal, "now," to flip the switch sending millions of volts of current into his coil.

Observers claim the coils flamed with fiery hair (which is consistent with Jung's dream of vril energy spewing from a copper column). A strange blue light then enveloped Tesla's tower.10 Sparks up to eighty feet long, blue as blue stars of Tula, flew out followed by rods of flame.

Then, mayhem. Jagged bolts of Tesla-created lightning leaped into the air from his 200-foot-tall mast. Tesla had succeeded in bringing fire down from heaven. Prometheus (*aka* the Pied Piper) had returned to steal fire from the Gods and give it to humanity.

From his experiments Tesla learned (or confirmed his theory) that the earth was alive with electrical vibrations. Theoretically, his advancements could have enabled humanity to take a quantum leap forward through working with the Planetary Grid of the earth to create a limitless supply of cheap, clean power.

This same technology was developed by the United States Air Force in the 1990's under the guise of Project HAARP,11 an advanced version of Tesla's technology.

Tesla did not have weapons on his mind. In 1929, Tesla proposed using his Planetary Grid technology to create a planetary wireless broadcasting system, a "scheme of intelligence transmission" as he called it, which he hoped would bring "enlightenment to the masses."12

In 1900, with funds provided by J.P. Morgan, Tesla set up shop on Long Island (home of the Montauk Indians) and built a massive 187-foot tall transmitter tower capped with a 55 ton, 68 foot metal dome. He called it "Wardenclyffe."13

Tesla told nosy oustiders his purpose was to build a mundane radio transmitter to signal England. However, as Tesla envisioned it, his tower on Long Island was the heart of a wondrous New Atlantis broadcasting (free) power to other Tesla inventions and conveniences, including the following devices, for many of which Tesla held patents:14

• anti-gravity, vertical take-off and landing airships,
• electric airplanes and submarines,
• ozone generators for curing cancer,
• a Wall of Light capable of manipulating time, space, gravity and matter (a.k.a. a stargate).

Tesla was convinced his technology would bring peace. The human family, it appears, was on the brink of having enormous gifts bestowed upon it by a man, who in name, and indeed, appears to have been a Shining One of Tula.

Instead...

In a panic for operating capital, Tesla revealed his secret intention to J.P. Morgan. Morgan, a shrewd financier and master of the universe wanna-be who was playing a chilling game for control of the world power supply, would have nothing to do with Tesla's humanitarian approach to this business, or, his utopian dream.

Fortune favored Tesla's rival, Thomas Edison, and his General Electric Co., which promoted his slower, less efficient, earth polluting DC power system.

In public demonstrations aimed at humiliating Tesla, Edison would force cats and dogs to stand on steel plates with AC current running through it and then would flip a switch. The animals would die an instant, dramatic death from electrocution.15

Despite the fact that virtually all electrical appliances are based upon Tesla technology, ultimately, it was Edison who was known as the wizard of electricity in America.

Denied acclaim and the power pack of fortune, from this point forward Tesla's life became a desperate search for financing, power, and sanity. Above all, he sought to prove his inventions to the world so that he might save it.

Tesla was perceived by his competition as something akin to a revolving, flaming, two-edge sword. His dreaded *Death Ray* technology,16 an early radio-wave-scalar energy weapons system, sealed this image. Newspaper interviews of Tesla were often accompanied by illustrations of his fantastic inventions: the antimatter ships, the Wall of Light, time machines, etc. But it was the Death Ray for which Tesla became renown.

Even Hollywood caught Tesla-mania, putting out several Death Ray movies, including *The Death Ray* (1938) starring Boris Karloff. Superman movies had the extraterrestrial Man of Steel battling the man of guile, the esoteric Tesla and his occult Death Ray. The man who sought to humanity had become its archetypal mad scientist. Fearing his Wardenclyffe Tower might be capable of producing death rays, the F.B.I. dynamited the tower in 1917.

Tesla was a peacemaker to the very end. At the age of 81, he pledged the Death Ray to humanity as a gift of peace. He died alone, save for his birds, in Manhattan's New Yorker Hotel in 1943.

FBI agents swarmed on Tesla's room and removed his personal papers from his safe on the grounds that they might contain details of another world-beating secret weapon. (This was highly unlikely since everyone knew Tesla kept the state-of-the-art of his inventions locked safely in his head.)

THE ATLANTEAN MOMENT

If ever there were a person whose life story imitated art, it would have to be Nikola Tesla. His life is a powerful example of how one man can completely alter the thoughtsphere of humanity and, in less than one generation, redirect the future of the human race.

Stories have circulated for decades stating Nikola Tesla was a reincarnated Atlantean priest/scientist or magician who was responsible for misusing the Atlantean light technology. This is quite interesting in light of the story of the Ana's misuse of vril force. If the Ana's story in *The Coming Race* is indeed the story of the destruction of Atlantis, is it possible history repeated iself in the life of Telsa?

The loss or prevention of the use of advanced Tesla technology in the early twentieth century is a clear Atlantean moment. We either missed the iceberg that could sink us, so to speak, or slammed into it. Nikola Tesla's single-handed impact on life in the New Age is beyond measure, or possibly the scope of comprehension. If we who crawl on the surface of the earth are ever to fly through the air it will be on the wings provided by Tesla.

As a matter of fact, there are rumors that there is a secret earthly civilization using Tesla's technology to do just that.

THE WILD SIDE

Throughout his career Tesla had only one peer, his best friend and all around big brain Gugliemo Marconi (1874-1937). Marconi (whose name combines Mars and On), was a student of Tesla. He won the Nobel Prize for Physics in 1909 for the invention of radio (which Tesla believed he deserved).

Marconi received other blessings that were denied Tesla. Marconi's family was filthy rich. He added to his wealth by cashing in on his inventions, including radio (credit for which a 1943 Supreme Court decision declared he shares with Tesla). Lucky for Marconi he didn't take business lessons from Tesla.

Marconi, like Tesla, enjoyed taking extensive trips to the wild side.17 Like a character out of a James Bond movie, he owned a yacht, the *Electra* (which happens to be the name of one of the seven stars of the Pleiades). Marconi's *Electra* was a floating mad scientist's dream lab. He sailed her around the world, stopping just long enough to perform an anti-gravity experiment here, or to beam energy into space then to power Australia there.

Echoing Tesla's peace jesture, in 1936, Marconi had a wild idea to contact Italian dictator Benito Mussolini with a plan to give the Italians *his* death ray technology.18 Mussolini was overjoyed. The year before, Mussolini had launched a failed attempt at retrieving the Ark of the Covenant, which the Old Testament stories reveal was a death ray technology, from Ethiopia. When the Pope caught wind of Marconi's world-beating idea he panicked. He immediately asked Mussolini to prevent Marconi from continuing the death ray project.

LOST IN SOUTH AMERICA

In 1937, in what may be another street myth,19 Marconi is alleged to have faked his own death, and sailed the *Electra* to South America. Along for the ride were ninety-eight of Marconi's favorite scientist friends. They all had one thing in common: they were filthy rich and believed the world was under the control of a military-industrial-religious complex that was not working in the best interests of humanity.

Pooling their immense capital, the scientists are alleged to have built a secret, underground compound in the jungle of South America. There, they perfected Marconi's and Tesla's anti-gravity and free (vril) energy technologies, creating an independent advanced nation which is said to be dedicated to the creation of world peace.

In his provocative book *The Mysteries of the Andes*, French author Robert Charroux tells the story of Marconi's self-sufficient super city. It is mostly underground, built at the bottom of a crater in a remote jungle, a breathtaking 13,000 feet in the rugged mountains of the Andes somewhere between Venezuela and Bolivia.

Charroux claims these scientists travel the world in discoid craft. They also fly to a sister city in the Cydonia Region on Mars.

South America is a hot bed of UFO activity. Suppose, as many UFO enthusiastists contend, that UFOs are not alien craft but advanced military technology. Is it possible these craft are those developed in WW II?

THE LAST BATTALION

On December 30, 1975, the *Landsat II* satellite took a series of routine photographs at 13 degrees south latitude, 71 degrees 30 minutes west longitude, over the thick jungles of southern Peru.20 When computer enhanced and analysed, these remarkable photos showed eight pyramids, each nearly the size of the Great Pyramid in Egypt.

More detailed analysis revealed that there are not eight, but actually twelve pyramids, all covered by the vegetation. Are these pyramids part of the Planetary Grid?

I mention these pyramids because it is just one more of the strange connections between the Nazis, Marconi, Tesla and South America. A number of military historians insist that a "Last Battalion" of Nazi soldiers escaped to South

America at the close of WW II. Were they in search of Marconi's city?

In his book *The Subterranean World*, Dr. Raymond Bernard claims an "Atlantean Noah" once came to South America and founded an underground kingdom. In Brazil this kingdom is considered the Garden of Eden. It is illuminated by a strange, green glow and its inhabitants are an advanced race which lives for thousands of years.

Could the Children of An be alive and well in South America today?

Notes:

1. Peter Lorie *Revelation* (New York, Simon & Schuster, 1994) p. 16
2. Jamie Sayen *Einstein in America* (New York, Crown, 1985) p. 58
3. Bruce Kuklick, *Puritans in Babylon.* (Princeton, NJ, Princeton University Press, 1996) p. 6
4. Preston Nichols & Peter Moon *The Montauk Project: Experiments in Time* (New York, Sky Books, 1992) p. 13
5. Ibid. p. 49
6. Stuart Gordon *The Encyclopedia of Myths and Legends* (London, Headline, 1993) p. 539
7. John J. O'Neill *Prodigal Genius: The Life of Nikola Tesla* (Hollywood, CA, Angriff Press)
8. Ibid. p. 178
9. Ibid. p. 181
10. Ibid. p. 186
11. Dr. Nicholas J. Begich & Jeanne Manning *Angels Don't Play This HAARP* (Anchorage, AK, Earthpulse, 1995)
12. Nikola Tesla & David Hatcher Childress *The Fantastic Inventions of Nikola Tesla* (Stelle, IL, Adventures Unlimited, 1993) p. 230
13. Margaret Cheney *Tesla: Man Out of Time* (New York, Barnes & Noble, 1981) p. 158
14. Ibid. p. 273-279
15. James Coates *The Chicago Tribune*, August 10, 1986
16. Ibid. p. 247
17. Ibid. p. 289-291
18. Ibid. p. 290
19. Ibid. p. 290-291
20. David Hatcher Childress *Lost Cities & Ancient Mysteries of South America* (Stelle, IL, Adventures Unlimited Press, 1983) p. 261

CHAPTER SEVENTEEN

ENLIL

Let us return to the Alien Book of Genesis and the Garden of Eden.

The Sumerian stories reveal Enki, one son of An, was vehemently opposed in his genetic experimentaion by his half-brother *Enlil*, who is called the "Lord of the Command."1 Enlil is managerial, hands on, and totally opposite of Enki, the dreamer. Ask Enlil to define human being and one likely would get something on the order of this. "Human being: an expendable component of a master colony; which exists as an unintelligent mass, concealed out in the middle of nowhere."

Known as the perpetually cranky, thunderbolt-throwing god *Zeus* to the Greeks, and Osiris' dark force brother, *Set*, to the Egyptians, Enlil also appears to be one side of Yahweh, the side which obviously despises humanity or fears that mankind will become like the gods.

Most incredibly, Romulus, the founder of Rome, had a twin brother, Remus, whom Romulus murdered, similar to the way Set murdered Osiris. Remus is *Sumer* spelled backward. From his name is derived such words as remove and remiss, as in remission or cleansing of sin. After his death Remus was carried into the heavens on a gleaming chariot driven by his father Mars. Obviously, Remus/Sumer was special to Mars. The same the way Enki was special to An.

Enlil ("Lord of the Command") is recognizable as the half of Yahweh who met Moses on Sinai and gave him "the Word" or "the Command," the "Ten Commandments": the penal code by which he demanded that his slaves live, i.e., "thou shalt not steal, thou shalt not kill," etc.

Enki wields "the Word" as the life force energy, or vril energy, upon which the world is built and which transforms homo sapien into homo angelis. In the stories, Enlil seeks to prevent Enki from using this Word or energy, similar to the way the greedy J.P. Morgan controlled Tesla and kept him from developing his two-edged energy technology.

The triangle formed by An, Enki and Enlil appears in the New Testatment book of John 1:1: "In the beginning was the Word, and the Word was with God, and the Word was God." Is the Christian holy trinity of the Father, Son and Holy Spirit duplicates of the original Sumerian An, Enki and Enlil, or the Assyrian An, Enki and Baal as has been suggested?

Enlil is completely at odds with his half-brother's way of doing things. The Sumerian stories depict him always trying to dig up dirt on his brother. The two are in competition for rulership of An when their father steps down. Enlil has the edge by birthright.2

THE MODEL MAN

When we last left Enki he and Ninharsag had created a prototype resurrection machine and was on his way to phase two of his plan to creation a model man.

When Enlil learned of this plan he aghast at what his half-brother Enki had done in creating the early earthling, the *lulu*.3 In response, Enlil probably dashed off a thermonuclear letter or two to Enki: "what the hell are you doing?"

This was nothing compared to Enlil's wrath when Enki initiated phase two of his stunning rescue plan and created an enhanced version of humanity, called the *Adapa*, or "the model man."4

This new biological entity or technology was capable of becoming a resurrection machine: a flow-er (or flower) of souls. Soon, the earth would be blossom with these advanced creatures.

In response, Enlil "phoned home."5 Anu, his father and ruler of An, was equally outraged at Enki's impetuous actions. "Let them fetch the earthling here!" he ordered.6

Enki got the word. Send the Adapa to the home planet. This of course, makes absolutely no sense if the Adapa is just some stupid primate who was lucky enough to have been bumped up the evolutionary ladder through artful genetic tampering.

It makes a great deal of sense if one of the souls animating that body is as spiritually advanced as the myths suggest: one a higher vibrational Christ soul capable of a vast array of spiritual capabilities, and the other a conquered soul from Tiamat, An's former enemy.

AN INTERGALACTIC SITUATION

There is virtually unanimous agreement in African and Mayan mythology. Adapa's advanced soul did not come directly from Tula by way of An.

According to Egyptian myth, this soul came from Sirius. Destinies usually are linked. If they were not already linked, did Enki enjoin the civilizations of Sirius, An and earth? Factor in the Mayan and Sumerian belief that the human body originated in the Pleiades (since Tiamat and her satellite Kingu were one of the Pleiades) and do we have an intergalactic "situation" on our hands?

Had Enki not only rocked the cradle, but also greatly disturbed the universe? Did he create the first melting pot society on earth?

Is the ancient belief that we have two souls within us, one of them a Christ soul, the single most explosive piece of information never disclosed to the public?

At this point, it should not go unnoticed that this suggests metaphysically there are two kinds (or planes) of souls: those of the extraterrestrials and the others. Certain Gnostic teachings hold that there are actually *three* planes of souls on earth:

• The *pneumatic* -- beings who have evolved to a spiritual level beyond earthly concern and whose motivation is philosophical peace, the co-creation of heaven on earth. These "guardian angels" guide the other souls in their spiritual and evolutionary development. They are the beings who make things happen in our universe.

• The *psychic*, who are the seekers on the path to ascension. They are beings who watch what is happening.

• The *hylic*, whose only awareness is purely physical and instinctive. These beings ask: "is something happening?"

In linking An with earth, had Enki also sealed our fates with that of the angels, those who make things happen? *This* state of affairs assuredly would have raised more than Enlil's blood pressure.

THE PLAN OF HEAVEN AND EARTH

The Sumerian texts describe how Enki unflinchingly fulfilled Anu's command to send the Adapa to the home planet (or Tula), behaving obediently, as did the Hebrew patriarch Abraham, whom Yahweh later ordered to set fire to his only son.

Fearing Enlil would intefere,[7] Enki conceived a plan to insure his son's safety. Before he allowed the Adapa to depart on his journey, he advised him not to eat the "Food of Life" or the "Water of Life."

Surely, Enlil would try to assassinate him.

"Then he made him take the road to Heaven, and to Heaven he went up."8 As the vehicle (rocket ship, rainbow bridge, light body?) carrying the Adapa lifted from the fiery altar of Mount Moriah in Jerusalem into the Heavens, all Enki could do was wait and wonder if he would have to take "the knife to slay his son." That is, would Enki have to destroy his genetics lab and all of his efforts?

If Anu were testing Enki's loyalty, Enki certainly passed. At the fateful meeting with his Anu, the Adapa impressed him with his intelligence and his understanding of "the plan of Heaven and earth,"9 which he had been trained by Enki. Perhaps more importantly, Anu wondered what to do with an earthling who knew the way to Heaven, knowledge reserved only for the gods.

Apparently, Anu realized the Adapa was like him -- after all, only gods live in heaven. The only fair action available to Anu, says Sitchin, was to invite the Adapa to join the ranks of the gods. Adapa was offered permanent residence on An by Anu.

To insure his survival "the Bread of Life they brought him," and "the Water of Life" was offered too.10

The Adapa was too smart for this.

He refused to eat or drink. This, however, was a genuine offer from Anu.

As a result, did Adapa miss his, and henceforth all of earth humanity's, opportunity for everlasting life?

The meeting over, says Sitchin, the Adapa is returned to earth -- a trip during which the Sumerian texts say he saw the "awesomeness" of space, "from the horizon of Heaven to the zenith of Heaven."11

EAST OF EDEN

The return of the Adapa to earth created a new crinkle in the relationship between man and the gods. After the Adapa passed the test of Anu, Enki appears to have been given permission to continue his plan for developing a new segment of humanity, continuing the line of the Adapa and his family. This would have been a real career boost for Enki. I speculate Enki would have pleaded quite a convincing case before Anu, perhaps securing additional technology, manpower and other resources to insure his success.

In the Sumerian story, Enlil was enraged by his brother's success. The generous cooperation of Anu made it even more infuriating. In retaliation, says the book of Genesis, Yahweh evicted humanity, along with the conniving, back-stabbing snake Enki, from the garden of the E.DIN, as the Sumerians called the abode of the Shining Ones. Enlil/Yahweh had to do something. After all, what would Enki do next?

As the book of Genesis records, Yahweh deployed a Flaming Sword and stationed Cherubim at the gate of Eden to prevent Adam and Eve, and the serpent, from returning.

This sword is linked symbolically with the *Sword of Destiny*, the fiery weapon which had caused the destruction of Tiamat.

From these two accounts are we to conclude that Enlil took control of the doorway to heaven?

Thus far, we have presented Enki as a benevolent and wise teacher, an advocate for humanity.

If he was a real person, and we have no reason to doubt that he was -- most myths are based upon a kernel of truth or actual events -- then we have to at least consider the possibility that before he led humanity down the Rainbow Bridge toward immortality he would have known that the only way for humanity to see this bridge would be to bring what we today call Christ-consciousness to earth.

Bringing these teachings to earth would mean Salvation for all, especially the condemned souls of Tiamat. These teachings are etched upon the *Stone of Destiny*.

Some say that a gem with the Messiah's name -- which floated with the wind until after the Altar had been built on Mount Mariah, and then came to rest there -- was the first solid thing God (Enki) brought to earth.

With the Sword of Destiny in Enlil's possession, and the Stone of Destiny in Enki's control, it appears we have a stand-off.

• One brother or group of beings (Enlil) has the Sword and control over the doorway to heaven.

• The other brother or group of beings (Enki) has control of the instruction manual for making it work.

• One brother (Enlil) leads a group of extraterrestrials who possess pure blood and enjoys using the human creatures as slaves and sex objects. He is interested in preserving his master race.

• The other (Enki), diluted the pure blood of the gods and is out to spiritualize the earth by mixing it with another soulsphere, making it a melting pot society.

The battle lines were clearly drawn in the ancient world. The esoteric battleground of WW II is plainly foreshadowed in the Sumerian story of two brothers, neither of whom would give an inch to the other.

Was this standoff between Enki and Enlil, later re-enacted in WW II?

Was WW II the continuation of an ancient rivalry over economics, politics and class?

THE CHOSEN FEW

Do Enki's intentions for humanity's development now become clear? Did they have to do with awakening humanity to the secrets of opening the door that reveals the Rainbow Bridge to everlasting life, which by his own ill advice to the Adapa had eluded humanity? Was Enki now out to deliver these teachings to humanity?

As Sitchin speculates,12 to do this Enki logically would have sought to remove the first advanced humans to a special place, another Eden, in which they might develop away from the counterproductive grasp of Enlil. The Adapa's family would truly be a "chosen people." Would not protecting them in this way be a natural impulse for one whose genes were running through humanity?

Would this impulse become evident if we could have evesdropped on the conversation between the God(s) and Moses? We know what Enlil would say: he delivered a penal code by which he could control humanity. Might the dualistic conversation between Enki and his chosen people have gone something like this?

"For you are a people holy to the Lord your God (Enki); the Lord your God has chosen you to be a people for his own possession (Enlil), out of all the peoples that are on the face of the earth."

Deut. 7:6

If the "chosen ones" were the family of the Adapa, the model man, there would have been a relatively small number of them as compared to the mass produced primitive workers. As Moses would later explain why they were chosen:

"It was not because you were more in number than any other peole that the lord set his love upon you and chose you, for you were the fewest of all peoples..."

Deut. 7:7

The lulu, left behind under the command of Enlil, would suffer greatly. The Mayan *Popol Vuh* offers stunning corroborative insights: "Let their sight reach only to that which is near; let them see only a little of the earth. . . *then the Heart of Heaven blew mist into their eyes* which clouded their sight as when a mirror is breathed upon. Their eyes were covered and they could only see what was close, only that was clear to them . . . In this way the wisdom and all the knowledge of the First Men (the gods) were destroyed."

It is astonishing to note that when Jesus (who is called the second Adam) appeared after his resurrection to perform his spiritual attunements to reverse this "fog," he did so by breathing on his subject.12 Developing the ability to "see" is obviously a top priority.

In Nazi Germany, the Gypsies were also marked for extermination. Superstitious Nazi leaders believed the Gypsies -- whom the Nazi doctors had proven were related to the Aryans -- possessed "second sight" and had access to a storehouse of occult information which could threaten the Reich.

Is this knowledge the knowledge Enlil sought to keep from the children of Atlantis?

Notes:

1. Zecharia Sitchin *The Stairway to Heaven* (New York, Avon Books, 1980) p. 101
2. Ibid. p. 101
3. Zecharia Sitchin *The Twelfth Planet* (New York, Avon Books, 1976) p. 348
4. Ibid. p. 348
5. Ibid. p. 104
6. Ibid. p. 104
7. Ibid. p. 104
8. Ibid. p. 105
9. Ibid. p. 105
10. Ibid. p. 105
11. Ibid. p. 105
12. John 20:22

CHAPTER EIGHTEEN

EXILES FROM EDEN

What happened to Enki and the Adapa? The book of Genesis skips over the remaining story. The thread is picked up in the *Timaeus* by Plato (427-347 B.C.), in which Critias tells Socrates how, visiting the Egyptian capital, Sais (Plato's) ancestor Solon (c.640-569 B.C) is told the legend of Atlantis, an island which lay just beyond "the Pillars of Hercules" (the Greek savior figure).

Plato remarked that ten kings gathered around a central enclosure ruled Atlantis, giving one cause to wonder if he weren't actually referring to the ten satellites of Tiamat gathered around Kingu.

Seeking to spiritually uplift a "chosen few" Enki and his female partner, the goddess Ninharsag, took the Adapa (Adam) and his offspring out of the "Garden of Eden." Led by Enki, the castaways of Eden went to a remote place, an island, where they could develop free of Enlil's harrassment. Their destination, of course, was Atlantis.

On their trek there the Adapa did not leave the Garden empty handed.

There exists an old Jewish legend. The Staff of God with which Moses performed many miracles, including the parting of the waters of the Lake of Reeds, was brought out of the Garden of Eden by Adam. Adam gave it to Enoch (who was called Thoth by the Egyptians): Enoch gave it to his great-grandson Noah, the hero of the Deluge.

Then it was handed down through the line of Shem, son of Noah, from generation to generation, until it reached Abraham (the first Hebrew patriarch). Abraham's great-grandson Joseph brought it with him to Egypt where he rose to highest rank in the Pharaoh's court. There the Staff remained among the treasures of the Egyptian kings; and thus it reached the hands of Moses, who was raised as an Egyptian prince before he escaped into the Sinai Peninsula.

In one version, the Staff was carved out of a single stone (likely the Stone of Destiny). In another, it was made of a branch of the Tree of Life, which grew in the Garden of Eden. This was the staff Enki used to bring the souls of man to earth. For this reason it is called the Key of Life.

The Messiah, it is said, will rule the earth "with a rod of iron" during the Millennium (Psalm 2:9, Revelation 2:27, 19:13).

A rod of iron, you say? In the Language of the Birds, "ir-on" is "ir" meaning light, of On or An. Does this mean the Messiah will rule with the light of An?

In two major quatrains Nostradamus alludes to the Key of Life... *He will fly through the sky, the rains and the snows and strike everyone with his rod ... One who is issued from the great Hermes.*1 Hermes is the Greek name for Thoth.

In another relevant legend it is said that God (An?) took compassion on Adam after he had been banished from Eden. He sent either the archangel Gabriel ("God's hero") or Raphael (later mistranslated as Raziel) whose name means "Secrets of God," to give him a book. Both angels are from the class of angels called *seraphim* or "serpent healers."2

The book they brought is *The Book of the Angel Raziel*. It contained all knowledge of the stars, the art of healing and the mastery of demons.3 It was given so that man might not only regain entry to the real Garden of Paradise, the heavenly Tula, but remember that he was, as the image of God, "the looker into the mirror of existence wherein he could perceive the Divine Face." This book "wherein all celestial and earthly knowledge is set down" has been handed down. An oral version still exists -- the *Kaballah*, the book given to Abraham by Melchizedek.

According to lore, *The Book of the Angel Raziel* was inscribed on a sapphire stone4 -- the stone of destiny -- and was once in the possession of Thoth/Enoch who, it is said, gave it out as his own work i.e., *The Book of Enoch/Thoth*. In *The Legends of the Jews from Primitive Times* we learn that that, like the Key of Life, Adam gave the stone to Seth, who gave it to Enoch, who passed it to Noah, where it develops that Noah learned how to build the Ark by pouring over *The Book*.

Like the Staff's journey, Shem, Abraham, Moses and Aaron were next in line. After which came Solomon who was thought to have derived his great wisdom and magical power from the Atlantean *Book of the Angel Raziel*.5

Here we link with the Koran, which tells us Solomon's wisdom came from his understanding of the Language of the Birds, the original language spoken by Adam in the Garden of Eden. Solomon's Temple, called Zion, is the spiritual home of Israel. Within her Holy of Holies was presumed to have been the Stone of Foundation, the secret Hebrew link to Tula. This stone is the *Stone of Destiny*.

ATLANTIS: THE SECRET PLACE OF THE STAIRS

Now we arrive at what may be the true earthly Garden of Eden of the human race. The Mayans, we are reminded, called this place, Aztlan/Atlantis, by its most sacred name, Tula, and recalled it as an island of creation with its City of the Golden Gates, at the center of which was a massive temple.

In *Critias or Concerning Atlantis*, Plato speaks of the capital of Atlantis as the central gathering-place for all her peoples, and her temple as the symbol and life center of their religion. Within the temple was a metal column on which were engraved in sacred language the teachings of the founder of Atlantis. This column was topped by a golden sun disk.

Could this Atlantean column be the original upon which the dream image of Jung and the copper column of Moses are based?

The Mayans are not alone in linking Atlantis with Tula. The Chinese, the Japanese, the Egyptians, Indians, Fijians, and others believed in the existence of an original island, particularly one associated with a serpent-god and goddess or dragon-god and goddess of the ocean. This, of course, reminds us of Enki.

The Sumerian myth confirms that the Tula was the place where the first generation of mankind came into being:

> *"The abundance of the goddess of flocks and*
> *of the Grain goddess,*
> *The Annunnaki in 'the holy chamber'*
> *Ate and were not filled . . .*
> *The Anunnaki in 'the holy chamber'*
> *Drank and were not filled"*
> **In the holy park, for their (the Gods') benefit,**
> **Mankind with the soul of life came into being.**
> *Then Enki said to Enlil:*
> *"Father Enlil, flocks and grain*
> *In 'the holy chamber' have been made plentiful.'*
> *In 'the holy chamber' mightily shall they bring forth."*

When mankind came into being in "the holy chamber," the Tula, a flowering of the celestial garden also occurred. Read the above lines in light of the flower symbolism. Is the human body a receptacle of the "abundance" of the creator and "the holy chamber" the genetics laboratory of Enki? If this laboratory is the same as the holy park in which mankind was brought forth from the heavenly Tula, does not the Sumerian myth take on a great deal of meaning? The blossoming of humanity in the Sumerian creation myth finds a counterpart in the Hawaiian genesis myth:

*"Man descended from the Sacred Shrine of
The King who created the heavens.*
**The Shrine of the King of Heaven who caused
that distant realm to bloom and flower**"

The Sumerians, Hawaiians and the Egyptians place the creation of man in the god's holy chamber, the Tula, which is likened to a flowering garden. This is quite amazing in light of the Roman legend that Mars was originally a gardener and the son of the union of the Queen of Heaven with a "mystic flower". The Song of Solomon, 2:8-14, gives us a further excellent description of this place.

*"My beloved spake, and said unto me, Rise up, my love,
my fair one, and come away.
For, lo, the winter is past, the rain is over and gone;
The flowers appear on the earth; the time of the singing
birds is come, **and the voice of the turtle is heard in our
land**."*

We have already heard the Native Americans tell us it was upon the back of the turtle, the survivors of the destruction of Atlantis, that civilization was brought back to life after the Flood.

According to Donnelly and others, *Tula* was the true site of Eden and all other earthly paradises, a great land where man and god once lived together in perfect happiness. It was the home of man's first civilization. Today, Atlantis stands for a land of great promise and of great warning.

As the Song of Solomon continues we learn an extraordinary detail of this place:

*"The vines with the tender grape give a good smell.
Arise, my love, my fair one, and come away.
O my dove, that art in the clefts of the rock,
in the secret places of the stairs."*

Through his half-human, half-divine creation had Enki created a doorway through which future souls could migrate to and from earth -- and also a resurrection machine? Can we think of this machine as both a flow-er or flower of souls and/or a *stairway* to heaven? Are we also encouraged to look for a separate doorway and stairway to heaven outside of the human body? Is this doorway and stairway that all succeeding generations would seek? Like Jacob's ladder, the top of which reaches into heaven, is this the place from whence angels ascend and descend?

ATLAS

As the link between two levels of civilization -- the earthly and the angelic -- is there any doubt that the Adapa carried the world on his shoulders? Is it mere coincidence that Plato called Enki Poseidon and that Atlas, the son of Poseidon, was depicted with the world on his shoulders? Poseid, Poseidonis and Poseidon were the ancient names for Atlantis. *Po* is also the Dogon name for Sirius. Poseidon is sometimes seen as *Poteidon*, Potei means "Lord," "Don" means wisdom.6

Atlas must have been a truly inspiring being. After all, the Atlanteans named themselves after Atlas. Did he actually exist though?

That a continent, a mountain range, and even an entire ocean should be named after him is a significant beginning point to prove his existence and the esteem with which Atlas was held. Like Hellas the "father" of the Greeks, Ingwe the English, Scota the Scots, and Romulus, the son of Mars, who sired the Romans, Atlas must have existed (the Mayans claimed he was Quetzalcoatl, their god of Tula). Like these other founding fathers, Atlas was the central light (sun or son) of his civilization. Only now, we know why he was called this.

In Greek mythology Atlas was the Titan who led his brothers in a war against Zeus (Enlil) and was punished by being forced to carry the world on his shoulders. From Atlas's point of view this was probably not viewed as a punishment.

Correspondingly, the Biblical Hebrews presents Christ as *"upholding all things by the Word of his power."* This connection of Christ with the "word" is found in several places in the New Testament where we learn God speaks in the Son and the son upholds all things by his word. The Book of John has two illuminating statements about this fascinating connection:

• *In the beginning was the word, and the word was with God, and the word was God.* (John 1:1)

• *Man shall not live by bread alone, but by every "word" that proceeds from the "mouth of 'God'"* (John 4:4)

The "word" has been interpreted as the life energy, the vril force, upon which everything is built. The word is also the power of the Key of Life, the Staff of Moses, as symbolized by the entwined serpents and the dove.

In Matthew 10:16 Jesus says "Be ye therefore wise as serpents and innocent as doves". In upholding the world (word) did Atlas, the first priest king of Atlantis, somehow play a role in delivering or representing the foundation of Christian teaching? Was Enki the originator of this teaching? More fantastically, did Carl Jung and Nikola Tesla understand vril energy this way?

THE FLOW-ERS OF SOULS

According to the Sumerian texts, Enki imported the blood of Kingu, the genetic material from the Moon, to elevate an early form of humanity. These new beings, the line of Adapa, theoretically had higher vibrational souls capable of more efficiently "flowing" this word or life force energy.

Their purpose appears to be two fold: to rescue the souls of the cataclysm of Tiamat, and to heal the remains of Tiamat, the earth, by bathing her in the light of Tula.

Is the mythology of the ancients clear? Are *we* the vehicles in which the two souls learned to dwell?

Do we have not one, but rather *two* souls within us? Is one masculine (solar), the other feminine (watery)?

Like the two entwined serpents of the caduceus, when the two merge into an ascended being, represented by the serpent-bird, will latent powers be activated within our souls?

Will a being of extraordinary power emerge which leaves the earth and returns home? Does this explain why the god-beings who walked around Egypt were depicted with serpents and birds on their head, and again, why Jesus is symbolized as a heron or phoenix-fish-man?

Unimaginable? What if this were so? What relevance, if any, does answering these questions have to WW II and New Age politics? Does the two soul theory help illuminate the mysteries of our time or the cause of WW II?

In part. I've already mentioned the ideas of Churchill and Hitler concerning the separate group souls of Britain and Germany. Now, let's talk about a third soulsphere our groupsoul involved in WW II. The one which was incarnate as the Jews who lived in Nazi Germany.

Rabbi Yanashem Gershom whose book *Beyond the Ashes -- Cases of Reincarnation from the Holocaust*7 documents stories of Jews who died at the hands of the Nazis and have now, he believes, returned with a special mission. According to Rabbi Gershom, the real reasons behind the imprisonment and persecution of the Jews in World War II are far more cosmically significant than has been previously apprehended.

Gershom believes that the Jews were a group of souls. They were called *Tikkun Olam*. Gerhsom translates this term literally to Repair the World. It could also be translated as "planetary healers." This soul group, says Gershom, have the job of keeping time and space in balance (exactly the mission of the Hopi people). They raise the vibrational quality of the earth in anticipation of the arrival of the Messiah.

By another rendering, are the planetary healers, in fact, a "collective messiah" or "Christ soul"? Is showing the lesser-evolved souls the way to the Tree of Life the task for which they are "chosen"?

Like Humpty Dumpty (or Osiris), was this cosmic egg of souls constructed or assembled in one part of our universe, transferred to earth, smashed to bits, implanted or blended into the human body/resurrection machine along with the victims of the holocaust on Tiamat?

Gershom maintains that Moses' Covenant on Sinai was a cosmic event in which the Planetary Healers pledged their allegiance to God and to uphold this world. After this pledge, they achieved victory over the Children of Darkness. Throughout history, whenever evil attempts to assert itself on earth, the Planetary Healers are the first to intervene. Is this the reason why Hitler and other dictators seek to persecute or destroy the Planetary Healers first? If the healers can be eliminated can they break down the spiritual energies or "thought sphere" protecting the planet?

If this rendering is correct, it forces a startling question. When Moses (Akhenaten?) ascended the nebulous "Mount Sinai" (the Moon? Tula?), was true his purpose to renew the agreement between one group of souls, the Planetary Healers, to come to earth to uplift the spiritual vibration to show the way home for their brethren, those souls who suffered the destruction of Tiamat?

If so, does the Stone of Destiny perhaps represent a remnant of the exploded planet Tiamat? Is it possible that the Stone's energy encodes powerful memories of this destruction and the fateful course chosen by this civilization?

Given that souls, no matter how advanced, are thought to take the vow of forgetfulness before reincarnating on the earth plane, does reacquiring this hunk of Stone serve as a "wake up call," triggering deeply embedded soul memories? In the Stone's presence do the Planetary Healers light up like a child reunited with its long lost mother?

BABEL

The basis for the conclusion that Enlil (Yahweh?) did not want the secrets of the Stone, the secrets of the doorway to heaven (Tula) taught to the Adapa and other earthlings is supported by an episode recounted later in the book of Genesis. In this story Yahweh's (Enlil's) temper would flare once again. This episode is called the Tower of Babel episode, the story of a *tower* with its "top in the heavens". This Tower is strangely reminiscent of Tesla's Wardenclyffe Tower. Babel means "gate". No one knows for certain when the first Tower of Babel, the first gate or door was built (or if Tesla's Tower was the last). Throughout time, gods can be found attempting to build (or destroy) a gate to God for their people.

As much of mythology appears to be based on original Atlantean stories, may we speculate that the building of such a gate was a focus of Atlantean civilization? Could misuse of the technology required to create it have led to its demise?

For example, long ago, Baal, the son of Enki, had installed a magical *"stone that whispers"*-- a talking stone -- in the temple at Baalbek, Lebanon. This is quite fascinating, as the runes were known as the "whispering stones," or "secret stones."

This temple was built upon an enormous pad supported by cyclopean stone slabs, some weighing between 500 and 1,200 tons each!8 Even today we do not have technology capable of lifting let alone moving, such stones. The Great Pyramid's largest weigh 200 tons. The volume of masonry of the temple at Baalbek may even dwarf that of the Pyramids.

Local legends claim this pad was built by Adam and his son Cain in cooperation with the "giants" (the Shining Ones) who were later destroyed by the biblical Flood.9 Does the involvement of the Shining Ones make Baalbek either an Atlantean outpost or one of Enlil's installations?

According to most Bible translators, the reason mankind built the Tower of Babel (which with the omission of the letter b becomes the Tower of Bael or Baal) was to make a "name" or "renown" for themselves:

"Then they said, Come, let us build ourselves a city, and **a tower with its top in the heavens,** *and let us make a* **name** *for ourselves, lest we be scattered abroad the face of the whole earth."* (emphasis added)

Genesis 11:4

In *The 12th Planet,*10 Sitchin claims that an error has been made in the translation of the word *shem,* or name, which when properly understood radically changes the meaning of the Tower of Babel episode. The Hebrew word *shem,* says Sitchin, originally signified not "name" or "renown," but *"that which goes up,"* as in a spacecraft or rocketship.

A similar misinterpretation occurs in Genesis 6:4 where it says: "The Nephilim were on earth in those days, and also

149

ONE FOOT IN ATLANTIS

afterward, when the sons of God came in to the daughters of men, and they bore children to them. These were the mighty men of old, the men of renown (*rocketships*)."

If Sitchin's interpretation proves correct, would not this difference in interpretation revolutionize earth history?

According to Sitchin, the *shem* was the cone-shaped command capsule called the *beth-el* ("house of God") by the Hebrews, the *betyl* by the Canaanites, the *ben ben* by the Egyptians.11 The ben ben is the phoenix or heron, the symbol of resurrection. What would it mean if the symbol for the Tower of Babel and the rocket launch tower of Heliopolis were the same thing?

It is interesting that *shem* is also the root for *shaman*, or divine intermediary. *Joshua*, the Hebrew name for Jesus, featured the *sh* sound. Obviously, Jesus did not come to earth to teach us to travel in rocketships. He was, however, known to travel around in his "chariot of spirit."12 Could this vehicle be the same as the fiery chariot, or Mer-Ka-Ba vehicle, of Ezekiel, which is described as the soul's light body or vehicle of resurrection and ascension?13

If so, this is where the Shem legends interface with the ancient Thule legends. If Enki was actually teaching the principles of ascension and resurrection to the chosen children of Atlantis, would they not have learned to jump into their light bodies and, like the Shining Ones of Tula, ascend to heaven? Was the "tower that reached into heaven" within?

In Genesis 11:5-9, we read Yahweh came to see the city and the tower, which the sons of men had built. Upon seeing humanity was united in its desire to ascend to the heavens, and that this was *"only the beginning of what they propose to do; and **nothing that they propose to do will now be impossible for them,"*** the Lord decided to *"confuse their language"* (emphasis added).

Confuse their language? That was only the beginning of Yahweh's wrath.

Yahweh (Enlil?) destroyed the Tower of Babel! Isn't this appallingly childish behavior for the supposed all-powerful, benevolent Creator of the universe?

Could the greater truth in the situation be in the statement "nothing that they propose to do will be impossible for them"? By destroying the Tower of Babel wasn't Enlil effectively closing heaven for business?

If he were managing the affairs of earth, Enlil, as one half of Yahweh, would have to plenty to worry about if Enki truly were teaching the keys to resurrection and ascension or awareness of Christ consciousness.

A planet full of Christs, or those aspiring to transform themselves into *homo christos* or *homo angelis*, had to be a repulsive thought for Enlil. Isn't a mass of humanity without a spiritual capability, or with empty or even false spiritual understandings, far easier to control?

What exactly this Tower of Babel was intended to be we will perhaps never know. If indeed the Tower of Babel incident is about ascension and the activation of the Planetary Grid, it is not the only story. Throughout the Scriptures, pseudipigrapha and the apocrypha, there are descriptions of ascension suggesting it is a recurring theme. In fact, this tower may even have reappeared today, and I'm not just talking about Nikola Tesla's tower either.

IS HEAVEN OPEN FOR BUSINESS?

Mythologically, is it possible the Tower of Babel has returned the New Age in the guise of the Hubble Space Telescope? *Hubble* is an astonishingly synchronistic name for a device of its power and purpose. Hubble is named after Edwin Hubble "the mariner of the nebulae." He was one of the towering figures of twentieth century science who made a series of discoveries that revolutionized humanity's vision of the cosmos.14

In 1923, Hubble was able to confirm the existence of other nebulae, or what are now called galaxies, beyond our own Milky Way. By 1930 Hubble had proven that the universe is expanding.

Hubble's discoveries were of enormous consequence to humanity. In fact, like Tesla's inventions, we can barely begin to comprehend the enormity of the universe revealed to us by Hubble. At one time astronomers believed there might be 10 billion galaxies in the Garden. Today, thanks to the Hubble Space Telescope, they believe the real total is more like a mind-boggling 450 billion galaxies and growing!

Something astonishing happens when we examine the word "Hubble" in the Language of the Birds. It is important to remember that in this strange language "reality" is never limited to one viewpoint or time period. The names of places and people derive their meaning from across time and space.

Beginning with the first two letters, *Hu,* what thought-provoking ancient linguistic connections may be illuminated from the word "Hubble"? Consider these:

• the Sufi Moslems considered the "Hu" sound to be the most sacred creative sound.

• in Chinese mythology, the human race came from Hu.

• Hu is the root for the words humane and hush, or breath. In the book of Genesis the first human came from the *breath* of God.

• in Egypt, the word *khu*, "Great Hu," meant the "shining, translucent, intangible essence of man."

• Hu is apparent in *Dyhu* or *Dyu*, the bright and heavenly divinity of India and Greece and in the Egyptian *HUHI*, or All-Father.

• *Hugh*, the Christian name, means "mind, soul, spirit."

If we added an "a" to *bble* of Hubble we easily render Babel, as in, the Tower of Babel).

Rendered in the Language of the Birds, the Hubble Space Telescope becomes our "gate to god," or the new Tower of Babel?

Remember, the Biblical Tower of Babel episode refers to the "gate" reaching into the heavens (possibly the Goddess Inanna's temple in Babylon) which at one time "God" did not want constructed. Babylon is associated with lust, prostitution and all things carnal. So too is Mary Magdalen, the representative of the temple of Inanna at Magdala (known as the "Tower of the Flock") which exalted Jesus.

Coincidentally, the name of Hubble's telescope was the *Hooker* telescope!

THE FIRST HOLY WAR BETWEEN GODS AND MEN

Does the Tower of Babel episode represent the first Holy War conflict between man and god over the ascension of the human species? Is this a recurring battle? Is this why the Babel story appears to recreate itself? Why is it necessary for this episode to repeat itself, or for humanity to re-invoke it?

As the theory goes, the early slave race multiplied very quickly. But then the situation took a turn for the worse. By the tenth generation, "men began to multiply" in numbers that apparently threatened or distressed the extraterrestrials.

Furthermore, a group of 200 rebellious angels (Genesis 6:1-4) lusted after the daughters of men. These were not the cuddly little cherubs on Hallmark greeting cards, or even the androgynous creator beings. These "angels" were embodied in flesh, with fully functional sexual organs. The Book of Enoch makes it clear these angels looked like humans.

The Nephilim had an insatiatiable sexual desire for earth girls. Against orders from the highers-up in their command structure, Enlil, who feared the dilution of the their blood, they began to procreate, willingly or not, with the earth girls. In some cases, the earth females preferred sexual relations with the extraterrestrials more than with Earth men.

The hybrid children of these two planets would have inherited their father's long life spans. Instead, Enlil saw to it that they lived only 120 years. These new creatures were known as "the Fallen Ones", whose evil ways God decided to wipe off the face of the earth.

Things were clearly out of hand on earth. This is the biblical age of Enoch and Noah.

In Genesis 6:3 we read:

"And God said to Noah, 'I have determined to make an end of all flesh; for the earth is filled with violence through them; behold, I will destroy them with the earth.'"

With this decision, says the Old Testament, humanity was destroyed. Here, it is important to note that the Book of Genesis is largely plagiarized from earlier Sumerian stories in which enormously important details later omitted from the Judeo-Christian tradition are supplied.

War developed between the beings from Tula and the earthly humans with Yahweh (Enlil) who was cast as being opposed to the Shining One's efforts to raise humanity to a higher level. The leader of these angels (Enki) was later was associated with the constellation Orion.

A Hebrew myth is relevant to our search for the four treasures of the Children of Dan. It is said that a group of angels asked God's permission to transform themselves into precious stones and other treasures, which were immediately stolen by mankind.15

The angels escaped from these treasures and attempted to teach men right living. While in human flesh the angels fell victim to human lust, were seduced by the Daughters of Men, and found themselves chained to the earth, unable to shapeshift back into angels. The Fallen Angels were stranded on earth until many years later, when they ascended Jacob's ladder and returned to heaven.

THE END OF THE BEGINNING

Just before the Flood, a command decision was made by Enlil not to save the earth humans.

Enki, however, had other plans. In the *Epic of Gilgamesh*, Enki warns the hero Utnapushtim (the Sumerian Noah) that the other gods led by Enlil, have planned the Flood, and that he must build an ark.

Enki gives him the blueprints for a six-decked ark *in the shape of a perfect cube*.16 When the rains begin Utnapushtim loads up the power tools and seals the ark.

The gods themselves leave the earth in terror. Packed into their space vehicles, they await the end of the deluge, cowering like dogs, say the texts.

When it is over, Utnapushtim releases all his people and animals, drinks a glass of wine (Noah is the first man to plant a vineyard and is the inventor of wine) and lights an aromatic fire. The gods smell the sweet odor of the wood and the delicious meat Utnapushtim is preparing for dinner and return to the surface of the earth.

As the story continues, Utnapushtim becomes an instant hero. Enlil is blamed for the flood. Enki confesses that he warned Utnapushtim of the flood and gave him instructions for building the perfect cube. Enlil tours the cube, blesses Utnapushtim and his wife, and makes them "like unto gods, and gives them two tickets to paradise where, later, they meet Gilgamesh.

In Berossus's version of the story Utnapushtim digs up sacred books which he has previously buried and these are his true tickets to paradise.

Notes:

1. Erika Cheetham *The Final Prophecies of Nostradamus* (New York, Putnam, 1989) p. 103
2. Malcolm Godwin *Angels: An Endangered Species* (New York, Simon & Schuster, 1990) p. 25
3. Ibid. p. 56
4. Robert Graves & Raphael Patai *Hebrew Myths* (New York, Anchor Books, 1964) p. 113
5. Ibid. p. 53
6. Brinsley lePoer Trench *Temple of the Stars* (New York, Ballantine Books, 1962) p. 132
7. Rabbi Yonassan Gershom *Beyond the Ashes: Cases of Reincarnation from the Holocaust* (Virginia Beach, VA, A.R.E. Press, 1992)
8. Zecharia Sitchin *The Stairway to Heaven* (New York, Avon Books, 1980) p. 178
9. Ibid. p. 181
10. Zecharia Sitchin *The Twelfth Planet* (New York, Avon Books, 1976) p. 143-148
11. Ibid. p. 147
12. Apochryphon of James 14:30-34
13. Charles Ponce *Kabbalah* (Wheaton, IL, Theosophical Publishing House, 1973) p. 35
14. Gale E. Christianson *Edwin Hubble: Mariner of the Nebulae* (New York, Farrar, Straus adn Giroux, 1995)

CHAPTER NINETEEN

THE SHINING ONES AWAKEN

Humanity was not finished. In Atlantis our evolution was accelerating. We were on our way to becoming god-like, say the myths. Then, things spun out of control.

Before the Flood did certain priests have knowledge or premonitions of the terrible approaching disaster and flee to safety?

Were the Shining Ones of Atlantis able to save more than one family, taking the big brain culture bearers, artists, engineers, scientists, educators, religious people, etc. and placing them in multiple rescue vehicles?

Did these ships carry these survivors to hidden relocation centers ala the United States government's Mount Weather, Va., facility, the massive, secret multilevel city hidden in the mountains 40 miles west of Washington, D.C., which is home to a parallel government in case of emergency?

After the catastrophe, did the refugees gather together to plan a new beginning, edging slowly into the light, taking shape, reinventing Atlantis again and again as the years went on?

During the cataclysm, say the legends, the Atlantean temples, including the Tula, were destroyed. The delicate cosmic balance was disrupted, the universe disturbed. The earthly connection to "home" was broken. Did this new beginning involve a plan for reconnecting earth with the heavenly Tula, the heart of heaven?

Did the "earth's other people" remember the greatness of their past? At the same time did they seek to provide warnings for future generations to avoid such a horrible fate? How else do we explain the ubiquity, the imagination, the immensity, the enchantment of Atlantis' second life: a great, constant craving cast in the light-encoded filaments of songs, art works, books, dreams, and sometimes more?

Do the voices of Atlantis remain?

Hitler entranced the Nazis with the belief that alliances could be formed with the remaining Shining Ones who live silently in mostly hidden cities.1 Soon, like another Flood, he believed, a new energy will sweep over the earth from the Sun. A new fire, frequency or vibration will envelop the earth. The Shining Ones will reappear to take dominion over the planet and all its inhabitants.

Hitler believed he personally was in contact with these Shining Ones. His goal was to "finish" humanity and create a new race of superheroes. As far as Hitler was concerned, humanity has a choice. We could learn the secret science of Atlantis which enables us to become gods (or make a pact with the Shining Ones to teach it to us) or become a slave to the new gods when they once again walk the New Atlantis.

As suggested by the prophecy on the back of the one dollar bill, was the belief in the existence and imminent return of the Shining Ones who dwell in the remote hidden cities fundamental to Nicholas Roerich and F.D.R. as well?

As contemptible as it may sound to a historian, is it possible the good guys and the bad guys of WW II shared the same occult trend of beliefs? Were F.D.R and Hitler pulling from different ends of the same golden thread?

It is this golden thread we are studying. It is hoped this study will not be ignored on the grounds that historians say it is occult. The historian may not be occult or New Age-minded, but history is.

Are we now entering a time in history when knowledge of long trampled occult beliefs will become necessary to assist us in understanding our "reality"?

2012

In the following pages we will trace the rebuilding effort after the Flood. Our hypothesis is that the inhabitants of earth of all Ages were seeking to re-establish communications with the Shining Ones and to establish vibratory kinship (or peace) with the galactic core.

Further, humanity did not drift rudderless without great leaders to set a standard and charge the imagination that fuels the rebuilding of Atlantis. The prophets of the New Atlantis were ever present in olden times just as their presence is at the heart of New Age politics, leading the faithful in the direction of the New Atlantis.

According to the Mayan calendar, earth will once again be in balance or direct alignment with the galactic core Tula in December, 2012.₂ Does this mean this time will be a new Atlantean moment?

2012, and beyond, is prophesied to bring not just a new era, but also a time when humanity redefines itself as citizens of the cosmos. Does this also suggest it may also be a time of a mass exodus of souls to or from the earth? Obviously, this time requires Moses-type teachers who can reconnect us with the Rainbow Bridge to Tula. Are these teachers in our midst now?

The Thule Society claimed they were in contact with the Shining Ones who survived the cataclysm of Atlantis as early as the 1920's. In 1934, F.D.R. searched Mongolia for Jesus to put him on top of the pyramid of civilization in America. They were also seeking his most treasured secrets, and as one of Henry A. Wallace's letters will show, the power tools for opening the gateways to the inner worlds. Our search, in part, is for these power tools:

• the Stone of Destiny
• the Cup of Destiny
• the Staff of Destiny
• the Sword of Destiny

Our understanding of these devices enables us to understand more of the occult secrets of WW II and the key piece of the puzzle of New Age politics, which had been withheld from humanity by the orders of Winston Churchill.

So, let us once again catch the cosmic wind, lift off from our political boss' cosmic mountain and take a heron's eye view of the ancient occult history of these power tools.

Our guide will be the Staff of Destiny, or Key of Life. The outline of our journey is the old Jewish legend. This wand of wonders (and the knowledge of how to use it) with which Moses and Jesus performed many miracles was brought out of the Garden of Eden (Atlantis) by Adam and passed to Enoch, Noah, and Shem, until it reached Abraham (the first Hebrew patriarch).

Today, a replica of this Staff sits behind the Capitol Rostrum as the symbol of the power and authority of the United States Congress.

By following the Staff, and the bloodline of Adam, we will follow the plan to rebuild the New Atlantis, the New Tula or the New Jerusalem after the Flood.

The story begins at the beginning.

WAITING FOR THE BULL TO RUN

10,000 B.C., can be considered year zero for humanity's effort to rebuild Atlantis and reconnect with the heavenly Tula. Astrologers call this time the Age of Leo. Scholars call this time "prehistoric," the Neolithic or New Stone Age.

This was the time when the earthly Atlantis was in ruins and when the planet An, in its 3,600 year orbit was tailing away from its recent rendezvous with earth. Sitchin claims the Flood resulted from the gravitational pull of the nearing An or Nibiru on the unstable ice sheet over Antarctica.3 An's tire tracks, frozen in the geological and climatic record, coincide with the abrupt end of the last ice age c. 12,000 years ago.

In the five millennia between 10,000 B.C. and 5,000 B.C., archaeology and paleoanthropology tell us, the earth was the domain of bands of primitive nomads and hunter-gatherers.

Archaeologists working in Anatolia have explored the major settlement of Catal Huyuk, inhabited between 6250 and 5400 B.C.4 Their iconography comprises two main symbols which reveal a Pleiadian connection: a goddess, and a male figure resembling a bull or sometimes a "bearded man riding a bull," a sign of things to come.

During this time period, astrologically the Ages of Cancer and Gemini, it is possible An made two more appearances, c. 8,700 B.C. and again in c. 5,100 B.C.

In ages past, we notice An may have made two encore appearances since c. 10,000 B.C. While 3,600 years may seem like an eternity to us, time goes by quickly if you're a Shining One of An making this cosmic journey. As Psalm 90 says:

A thousand years, in thy eyes,
are as a day past, gone by,

Many texts, including the Hindu, speak of enormously vast time periods and gods who live hundreds, even thousands of years.

The key is to realize these texts were written by beings which did not live on earth time. They lived on divine-time. One divine year -- the time it takes for An to orbit the Sun -- equals 3,600 years on earth. That's a ratio of 1:3600.

This means the being we knew as Enki in Atlantis could reappear today. To him, only four divine years would have elapsed. This also means that while thousands of years have elapsed on earth, in divine-time the cataclysm of Atlantis just happened. The rescue is still underway.

According to historians, during the Age of Gemini, c. 6000 B.C., man is supposed to be a primitive creature with the approximate cosmic awareness of a monkey.

Tell that to the Aryans of India whose myths and hymns including the *Rig-Veda* detail astronomical events from this time period. These ancient Hindus shared the Egyptian obsession with Orion and Sirius. Their hymns also speak of ancestors coming from across the sea, survivors of a great flood.

EGYPT: THE TIME CAPSULE FOR THE AGES

Around 4,000 B.C., Egypt, the time capsule for the ages, began to open. The rapid, untraceable advances in human culture that took place in Egypt at this time have astonished archaeologists. Civilization simply exploded in this area. It was as if Egyptian civilization were a mighty seed that pushed and pushed until finally it blossomed from underneath the desert.

With this blossoming, the New Age of Taurus the Bull was off and running.

Suddenly and inexplicably there appeared sophisticated agriculture, art, religion, temple building, and other elements of high civilization. To some observers, such as Graham Hancock,5 these phenomenal advances are difficult to account for unless there was a group of people who preserved the basic seeds of advanced civilization (as in a time capsule) and were responsible for unearthing this capsule and helping its seeds to blossom.

The Egyptians plainly state they were the children of Maat.6 Sirius was the Great Provider. If we take them for their word, that they are the children of Tiamat, and their gardeners and teachers came from Sirius, does this explain how Egyptian civilization could appear to have simply blossomed out of thin air?

The Age of Taurus is the beginning of Biblical time. It is also when time began to be measured in earth time. Events and life spans began to be recorded in days, months and years which were now tied to the cycles of the Sun and Moon, rather than the 3,600 year cycle of An.

Sunday school teachers, historians and Hollywood have interpreted Biblical times as a period of tribal wandering, clan warfare and nomadic existence. It could be this was the lot of the majority of civilization after the Flood. With only the meagerest remnants of civilization left, they were forced to fight for a living and to live off the land.

What if, however, Biblical characters were more like the characters in *Mad Max* who once lived in a post-industrial world and suddenly found themselves in the process of rebuilding after a global cataclysm? Scattered around them were massive temples and artifacts they likely only dimly recognized. What stories might they invent to explain these strange monuments?

There may be only one way for us big brain Aquarians to appreciate their harrowing predicament. Imagine if suddenly we faced another Atlantean moment when all "the goods" of western civilization, our advanced technology and life's necessities -- space shuttles, satellites, automobiles, airplanes, computers, the Internet, telephones, televisions, microwave ovens, refrigerators, hair dryers, CD players, shopping malls, grocery stores, plumbing -- suddenly evaporated and we were forced to live off the land. How many of us would survive? How long would it take for us to climb back to this level of civilization? Could we do it? (Would we want to?)

Despite all the hardships, a segment of the population had retained enough civilization to record what happened and to lead humanity off the death march trail step by step onto the golden path to a New Atlantis. By all accounts the initiates knew humanity would make a quantum leap to a new rung of evolution's golden spiral during the Age of Taurus (c. 4,000 B.C.) and another six thousand years later in c. AD 2000, at the beginning of the Age of Aquarius.

That appears to have been the plan anyway.

These key dates were fixed by the four beasts of that sublimest of all sublime creatures, the Sphinx, which open-minded scholars now believe was constructed in 10,000 B.C.

The Sphinx -- the lion, bull, eagle and human adorned with the uraeus snake (the Egyptian symbol of mastery of time and space) -- has captured the imagination of humanity for millennia. Astrologers believe it is symbolic of the four New Ages in which the human race would make quantum evolutionary jumps: Leo the Lion, Taurus the Bull, Aquarius the Human (2000 AD) and Scorpio the Eagle (c. 9000 AD).

LAND OF THE MOON

The early Egyptians called Egypt *El Khe-menu* or the Land of the Moon after the Lord of Khemenu, Thoth.[7] Earth herself was called *Ta-Meri*, possibly after Mer or Tiamat.[8] (Fascinatingly, when the Arabs in the tenth century AD they inexplicably referred to Cairo as *El-Kahira*, or "Mars."[9])

Before the Flood, Thoth (whom the Hebrews called Enoch) was called to heaven.[10] During a personal meeting with "the Lord" he was instructed to build the Great Pyramid and (along with his wife Seshet) to begin gathering artifacts and important books of knowledge. These items would be stored in a Hall of Records underneath the Great Pyramid and the Sphinx. They would be located in future generations and be used to spiritually initiate and uplift the human race.

The enormity of this undertaking is virtually off the occult Richter scale. Global in scope, psychic and physical in actualization, this was a titanic effort to preserve and protect what had taken thousands of years to create.

According to Egyptian myth, Thoth had more than an engineering miracle to perform when building the Pyramid. Egypt was a land fraught with challenge. The Egypt that emerges from the remarkably consistent and cohesive Edgar Cayce psychic readings is one of a new nation disintegrating under the sudden stresses and strains of massive planetary changes, earthquakes and sinking continents, mass migrations of people, the shifting of the earth's poles and an impending Great Cataclysm.

If prophecies and forecasts are correct was it not a time very much like our own?

Something or *someone* had to unite the people. If there were ever a time for a great messenger to appear and bring to mankind an important vision for the future, this was it -- and his name was Thoth.

His role as Peacemaker is shown most movingly in a hymn contained in Chapter 183 of the Egyptian *Book of the Dead* where he is referred to as Thoth, the Peacemaker.

Since Egyptian cosmology was dualistic we know that "peace" refers to the uniting of heaven and earth.

Does the cataclysm of Tiamat or Atlantis explain why the entire social philosophy of Egypt was geared toward effecting a mass transmutation (or rescue) of their civilization from a lower state to a higher state which enabled the soul to return home?

Was this transmutational focus so prominent that it compelled the Greeks to call the land of Egypt, itself, the land of Khem, the land of alchemy or transmutation?

TEMPLE SCHOOLS

Archaeologists who have followed this line of thinking have inevitably found the center point of the reemergence of civilization at Egyptian temples that also doubled as schools.

These ancient temples appear to be a means to preserve the sacred teachings of the Egyptians.

By traveling down the Nile from temple to temple, the neophyte would experience the religious teaching each school offered in preparation for the ultimate initiation at the Great Pyramid.

Evidence of this network of temples of initiation is found in the Building Texts, discovered among the ancient hieroglyphic inscriptions on the inner enclosure wall of the temple of Edfu, an ancient Egyptian holy city that was dedicated to the god Horus.

The Building Texts contain references to such astounding records as "The Sacred Book of Temples," which is an inventory, or perhaps a travel log, giving a list, history and description of shrines and sacred places dating into remote antiquity.

Is it possible these sacred places were known in Atlantean times?

THE EGG OF CREATION

"And God said, Let the waters under the heaven be gathered together unto one place and let the dry land appear: and it was so."

Genesis 1:9

Astonishingly, the Edfu inscriptions tell us that *before* the Flood an enormous mound or island was raised out of the Nile waters in the area of present-day Saqqara, Giza and Heliopolis. This artificially raised mound, which scholars now suspect was a *twelve-acre, thirty-foot high megalithic platform* -- was called the Egg of Creation.11 Upon it sits the Great Pyramid. Thoth, or his followers the Peacemakers, were credited with this breathtaking engineering feat.

Now, a *twelve-acre, thirty-foot high megalithic platform* called *the Egg of Creation* provokes more questions than can be answered in this book. Was this Egg of Creation the original Tula on earth? Was this Egg a womb constructed to work in conjunction a human resurrection machine?

The Sumerian tale, *The Epic of Gilgamesh* (c. 2000 B.C.), describes the Flood and the king's search for the lost secrets of immortality and the way to ascend into the heavens, the "Land of the Living." His destination is a place which turns out to be the secret home of the An which features:

• an enormous wall with
• a gate which stuns all intruders, but which opens to
• a tunnel system leading to
• a holy enclosure
• in which stands a Tree of Life or ladder ascending to heaven
• beside which a "god" speaks.

This description matches the mythological descriptions of the Garden of Eden, the Egg of Creation, Solomon's Temple, and the New Jerusalem or New Atlantis.

In his excellently researched *Giza One*,12 Dr. Joseph Jochmans explains how the Egg was raised by planting sacred power tools. One was called the "Member of Progenitor," another the "image of the Arm," apparently in relation to the ability of this device to uplift or separate the earth from the waters of the Nile.

Once the Egg of Creation was habitable, say the Edfu texts, *djed pillars* were set up on the Egg.13 In my book *The Gardener and the Tree of Life*, I make the case that these djed pillars were the Trees of Life used to channel and balance the soulsphere.

In confirmation of this theory, the enigmatic Egg of Creation reappears in the Edfu inscriptions *after* the Deluge. In this gruesome chronicle we learn this time the Egg is in darkness. The waters (souls?) surrounding it are no longer the waters of primeval creation, but the waters of the *dead spirits*.14 The Egg is described as being submerged, split apart, as if by cataclysm! The soulsphere had collapsed. It needed to be revived.

The Edfu texts continue to offer illumination, informing us the Peacemakers have survived the destruction of their once great civilization (Atlantis?).

They have returned to claim their sacred books, power tools and the power words which enabled them. These items were stored in a protected site named the *bw-hmn*, the "deep place that is constructed" -- the Hall of Records.15

In the inscriptions it becomes clear that it was only the Peacemakers who had knowledge of this repository and its contents, including the power tools. They were also charged with its care. The texts make enigmatic reference to the Sphinx or a Winged Gateway as the marker for this sacred cache. In connection with this place, Thoth is identified as the "Overlord of the Image," meaning the "face, head, statue or sculpture" i.e. the Sphinx.16

According to the temple inscriptions, at each of the post-Flood temples they created, the Peacemakers established a priesthood. Once the area was sufficiently reestablished, the sacred books and power tools were returned to the Hall of Records. From this point forward the Hall became known as the "Place of the Throne of the Soul," the place where knowledge of resurrection, ascension *and* embodiment of the soul was housed.17

THE KING OF TERROR

As I discussed in *The Peacemaker and the Key of Life*, Nostradamus left numerous prophecies suggesting that the Sphinx and Pyramid complex is the place where the current era Peacemaker will return to recover crucial power tools used to resurrect the King of Tula sometime around the year 2,000.

In my book, I offer explanations for why Nostradamus called the Peacemaker (who may be Jesus) "the King of Terror." His mission is to resurrect the King of Angolmois, an anagram for Mongolia. Earlier we explored this region's connection to Tula and to WW II. It may be the earthly home of the Gardener, the King of Tula, whom F.D.R. was seeking in 1934. Why call this figure's herald "the King of Terror"? Consider:

• The Arabs call the Sphinx the Father of Terror.18

• The Sphinx faces to the east, indicating its creators intended it as a symbol of the sealed Eastern Gate (through which the messiah enters).

• In addition to calling the Shining Ones Nephilm, the Hebrews called the Shining Ones the Emim, "terrors".19

• In a Grail legend popular in Nostradamus' home in Southern France, Jesus appears to a young Frenchman and dictates his book to him: "Here commences the first telling of the Holy Grail," says Jesus. "Here commences terror."20 The young Frenchman is instantly terrified, then enlightened.

From this moment forward, at least in Southern France, Jesus, terror, enlightenment and the Holy Grail (the Cup of Destiny) were linked.

According to Nostradamus' King of Terror prophecy, the reappearance of this Shining One and the recovery of the cache of sacred Atlantean science and power tools hidden within the Sphinx, will rock the cradle of New Age politics.

Is it possible F.D.R. and Hitler knew this secret science would also put us in touch with the god-beings of Atlantis and their stunning array of soul capabilities?

Nostradamus predicted that the rediscovery of this sacred knowledge would cause the clock on the existing Big Four religions to grind to a halt. Played out, they will either be made obsolete (or transformed) by proof of the existence of an advanced pre-Flood civilization and the unveiling of the original religion and language.

According to Nostradamus, in the King of Terror's hand (or perhaps his wife's) is the Key of Life -- the teachings which enable the human soul to blossom and for earth's spore to spill into the cosmic ocean.

With this "rod of iron" as the book of Revelation calls it (aka the Staff of Destiny), the messiah rules from atop the pyramid of human civilization (just as depicted on the back of the one dollar bill). With a single wave of his wand, like the strum of a harp, will this figure send out shockwaves that instantly change the rules of New Age politics?

The appearance of this Shining One promises to be the fulfillment of the dream of all history which began after the Flood and began to pick up momentum with Jesus' ancestor, the Hebrew patriarch Abraham. It promises to be a victory of and for the human race, bringing enlightenment.

Make no mistake about it. Some will see this triumph of the human spirit as a terrible event.

To fully understand the Secrets that may soon be coming out of the ground in Egypt we must get to know Abraham. For most of us, Abraham is one of those Biblical characters we used to watch Sunday school teachers put up on felt boards and wax poetic about. He is most famous as the obedient son of God and the patriarch of Israel.

In addition, Abraham is a hyper-mysterious figure, a man of light draped in a thick blanket of secrets standing at the edge of the gate to the Promised Land. That is to say, secretly Abraham may be one of the architects of the New Atlantis. He, perhaps more than any other Biblical or other historical figure, possessed the deep occult Secrets the Nazis sought to possess. This alone makes studying him worthwhile.

Abraham came to earth four millennia ago to usher in humanity's first true post-Atlantean New Age. By taking a few moments to understand the politics of his New Age we will learn a lot about what may come in our own.

Notes:

1. Louis Pauwels and Jacques Bergier *The Morning of the Magicians* (New York, Stein & Day, 1960) p. 146
2. John Major Jenkins *Maya Cosmogenesis 2012* (Santa Fe, NM, Bear & Co., 1998) p. xlv
3. Zecharia Sitchin *The Twelfth Planet* (New York, Avon Books, 1976) p. 401-405
4. Julien Ries *The Origins of Religions* (Grand Rapids, MI, William B. Eerdman Publishing Co., 1993) p. 58
5. Graham Hancock *The Fingerprints of the Gods* (New York, Crown Publishers, 1995)
6. E.A. Wallis Budge *The Gods of the Egyptians* (New York, Dover Publications, 1969) Vol. 1. p. 423
7. Barbara G. Walker *The Woman's Encyclopedia of Myths and Secrets* (New York, HarperCollins, 1983) p. 671
8. Bruce Rux *Architects of the Underworld* (Berkeley, Ca., Frog, Ltd., 1996) p. 277
9. Ibid. P. 262
10. *The Book of Enoch*
11. Dr. Joseph R. Jochmans *Giza One -- Keys to the Hall of Records*, p. 61
12. Ibid. p. 61
13. Ibid. p. 62
14. Ibid. p. 62
15. Ibid. p. 62
16. Ibid. p. 62
17. Ibid. p. 63
18. Ibid. p. 276
19. Robert Graves & Raphael Patai *Hebrew Myths* (New York, Anchor Books, 1964) p. 106
20. Norma Lorre Goodrich *The Holy Grail* (New York, HarperCollins, 1992) p. 5

CHAPTER TWENTY

ABRAHAM: HE WHO HAS RAM

Descended of Shem, the oldest son of Noah, Abraham was born some 4,000 years ago (c. 2,200 B.C.) in the city of Ur ("light," "fire").[1] He arrived precisely at the time when the New Age of Aries the Ram replaced the Age of Taurus the Bull.

Abraham means "the father of the Ram," or "he who possesses ram." He could have been a holy warrior (or holy-roller) from any country from Tibet to Egypt:

• In Egypt, "Ab" means heart-soul, the soul weighed in the balance by the Goddess Maat or Tiamat.[2] The heart-soul was symbolized by a tiny dancer in the middle of the body.

• In Tibet, "ram" means "basis of the world" and is used as the symbol for all that radiates from the Sun: the Central Spiritual Sun, Tula, that is.

• In Egypt, the ram was also the symbol for the savior, the fire of the sun, and was expressed by the pyramids ("fire within").[3] In Arabic, pyramid is *ashram*.

These connections link Abraham with the Egyptian savior archetype, the heron. Perhaps he looked the world over looking for just the right place to descend. He had many choices.

Even the briefest survey of global history in Abraham's time reveals that the Planetary Grid, at long last, was preparing to blossom. Egypt, Israel, Syria, Tibet, India, South America, and Mexico were all experiencing growth as if the entire planetary mind was somehow waking up after the nightmare of Atlantis.

166

Our attention is drawn in particular to Mexico and Egypt. The deep kinship between the Maya in Mexico, who claimed they were former Atlanteans and called Tula the "place of herons," and their brethren in Egypt has been hinted several times here.

This connection is obvious even to the untrained eye in the technology, geographical knowledge, and observational astronomy the Mexicans built into the masonry of their great city Teotihuacan.4 Scholars date the beginnings of this city to 4,000 B.C., the beginning of the New Age preceding Abraham, the Age of Taurus the Bull.

It is no coincidence that Jose Arguelles, author of *The Mayan Factor*, has called Teotihuacan a Tula. Interestingly, the Teotihuacan complex (pronounced *Tay-oo-tay-wa-can*) is a mirror image of the Great Pyramid complex on the Giza plateau. Here, as in Egypt, there are three principal pyramids: the Pyramid or Temple of Quetzalcoatl, the Pyramid of the Sun and the Pyramid of the Moon.5

Quetzalcoatl was revered by the Mayans as a god of Peace and King of Tula.6 His name means "the feathered-serpent." He was frequently depicted as a man with a fish mask, a bird-fish-man. Like the Egyptian heron, he was shown perched atop the Mayan pyramids.

Is it possible Quetzalcoatl is the same serpent or fish-bird-man who simultaneously appeared in Egypt as Thoth?7 Based upon these remarkable correspondences, numerous scholars have asked this question.

Intriguingly, from the occult point of view, Abraham's story in 2,200 B.C. is the same as Thoth's and Quetzalcoatl's. His assignment is the same -- to kickstart the Planetary Grid and usher in the New Age -- in this case the Age of Aries. Is it possible Abraham, too, was one in a line of these fish-bird-men?

Three world religions blossomed from the seeds Abraham planted: Judaism, Christianity and Islam. These are the Big Three religions with the most to gain (or lose) in New Age politics upon decipherment of his secrets (or release of "the goods" stored in the Hall of Records). We can begin to see the value of taking a fairly detailed, but thrilling, peek at this heroic past New Ager.

THE BLOODLINE OF ABRAHAM
AND THE BEGINNING OF ISRAEL

According to esoteric tradition, the Key of Life given to Adam (the Adapa) by God (An) in the Garden of Eden (Atlantis) was handed down from generation to generation of key-holders and Pyramid keepers, until it reached the family of Abraham.

Practically all of the previous key-holders have been fish-bird-men.

Abraham was no exception.

These fish-bird-men are most easily identified by their trademark fish suits and by their water myths.

* They walk on water (as did Jesus),
* Are rescued from water (like Noah, Moses and Deganawidah),
* or, in the case of Jonah, are rescued from the belly of a great fish. (Jonah is Oannes, the Fish Man of the Dogon, from which came the common name John.)

Could it be the water motif is a symbolic tip-off that these individuals are members of a priesthood who have mastered advanced spiritual knowledge which was rescued from the catcslysmic destruction of Atlantis by water?8

Mythologically speaking, the three days Jonah spent in the belly of the whale9 are the three days Jesus spent in between crucifixion and resurrection.

Jonah was spit from the mouth of the whale onto dry land of Tarshish or Tartarus, aka Turtle Island (the New Atlantis).

Hercules, the Greek savior whose Pillars symbolize the (star?) gateway to Atlantis, was the son of the moon-virgin Alcmene (the Greek version of the Hebrew *almah*, "moon-virgin," a title later given to the virgin Mary).10 He too was rescued from the belly of a whale.

The fish, we have seen, is an ark symbol, which points to a rescue from water.

This takes us back to Tiamat, the heavenly Atlantis.

The Great Fish was one of the evacuation vehicles or arks from Tiamat or Mer (Mary) whose freight represented the seeds of life passing from Tiamat to the Moon to earth.

In the Bible, the "blossoming" of these seeds is heralded by the arrival of the dove (Genesis 8:12), the symbol of Mer or Tiamat, and later used to represent the Holy Spirit of Jesus. Symbolically, "Jesus son of Maria" also means Jesus son of Mer or Tiamat, the Fish-mother.

In addition to the Hebrew terms bethula ("vessel of Tula") and almah, Mary often received the title of "Ark." The word ark is thought to mean vessel, chest or box for preserving sacred things.

This meaning is reflected in the Argha of the Hindus and in the ship the *Argo* of Jason and the Argonauts who daringly sought the Golden Fleece of a magical flying ram.

Serious Ark raiders, like the Nazis, pay attention to these mythological connections for, as we shall see momentarily, they point to the true nature of the Ark of the Covenant.

ABRAHAM: "FROM THE OTHER SIDE OF THE FLOOD"

The Bible tells us Abraham lived in a town called Ur, located in present-day Iraq. This was also the home of the Ur-religion and Ur-language. For centuries Ur lay undisturbed. Then, as dawn arose on a New Age, it became favorite digging grounds of the German scholars who were looking for the original Atlantean language, and American Bible scholars who were seeking to prove the Bible true.

In Joshua 24:3, in a gathering of the Israelites at the sacred oak at Shechem, we learn the first Secret of the father of the Jews. God took Abraham from "*the other side of the Flood.*"

What does *that* mean?

Did Abraham, or his gene pool, wash up at Ur from the same place as Noah, as in Atlantis? Could Abraham be Noah reincarnated? Or, instead of his grandson or his reincarnation, could Abraham be Noah with a new name? What would this suggest about Ur? Could it be an early Atlantean outpost?

We may not be too far out of touch with Biblical reality in suggesting so. In fact, are we just far enough out to be in?

"Noah" is the Hebrew name for Nu, or Nun, the "Fish," originally the god born of Ma-Nun, the Egyptian Goddess of the Deep whose name turns up in the Sumerian, Egyptian *and* Aryan creation-flood myths.11

Egypt, we noted, was called El Khe-me-nu, the Land of the Moon. Here is one explanation why;

"Ma" or "Me" was another name for the Sumerian Womb of Chaos, or Tiamat. "Nu" was the embryonic seed of life that was associated with the Moon. Putting this all together, could Ma-Nun be Man-Un, Ma-Un or the Moon?12

If so, this suggests two very strange, but illuminating, possibilities. One, Abraham, like Thoth, may be one of the Moon men. Perhaps even *the* healing moon man, or *christos*.

The fact that the people of Ur worshipped the Moon god (whom they called Sin), supports this idea. As in Egyptian tradition, were the Urians awaiting the arrival of a heron or christos at the beginning of the New Age of Aries? Was Abraham recognized as this figure?

Similarly, 2,150 or so years later, the Essenes awaited the arrival of the christos (Jesus) at the beginning of the Age of Pisces, our year zero. This set the clock ticking for the next appearance at the beginning of the next New Age.

Today, two thousand years after the appearance of Jesus, millions are looking to the sky (or beyond to the cosmic ocean) for the incredibly exciting appearance of the new fish-bird-man. According to Egyptian myth of the return of the heron and the prophecy of Nostradamus, this figure will land on top of the pyramid, open the Hall of Records and share a phenomenal teaching with humanity.

Many believe this will be Jesus. Only instead of being crucified, this time he will reign during a Thousand Years of Peace. Since Jesus' signature, the fish or 8, is the Egyptian hieroglyph for the heron, is it possible the modern world is on the verge of experiencing the same series of events as the people of ancient Egypt, Iraq and Palestine?

A second strange possibility suggested by the connection between Egypt and the Moon emerges. The Aryans recall that after their victorious king *Ma-nu,* also called *Ra-ma* in Hindu tradition and later identified by the Greeks with their green-faced god Dionysus (the Gardener), the Aryans flooded into India.13

Are we to conclude Manu, aka the Aryan Moon man and Gardener, was not just a Hebrew savior, but also an Aryan savior as well? Were the Jewish and Aryan religions originally intertwined?

The new Aryan world order Manu or Rama founded, the Rama Empire, is believed to stretch thousands of years into antiquity. It was founded by the ancient serpent/fish-bird-men or *mer-men,* who worked for the mother goddess Ninharsag, guarding her treasure in underwater palaces and keeping books of mystic knowledge.

We have traced the origins of these mermen and the knowledge they preserve to Tiamat.

Connecting the mythological dots between the Aryan Manu and the myth of Tiamat leaves me wondering: did the Aryan empire initiated by Rama originate in the Pleiades too?

Scholars can't say for sure. However, they do know its earthly, but no less ethereal, focal point was the Indus valley of India. Some believe this civilization's cultural links with the Sumerian civilization are so close that the Indus civilization is the offspring of Sumeria, specifically Enki, the *original* Fish Man and Gardener. Others believe it co-existed with Atlantis (which I proposed was founded by Enki).

Reflecting on the dots we have connected between Enki, Thoth, Abraham and Noah, and Noah and Manu/Rama raises an astounding (surprise) question:

Did the Jewish people borrow their mythology from the Egyptians, as is commonly stated, or the Aryans (Sumerians) of India who were former Atlanteans?

To us this question may seem astounding. However, were HPB here she'd pull a long drag from a cigarette, blow a big puff of smoke, and tell a whale of a politically incorrect tale.

The Jews, the Mongolians and the ancient Akkadians (Sumerians), she'd say, are *all* descendents of the Aryans. And yes, they were Atlanteans. This was obvious.

As evidence she might display a Tibetan Buddhist yantra popular in Hindu mysticism which features a six-pointed Jewish Star of David with a swastika at its center. The crossed swords of the swastika, she'd comment, symbolize the ether or blue air.

HPB would also say, as she did at the turn of the 20th century, that the Aryans would soon be replaced by a new and improved race, which was evolving not in Nazi Germany, but in America. (Though Hitler generally subscribed to tenets of HPB's Theosophy, this thought would no doubt have been repulsive to him.)

Now, the fact that the Nazi swastika and the Jewish star were once unified may be disturbing for some. I'm not out to defend HPB and her politically incorrect ideas. I'm out to follow the golden thread of Atlantis.

In following this thread we take note that in the name Abraham we have mythological proof that HPB was not pulling her ideas out of thin air. The mythological strands linking the Aryan and Jewish religions and peoples are there. These strands, more of which we'll explore now, may be perceived as heretical to some. However, they are among the most relevant pieces to the occult puzzle of WW II. They show us, once again, that WW II was a family squabble between the gods and their children.

H

When we first meet the father of the Jews he is Ab-ram. Isn't this the Aryan Brama, with the *a* as prefix instead of suffix? Brama ("First Born") was the name of the Hindu creator god (which was imagined as a cosmic egg or cave). Later the letter *H* was added, making it Brahma.

Why was the "H" added? The Bible goes to great pains to make the explicit point that after his "initiation" by the Gardener Melchizedek, Abram became the new and improved role model of the Jews, Abraham.14 Mystics claim the *H* signified Abraham's acquisition of the "breath of God" or "soul of God." Simultaneously, his wife Sara became Sarah, suggesting she too received this "breath."

H symbolizes the soul of God you say? *H* is also the 8th letter of the alphabet.

As noted, 8 is the number of infinity, Tula, Thoth, the Key of Life, and Jesus. Erase the very bottom swell of the 8 and we're left with the Egyptian hieroglyph for the heron. Turn it sideways, and don't we have Jesus' symbol, the fish swimming sideways?

Some believe the H represents the soul of Melchizedek, *the* Fish Man, which some mystics believe inhabited the body of Abraham just as it later did Jesus, who was a priest forever after the Order of Melchizedek. This suggests Jesus also acquired the H (and lends occult authority to the slang declaration "Jesus *H.* Christ!"). Do the words "after the order" make Jesus one in a line of other key-holders?

If the key the mystics are holding is the soul of the savior, does this mean Jesus' ancestor Abraham was one in the line of 8's before him?

Or, is Abraham actually the soul of the Gardener incarnate? Should we take one of F.D.R.'s one dollar bills with the Gardener's logo stamped on it and stick it on Abraham's or Jesus' name tag?

It is hard to say. Interestingly, however, in the Babylonian tale of Abarama, we learn of a gardener, who lived at the time of Abraham. This is intriguing. It seems unlikely to me that a mere gardener would be memorialized in myth: a star being, perhaps even a New Age savior figure, would.

H RETURNS

In Germany, the runic letter *H* was revered by the inner core of the SS.15 This fact may reveal more about the Nazis, and their mastery of messianic occult legend, than any other fact.

In SS-land the four arms of the H were related to the four points of the ss-wastika, which to Himmler and his goose-ss-tepping goon-ss, ss-ymbolized the cro-ss ss-ection of the caduceu-ss or (SS) taff of Destiny, which was powered by the ss-oul or hi-ss of the ss-erpent god and godde-ss.

Each point of four points of the H (plus the center point) also represented the five men who ran Nazi Germany, all of whose names began with an H.16 These men were Hitler, Himmler, Hess, Reinhard Heydrich (head of the Gestapo), and Dr. Karl Haushofer, the founder of the occult Vril Society and member of the inner sanctum of the Thule Society.

As any green Freemason, including F.D.R., would have observed in an intelligence briefing on this subject, H also stands for the Greek Savior and Sun god *Helios* and was used by the Freemasons to indicate the two pillars of Solomon's Temple joined by the golden thread.

There's your trouble. Occultists appear to believe the curiously popular H stands for the ladder or gateway to Tula.

Were the Nazis on the verge of opening this gate? Yes indeed! This may be the greatest occult secret of WW II.

ABRHAM:BRAHMA

In Aryan myth and scripture we learn Brahma had his source in Ahriman, the Great Serpent who tempted man and woman, and, who revolted against his mirror or twin brother, the Heavenly Father, in a war in heaven.17

Isn't this the basic story of Enki and Enlil?

The Persian Magi (the cult of famous Wise Men who later greeted Abraham's descendent Jesus) considered Ahriman the source of their magic power. He was the Hindu god Aryman, maker of "Aryans"18 -- the Atlantean people he created from clay (just like Adam in the Bible).

Welcome back, my friends, to the show that never ends.

We have, once again, entered the alien mirror world that is the study of Atlantis. There's a funny thing about this occult mirror. It sometimes puts us face to face with which we don't want to face.

In this case, the Atlantean mirror shows us the Aryan Brama is obviously Enlil. Abram, his mirror image, is Enki or his offspring.

In our Atlantean mirror we find the truth behind the myth behind the story behind the legend of Abraham. His story marks the start of the post-Flood antagonisms between Enki ("Mr. Melting Pot") and Enlil ("Mr. Eugenics").

As Rome had its founder Romulus (Enlil) who murdered his brother Remus – Enki's *Sumer* spelled backward – Abraham's New Age of Aries witnessed the epic drama between Abram, the founder of Israel, and his twin Brama, who are mirror images of one another.

As Roma (or Rome) did battle with its mirror image Amor (the Cathars of Southern France), Atlantis (Enki's kingdom of light) did battle with Rama (Enlil).

These ancient war games are shockingly relevant to New Agers today since this mirror world effect is *the* occult pattern that continually repeats itself throughout history and was even reflected in the Holy War of WW II.

THE EYE OF THE STORM

If the Nazis were holding on to this wildly bucking bull, they would have realized the occult interpretation of Jewish mythology suggests that while Abraham is called the father of the Israelites, he just as easily (and properly) could be called the father of the new Atlanteans.

Abraham was.... Atlantean? Surely the Nazis weren't so arrogant or stupid as not to question this.

This question would have put the Nazis precisely just above the dip in (Taurus the Pleiadian) bull's back -- the place the riders call the "eye of the storm."

This wild bull does not give up its secrets easily. A powerful leftward step followed by a thrust skyward sends us flying headlong into Atlantean politics at the beginning of the New Age of Aries.

Abraham's story, as well as his tight mystic relationship with Melchizedek, indeed implicates Abraham as one of the

ONE FOOT IN ATLANTIS

Planetary Healers, who were the founders of Atlantis. Did they return to earth to create a New Atlantis and continue their rescue mission of the souls of Tiamat during the time of Abraham?

Perhaps even more incredibly, when the Nazis joined this Aryan rodeo did they too realize that looking at Abraham's activity in the dualistic Atlantean mirror reveals another strange reflection? Did they ask if Abraham's home, Ur -- the home of the original language and religion -- was actually on earth?

In the dualistic cosmology of the ancients, earthly cities and temples are copies of heavenly originals. By this line of thinking, is it possible that Ur, the *original* Kingdom of Light, is in the stars?

Is Ur actually Urion, or Orion, the Aryan or Atlantean homeland in the stars?

By this interpretation we could easily accuse Abraham, the father of the Israelites, of not being human.

So let's accuse him. Carried to it's extreme, as no doubt the Nazis did, we may posit that when the Bible tells us Abraham was brought from "the other side of the Flood," it may mean he is a Shining One (possibly not a human being) who was brought from Orion.

According to Sumerian myth, this is where a fortunate group of survivors who fled in arks from the destruction of the Pleiadean planet Tiamat were residing.

Some of these Shining Ones are the heroic cowboys on white horses of the ancient world. The deviant ones wear black hats. When they get together it's a real rodeo in which the winner takes all.

Once freed from his shroud of secrecy, does Abraham emerge as a shining holy *star* warrior engaged in the bitter Atlantean family struggle between Enki and Enlil? What is the crux of this family struggle?

What else, but control of humanity and their right to use the power tools of Atlantis to return home.

Perceived through our occult Atlantean mirror, do our orthodox interpretations of Abraham's life appear hopelessly inadequate? If Abraham is Atlantean, does it then also follow that the Bible is *Atlantean* too?

If we answer these questions affirmatively, wouldn't this overthrow or destroy *any* Nazi belief in the superiority of the blood of one race of humans over another?

Hasn't our investigation into Tula myths revealed that *all* souls came from the same pure place?

Isn't it possible that *all* people on earth, not just the Aryans, have the ability to achieve the holy blood?

174

Are we not all children of the Shining Ones? Don't *all* Abraham's offspring, Jews, Muslims, and Christians alike, carry the soul of Atlantis, the soul of the gods, awaiting a time when they awaken and blossom?

With the possibility in mind that we all carry the potential to become gods, and some carry the Christ soul. Does this help to explain why Hitler would seek to exterminate the children of the Shining Ones?

THE OAKS

Let us continue exploring Abraham's strand in the golden thread. In so doing we will reveal additional startling occult secrets.

One day c. 2200 B.C., "the Lord" appeared to Abraham at the sacred oak of Shechem, where Abraham built an altar. Later, Abraham built another altar to the oak god at Mamre.

Talking about the mystic Abraham without mentioning his incredible oak fetish is like talking about Jack without mentioning a thing about the importance of beanstalks. Three facts offer insight:

• first, the oak god is the Green Man,[19] aka the Gardener and Fish Man Enki,

• second, the oak is sacred among many ancient peoples, primarily because of its powerful and majestic form and its habit of attracting lightning[20] or the blue fire of heaven (like the copper columns of Moses and Jung and the Tula tree of Tesla),

• third, in the 4th century A.D., Constantine (who saw fit to torture and twist Christianity to fit his political needs) said Abraham's home at the Oak of Mamre was still a pagan shrine: "It is reported that *the most damnable idols are set up beside it.*"

There's your trouble.

In the Language of the Birds, the oaks could connect Abraham with the Druids, the men of the oak trees who communicated with the Children of An, for the reason that "false idols" or "damnable idols" is Enlil-speak for the Atlantean power tools.

Calling these power tools which allow the exit from the earth "false idols" appears to be a grotesque, but effective, literary ruse of priests who wished to dominate the fledgling human race that was still painfully smarting from hitting the unforeseen iceberg during the Atlantean cataclysm.

Careful decoding of the events which transpire around Abraham's "oak tree" reveals this may be the profound moment when the torch of Atlantean and Egyptian legend and religion is adopted and transformed by a new group of peoples, the Israelites.

Their ascendancy exalted the Israelites in the eyes of big brain Freemasons like George Washington, Thomas Jefferson and Benjamin Franklin, who read their stories like architects, read blueprints.

The Israelite's powerful potential also marked them for persecution by dictatorial regimes throughout their history, including the Ceasar's Rome and Hitler's Nazi Germany, who read the same codes but came up with a different membership plan for entrance to their racist version of the New Atlantis.

THE LAND OF HOLES

According to Hebrew legend, Abraham was a child of destiny whose life's mission was to overthrow the gods21 (which is why King Nimrod ordered him killed at birth). His mother's name, *Ami-tla-i* (*ami* is the root for "friend," *tla* is Tula),22 points to her and her son's connection with Tula or Atlantis.

Things began to heat up for Abraham when his father, Terah, an astronomer and noted idol maker, suddenly picked up and moved his family to Haran, a town five hundred miles from Ur. Like Ur, Haran was devoted to the worship of the Moon god whom they called Sin, but who was the same as the Egyptian Thoth and the Sumerian Kingu.

Har-An, says Philo, means "the land of holes."23 This is an interesting name (especially given the connection to the life-altering trans-dimensional hare or rabbit hole (stargate) in *Alice in Wonderland*). Cross-checking Hebrew and Aryan myth, in India we learn of Fohat, who digs holes in space.

Holes in space you say? Possibly in Haran? Hitler and the Nazi monsters were ridiculed by historians for believing the universe was an infinite rock (or cube) with hollow areas -- like a piece of Swiss cheese -- solid with holes. They claimed there were passages that allow travel between hollow areas.

Did the Nazi occultists learn this cosmology from Jewish or Aryan mythology? Or both?

I have endeavored to show that the Shining Ones of Tula, are essentially a rescue team of cowboys on white horses charged with opening "beam me up Scotty-type" gateways out of the so-called "Pit" of earth to Tula. Control of the power tools that dig these holes in heaven insures control of the destiny of the human race.

At crucial moments in human history (typically at the beginning of New Ages) these power tools (or the technology to recreate them) are located and used.

There is a need on the half of one faction of the Atlantean family to hide the star origins of branches of the human gene pool, and to prevent them from opening the hole or door to the Promised Land. Did Abraham represent the other half of the family, the one that sought to beam humanity into the Promised Land?

Where is the Promised Land? I have outlined myths that tell us it is the heavenly Atlantis, aka Tula, the Central Sun.

In corroboration, the Hindu "hole in space" theorists tell us that "below" the earth are seven intermediate points or cavities: Atala, Vitala, Sutala, Talatala, Mahatala, Rasatala, and Patala24 -- all names with the T-L-A significator letters indicating they are... Tulas.

These seven Tulas are described as unearthly (as in heavenly) holes.25 They contain cities built by Maya (one of the Pleiades) whose inhabitants live lives of utmost perfection amidst palaces, gardens and playgrounds.26 In Patala dwells the Lord An-an-ta, the primeval Hindu god, intoxicating all with drops of fragrant honey from his fresh *tulasi* flower!27

Interestingly, Abraham settled in a place called Beersheba or "Seven Wells." Beersheba, says Zecharia Sitchin, was a town controlled by Enlil. Of course it was! It makes sense for Enlil to want to control these holes. His life's purpose appears to be keeping the souls of Tiamat from returning home.

Following the golden thread as it weaves itself through the life of Abraham has led us not only to the possible origins of the bizarre Nazi "Swiss cheese" theory of holes in space, but also to either the inner earth world of the An (the reputed survivors of Atlantis), or the seven stars (holes) of the stargate to Tula, the Pleiades.

I tend to think it is the inner earth that is described due to the observation that the flow-er of life, the tulasi flower, is found there. However, since as the book of Revelation claims, one of these Tree of Life devices is on earth and the other is in heaven, could it be that the "holes in space" theory has led us to the *heavenly* Atlantis or Tula?

Continuing to follow this enigmatic golden thread leads to even more big-time Secrets and proof that the Atlantean ancestors of the Nazis had been in conflict with the Israelites -- which turns out to be another Atlantean alliance -- for at least the last four thousand years before WW II. This family squabble was over control of the power tools and the means to open the stargates and tie the thread (the Rainbow Bridge) between earth and Tula.

In the next chapter we'll stay tuned to Abraham's story. You won't want to miss how the Nazis twisted this occult knowledge.

Notes:

1. Reader's Digest *Who's Who in the Bible* (Pleasantville, NY, Reader's Digest, 1994) p. 16

2. Barbara G. Walker *The Woman's Encyclopedia of Myths and Secrets* (New York, HarperCollins, 1983) p. 2
3. Bruce Rux *Architects of the Underworld* (Berkeley, Ca., Frog, Ltd., 1996)p. 276
4. Graham Hancock *Fingerprints of the Gods* (New York, Crown, 1995) p. 168
5. Ibid. p. 169
6. Moira Timms *Beyond Prophecies and Predictions* (New York, Ballantine Books, 1980) p. 258
7. Zecharia Sitchin *When Time Began* (New York, Avon Books, 1993) p. 293
8. Graham Hancock *The Sign and the Seal* (New York, Crown Publishers, Inc., 1992) p. 323-328
9. Jonah 1:17
10. Ibid. p. 393
11. Ibid. p. 730
12. Ibid. p. 730
13. Edouard Schure*From Sphinx to Christ: An Occult History* (San Francisco, Harper & Row, 1970) p. 77
14. Genesis 17:4
15. Col. Howard A. Buechner and Capt. Wilhelm Bernhart *Adolph Hitler and the Secrets of the Holy Lance* (Metairie, LA, Thunderbird Press, 1988) p. 92
16. Ibid. p. 93
17. Ibid. p. 14
18. Ibid. p. 15
19. Ibid. p. 75
20. Barbara G. Walker *The Women's Dictionary of Symbols and Sacred Objects* (New York, HarperCollins, 1988) p. 468
21. Robert Graves & Raphael Patai *Hebrew Myths* (New York, Anchor Books, 1964) p. 134
22. Ibid. p. 135
23. Lloyd M. Graham *Deceptions and Myths of the Bible* (New York, Carol Publishing, 1994) p. 113
24. Cornelia Dimmitt & J.A.B. van Buitenen *Classical Hindu Mythology: A Reader in the Sanskrit Puranas* (Philadelphia, Temple University Press, 1978) p. 348
25. Ibid. p. 348
26. Ibid. p. 348
27. Ibid. p. 350

CHAPTER TWENTY ONE

THE STONE OF DESTINY
AND THE LADDER TO HEAVEN

The book of Genesis tells us Abraham was ordered out of Haran, the place of holes, into the wilderness of the land of Canaan by Yahweh (Enlil?)[1] Upon arrival, he set-up two command and control centers: the *Oaks of Mareh* (Ma refers to Tiamat) and *Bethel*, which is an Egyptian term for House of An or House of God.[2]

It is important to realize that Abraham is the grandfather of Jacob, who talked with the birds, feuded with his twin brother Esau even in their mother's womb,[3] and then pulled a fast one as an adult to get control of the power tools. Jacob is one of the bravest of all Biblical superheroes who appears to have possessed the profound occult knowledge the Nazis were after in their quest to develop their "Swiss cheese" universe theory into practical military and spiritual applications.

Genesis 28:11 tells us Jacob, this cunning bird-speaking commando, swooped in on Haran and took the *stones* that were hidden there.

What stones? Why were they hidden? What did Jacob use them for? What do they have to do with Abraham? What do they have to do with the crazy Nazis?

Buckle up. We're about to take-off on a journey that may well lead us to the answers to these questions.

JACOB'S LADDER

As he rested in exhaustion after his get-away flight from Haran, Jacob used one of these stones for a pillow.[4] He dreamed that he saw angels ascending and descending a ladder or supernatural stairway that was suspended between heaven and earth.[5]

179

Standing at the top of the stairway was the "Lord God of Abraham."6 (Would that be Enki, the Gardener?") When he awakened the morning after what appears to be an extraordinary journey into heaven, Jacob looked at the earth around him. "Terrible is this place,"7 he exclaimed. This is not surprising. Throughout the ages, people who have experienced a Near Death Experience, an Out of Body Experience, or have read the Tibetan, Hindu, Christian, Buddhist, or Egyptian writings on this subject all say the same thing: the glorious beauty of the "other side" is as sweet as honey.

Then, Jacob realized where he was. "This is none other than the house of God, and *this is the gate of heaven*".8 Did Jacob already know this? Is this why he picked this spot? Was Jacob in possession of a technology capable of knocking a hole in heaven? Is this what is meant when it is said he set the stone which enabled his magical journey into heaven as a pillar?

Was the stone in question none other than the Stone of Destiny?9

If so, why did Jacob, one of the brightest stars in the Lord God of Abraham's elite army, pour oil on top of it?

Ancient texts are loaded with stories of healing pillars or obelisks.10 Since the ultimate healing for the soul is escape from earth life and a return to Tula, does Jacob's "oil" perhaps have something to do with the journey to heaven?

This may be more than just a possibility. In the ancient Egyptian world, hieroglyphic inscriptions -- possibly the secret words of power or "open sesames" for the gateways to heaven -- were inscribed on the reverse side of healing pillars. In order to be healed, the initiate poured water over the texts. The water became charged with higher vibrational power and energy. Blessed, it was caught in a bowl and used by the initiate in the form of a baptism.

The golden pillar, one of the two pillars from Solomon's Temple, likely operates the same way. The heron travels to Tula, golden thread in hand, makes the cosmic connection, returns to earth and inscribes the coordinates on the Tree of Life, the healing pillar. The initiate "drinks" the living waters and absorbs the teaching orally.

This process may explain why, immediately following his stargate experience at Bethel, Jacob backtracked to Haran, and returned the stones. In fact, we learn he placed the Stone of Destiny over a "well" to "water the flock."11

There are several startling points in Jacob's story:
• he recovered a (s)tone with which
• he opened a hole in heaven
• where he saw god-like beings

- who were ascending and descending a ladder
- which stretches into Heaven
- which Jacob did not see the night before,
- but was revealed when he lay his head on the (s)tone.

According to renowned French mythologist and occultist Rene Guenon, the original name of the place where Jacob saw the hole or gate to heaven was *Salem* ("peace") or *Tula*.12

This is startling, but is it surprising? A moment ago I mentioned the myth of the group of angels who, before the Flood, asked God's permission to turn themselves into precious stones and other treasures.

In this story, which sounds like something straight out of *Aladdin*, the angels popped out of these treasures, implanted themselves in human bodies and attempted to teach men right living. While in the flesh the angels fell for the daughters of men, and found themselves chained to the earth, unable to shapeshift back into angels. These "Fallen Angels" were stranded on earth until many years later....when they ascended Jacob's ladder and returned to heaven. Does this suggest Jacob was not alone in his stargate maneuver?

Are we to also learn from Jacob's experience that:
- The angels of the power tools are involved in this process of opening the gateways?
- The angels have the god-like ability to take the quantum equations of the three great German philosophers Einstein, Heisenberg and Plank and dissolve solid, molecular-atomic matter into cluster-waves of information and reassemble these waves into alternate forms?
- Making a pact with these Shining Ones, as Hitler and F.D.R. apparently sought to do, can be a mutually beneficial arrangement?
- Acquiring the (S)tone of Destiny is a prerequisite for making this pact? Is this why Nicholas Roerich, who claimed he was in possession of this Stone, rose to such prominence in the F.D.R. Administration?

Y

I tend to think the (S)tone is the critical power tool. As we have seen in the Asian terma tradition, a (s)tone is capable of holding enormous amounts of data or teachings that can alter brain waves. Did decoding the whispering rune stones enable the Nazis to communicate with the god-beings of Atlantis?

Did Nicholas Roerich possess this same ability, possibly acquiring this talent during his travels in Tibet?

Further, a (s)tone played a key role when Moses, whom we've already identified as the serpent-holding link with Tula, channeled the Holy Spirit to achieve victory during a battle. "But Moses hands were heavy; and they took a *(s)tone*, and put it under him, and he sat thereon; and Aaron and Hur stayed up his hands..." (Exodus 17:12).

Would God give the Israelites victory just because Moses held his hands up? Possibly. Moses is described invoking a sacred ecstatic body posture or prayer position -- a Y. This posture was known to have been used by Atlas, Hercules, the goddesses of Egypt, Osiris, Quetzalcoatl and his other co-workers from Tula, including Jesus. This posture transformed their bodies into a pillar or antenna to channel the Holy Spirit, or the healing energies from the Central Sun. The Y was also the symbol used by Dr. Wilhelm Reich to represent orgone energy.13 (For a further illustrated treatment of this ecstatic body posture, please see my video *The Secrets of the Bird Tribe: Lost Stargate Artifacts and Spiritual Teachings and the Fulfillment of Millennial Prophecy*.)

ISRAEL

Not long after his stargate maneuver Jacob returned to Beth-el. One night he got into a shoving match with an angel (Genesis 32:24). After this, Jacob wanted to call the place "Peniel," or the Face of God, because in the morning he realized the angel whose face he could not see in the dark was God's.

Upon his victory, Jacob was given a mark on this thigh and a new name, *Israel* or "he who wrestles with God." (Jesus has a similar word of power symbol tattooed on his thigh at the Second Coming.)

As we have learned, the El suffix means "Shining Ones" or "God". *Is-Ra-El* rings of the combined Egyptian Shining Ones Isis and Ra, or possibly Osiris and Ra.

Was the name Is-Ra-El selected to connected Jacob with the gods of Egypt, and hence, with god-beings who claimed they came from Orion (or Aryan) and Sirius to deliver the power tools to earth?

ABRAHAM GOES TO EGYPT

As Jacob was in possession of the Stone of Destiny before his stargate maneuver (if not having to steal it to facilitate his experience), and Moses later used a similar, if not identical, key (s)tone (which indicated that God was with him), can we also link the Stone with Jacob's grandfather Abraham too?

According to the Egyptian accounts,14 in the time before Abraham, the Stone, along with the other power tools, was stored in the Great Pyramid. After a devastating famine swept through Canaan, says Genesis, Abraham took his family to Egypt.

There, something magical happened.

In a Hebrew legend, Abraham and Sarah were out in the wilderness when they came upon a strange "cave (read "the Great Pyramid" or "Hall of Records"?).15

Inside, they found Thoth in suspended animation. At his feet were his prized Emerald Tablets or (S)tones of Destiny and his Key of Life aka the Staff of Destiny. Sarah, a woman whose extraordinary beauty could charm a cobra (a handy asset for getting past the guardians of the key), took these treasures.

What did these early raiders of the lost Hall of Records get for their effort? It could have been the remote control for opening gateways to other parts of the universe.

Let me offer an explanation for why this may be possible. Thoth's Emerald Tablets are associated with a shape Charles Hinton called the *tesseract*.16 Popular women's magazines of the late 1890's featured articles and advertisements featuring this curious cube.

The *tesseract* is a three-dimensional "shadow" of a four dimensional hypercube -- a figure having a fourth dimension *at right-angles* to the three with which we are familiar. By simply adding a fourth dimension to this three-dimensional cube we approximate the empowering mind shift from three dimensional to four dimensional and beyond to hyper-dimensional thinking, exemplified by the tesseract.

In their excellent work, *Secrets of Rennes-le-Chateau*,17 Lionel and Patricia Fanthorpe note that members of some ancient mystic cults have been said to meditate for hours upon the tesseract until they experienced a shift of perception followed by the opening of a gateway to another dimension. Once through this doorway, the individuals are greeted by beings from this dimension.

KNIGHT MOVES

In his obsessive search for the missing pieces of Atlantis, and the means to become a master of the universe, Himmler aggressively pursued all angles. He authorized archaeological expeditions all over the world including the Near East (1938), two expeditions to Tibet (1939), and multiple expeditions to Antarctica between 1938 and 1945.18 (As we'll see in a later chapter, Heliopolis, the Egyptian city of 8, also offered an obvious allure.)

The "pieces of Atlantis" Himmler was seeking were not just geographical hunks of real estate. He was seeking the power tools of the Children of An, especially the Stone of Destiny. As New Age warrior monks, the SS were highly educated on the history of these pieces. Like the Freemasons, they envisioned themselves as knights on the great checkered chessboard of life, the Planetary Grid.

Acquiring the power tools or game pieces of Atlantis makes players out of warrior-wannabes. These players don't become masters of the universe, but they do become Grail Knights who can make Knight Moves on the universe. What is a Knight Move?

An L. In the game of chess the knights move in L's, or right angles.

From the stories we have encounteed, it appears one of the abilities of L's, Els or Shining Ones is the ability to interact with the fourth dimension at right-angles to our own and to make ninety-degree turns in hyperspace in order to go there.

How do we find these power tools of the Shining Ones? Himmler believed he would find them by mastering the runes, the "secret" or "whispering (s)tones," and Teutonic lore[19] (which we'll also discuss momentarily in connection with Heliopolis).

He didn't do it alone. Himmler set-up the *Ahnenerbe*, the branch of the SS responsible for looking into the ancient Atlantean heritage. This group spent enormous resources on esoteric research projects and archaeological digs; especially as we have noted, those which concerned the original Aryan homeland Ur, (aka Orion/Aryan). As part of his personal staff, Himmler had experts on ancient sacred texts, mythology and Sanksrit scholars. As Himmler well knew, language, especially the Language of the Birds, is power.

"UNION"

After his mission in Egypt, (S)tone of Destiny and Staff of Destiny in tow, Abraham moved his family to Hebron (or is it heron?), beside the oak trees at Mamre (Abraham just can't get enough of those enlightening oak trees).[20]

The oak trees may not have been the only attraction. The Old Testament tells us Hebron ("union") was built c. 5,500 B.C. Originally it was known as the "Town of the Four." The tribe that lived there was none other than the Anakim, the An-nun-aki or Shining Ones of An.

There's your trouble. No sooner is Abraham settled in at home when suddenly four powerful kings from the East form a coalition force. They are out to storm a place in the middle of the desert called El-Paran,[22] literally "God's Glorified Place."[23] El-Paran was a well-fortified desert garden or oasis which archaeologists place near the center of the northern part of the Sinai, the 24,000 square mile link between Asia and Africa (East) and the Holy Land (West).

The Bible does not explain why the Four Kings were seeking to control this remote location more than a thousand miles from their home. However, an enlightening explanation comes from the Muslim legend of Parwan, aka *the White Mountain*, where the Koran states John the Baptist went to school after being lifted up from Ur-Salem or Jerusalem by a "splendorous cloud." The "white" or "pure" mountain is a symbol for Tula. Interestingly, Mount Paran is listed in the first paragraph of Deuteronomy as the site where Yahweh appeared to the Israelites.

Does the composite description of El Parwan, an isolated garden surrounded by mountains, sound familiar? In the Egyptian Pharaoh's journey to land of immortality, which is virtually identical to the Sumerian *Epic of Gilgamesh*, he seeks a glorious "Mountain of Light" beside an egg-shaped valley enclosed by mountains -- the Tuat, the inner earth gateway to Tula.

This egg is depicted with the "streams of Osiris" (the Gardener) watering a garden area. The Assyrian depiction of this place shows a god being beside a Tree of Life, and flanked by a bull, the symbol of the soul, the Pleiades and Tula.

ABRAHAM: GUARDIAN OF THE GATEWAY TO ATLANTIS

In *The Wars of Gods and Men*,24 Zeharia Sitchin relates this Biblical event, which is woefully lacking in details, to an eye-opening, fact-filled Babylonian text concerning an invasion by kings of similar names, at the same place, at the same time, with the same outcome.

A Sumerian cylinder seal that depicts this face-off (or rodeo) contains another breathtaking detail also omitted from the Bible. It depicts a crowned cowboy on horseback (Abraham) standing between a Winged Gateway and two armies, one led by four kings.25

The Winged Gateway (ala the Sphinx) is universally connected with the Key of Life and places where the gods toggle between earth and heaven. The crowned cowboy is symbolically equivalent to the Christ or Messiah who rides in on a white horse in the book of Revelation (19:11), and who also enters Ur-Salem through a sealed gate.

Based upon the stunning corroborating details found in these stories, does it not appear likely the "garden" the Four Kings were hell bent on controlling was a secret Mt. Sinai, a gateway to Tula?

Was the christos about to enter this gateway?

The one who stood in the Four King's way -- the birdman protecting the egg -- was Abraham. He was seeking to clear the way for the heron.

And he was successful in doing so.

THE SECRET LOT IS HIDING

After turning back the Four Kings, Abraham returned to his command center by the oak of Mamre. Unexpectedly, the retreating Kings turned around, ambushed neighboring and apparently defenseless Sodom, where Abraham's nephew Lot was living, seized the city, and took Lot hostage.26

Now, hang on just a second.

Why take Lot hostage? His only obvious strategic value to the Four Kings was his closeness to Abraham.

Does Abraham possess something that the Four Kings hope to exchange Lot for?

Could Lot's value stem from something more impressive than a genetic linkage?

My suspicion is aroused by the fact that in Hebrew Lot's name means "covering."27

Covering you say? Is Lot a cover, a false story, or a protector for something? If so, what Secret is he hiding?

Given that Abraham is the spiritual father of Islam, the religion of *Allah*, who began his career as a male Moon god in Arabia, one highly combustible occult Secret Lot could be hiding may be that he is actually *Allah, Allot, Alat* or *Tula*.

In Greek myth, Laton (or Lot-An) is the name of the dragon which guards the Golden Apples sought by Hercules *and* the Golden Fleece of the magical ram sought by Jason.26 Laton's name comes from the Greek word meaning *to be hidden, unknown, ignored* -- or covered, like Lot.

Laton is also the mother of Apollo (the sun god who in myths made frequent educational trips to Tula and who is believed by his followers to have reincarnated as Pythagoras).

Does Lot serve as a literary double-edged (s)word?

Is he a literary cover for Tula and the power tools that take us there? Or, more fantastically, is Lot a representative from Tula?

If you're Nazi, Jewish, Muslim or Christian, and you believe your religion is isolated from or even superior to the others, you may share the same fate as the *Titanic* and the answers to these questions may be your iceberg.

Upon closer inspection, it appears all four of these religions, once stripped of their blanket of secrets, are from the same Source.

Until now, the original name of this Source has been hidden: Tula/Atlantis.

All New Age politics revolves around the bucking bull of God. Millions argue the question whose God is greater, Yahweh, Allah, Christ or whatever?

What happens when it is realized all these gods may be the same with different names?

ABRAHAM'S INITIATION

In a scene that smacks of the Three Kings who came to greet the baby Jesus, Four Kings came to "greet" Lot. Was this due to what he represented: a threat to the New World order of the Age of Aries?

If word got out that a gate to Tula was operating in Sodom, wouldn't it create pandemonium in the ancient world sure as word of a stargate opening and the emergence of Jesus in our modern world would rock the cradle of New Age politics?

From Enlil's point of view, this dragon had to be slayed.

Rather than greeting Lot with treasure (as was the baby Jesus), the Four Kings seized him and confiscated the goods of Sodom (which may be what Lot was hiding).28 The citizens of Sodom fled into a mountain. One of them escaped and ran to tell Abraham, who gathered a posse of 318 men, like the Green Berets or Special Forces of the Age of Aries, and pursued the kings into Dan, a city north of the Sea of Galilee, controlled by the tribe of D'an,29 or the Tuatha de' Danann. There, Abraham defeated the pesky kings and returned all "the goods" of Sodom and Gomorrah.

This would prove to be a big mistake.

Upon his retrieval of "the goods" of Sodom, Abraham was initiated (or promoted) by Melchizedek the King of Salem (Tula). He got his "H". Abraham may even have become *the* Peacemaker as Melchizedek blessed Abraham saying "Blessed be Abram of the most high God, *possessor of heaven and earth.*"30

We have already discussed Melchizedek's connection with the Fish or serpent man Enki, and the subject matter one learns when going to class with him. When Lord Melchizedek tells someone they possess heaven and earth, he doesn't mean maybe. He means they are Peacemakers, connectors of the golden thread between heaven and earth, who know:

• the whereabouts of the Atlantean power tools,

• the instructions for making the power tools work,

• the coordinates or codes used to open the doorway and the rainbow bridge connecting earth with the Central Sun, and

• the teachings which enable initiates to raise themselves, or ascend, to the spiritual level of the Shining Ones so that they might see and then enter the doorway home.

These are exactly "the goods" Enlil and his priests seek to keep out of the hands of humanity. If these are the goods the Bible says Abraham recovered for the Jewish people, are we witnessing the not so pretty changing of the guard at the beginning of the New Age of Aries?

Was this a time when the air was thick with thieves and intriguing New Age politics?

ABRAHAM AND THE RACE TO CONTROL HYPERSPACE

Did Abraham really avert a hostile take-over of the power tools? For his reward did he receive the Gardener's advanced (and revolutionary) training? Is this the ultimate occult Secret the Nazis were after?

Any lingering questions may be answered by careful scrutiny of the utterly chilling account of Abraham's meeting with "the Lord" some fifteen years later. One day, in Genesis 18:1, our two Pyramid raiders and occult initiates, Abraham and Sarah, have pitched a tent and finished the preliminaries. Everything's ready. Abraham is *gazing out the door* of his tent *beside the oaks* looking into the plains of Mamre at noon.

Then, Abraham "raised his eyes" and, out of nowhere, "there were three *men* standing by him." Abraham bows and calls them "My Lord". One of the men is actually *the* Lord.

The other two men turn out to be the Lord's two messengers called *malachim* by the Sumerians. Interestingly, the Sumerian depiction of the malachim shows extraordinary beings, which are obviously not human. In fact, they are strikingly similar in appearance to the three-foot-tall, almond-eyed beings extraterrestrial investigators call "the Greys." This is our first tip-off that all is not as it seems in this story.

Let us suppose that as a result of his initiation by the Gardener, Abraham became an El, able to wield the Key of Life like the remote control to a television, changing channels on the Planetary Grid. Or, let us suppose he learned how to make Knight Moves on the universe. Instead of gazing out of a physical door, could Abraham have been gazing into the (s)tone of Destiny, or be using the Key of Life to open the doorway to other dimensions, to hyperspace?

As soon as he sees the Lord, Abraham runs in the tent and asks Sarah to cook dinner for him and his angels[31] (that these beings eat human food at all is striking).

The events that follow are some of the most massively covered-up Biblical events I have ever read, but the most relevant to our search for the occult beliefs of WW II and New Age politics.

While eating under the branches of the ole oak tree, the Lord has a chat with Abraham.[32] He tells him that when he returns this time next year, Sarah will have a son. Ten years previous to this event Abraham had been promised a child,[33] but God did not deliver. Isn't this like telling a man he can stand at the door of the Promised Land but can never go in?

Sarah, who is barren, beyond child bearing age and generally uncooperative, laughs.[34]

Sarah's laughter is a slap in the face to the Lord.

He curtly informs her in no uncertain terms that nothing
is impossible for him.35 She will have a son whether she likes
it or not. (When the child is born he is named Isaac or "h e
laughs." Undoubtedly this name was not Sarah's idea,
hinting that this story has a political agenda.)

Sparring with his wife and informing Abraham of his
impending miraculous paternity are not the real reasons for
the Lord's visit, however. It is the New Age and the Lord has a
sensitive political problem to talk over with Abraham.

SODOM

At this point the two angels are dispatched to the nearby
town of Sodom.36

There waiting is Abraham's "nephew" Lot, who was
"sitting at the gate of Sodom."37 (Does this suggest Lot
either watched at the gate of Sodom quite often, or the arrival
of the Lord's messengers was a planned event, and not the
surprise the Bible makes it out to be?)

Upon their arrival, Lot takes the angels to his house for
dinner.38 These visitors cause quite a commotion. The town's
people surround Lot's house and demand that Lot hand over
the two angels.

For some reason, they want to "know" them,39 the
Biblical term for having sex with them.

In response, though the weapon is never identified, the
two angels of the Lord "smote the people at the entrance of
the house with blindness... and they were unable to find the
doorway."40

Which doorway, the one to Lot's gate?

Why all the emphasis on gates, doorways and vision with
this family?

What is going on here?

While in Egypt (possibly the Great Pyramid), or during
his career-boosting skirmish with the pesky Four Kings at the
Winged Gateway, did Abraham recover (or did the Gardener
give him) the power tools, the means to open the gateways to
Tula?

If so, was the Lord taking a page out of Enlil's playbook
and seeking to recover these power tools?

Or, are the Lord and the two angels who popped in on
Abraham actually Enlil and his henchmen?

Were Abraham and Lot involved in a race to control
hyperspace at the beginning of the Age of Aries?

These possibilities are more than strongly reinforced by
the horrifying event that happened next.

FACE-OFF

Abraham learns that the New Age political problem "the Lord" has come to personally discuss is the sudden outbreak of "wickedness" in Sodom and Gomorrah. He plans to splatter this wickedness like a big ugly millennial bug by baptizing these sinful cities with an explosion of fire and brim (s)tone of atomic proportions.

He assumed this was going to be no contest.

Abraham, however, pleads with the Lord for the lives of the righteous souls who dwell in Sodom and Gomorrah,41 including his nephew Lot. During their visit the angels tell Lot the Lord is about to roll up his town in a heavenly assault. If he's smart he won't try to run with this bull. He'll take his wife and family and evacuate the area immediately.42

The reason for the Lord's extermination of the citizens of Sodom and Gomorrah are preached about from pulpits every Sunday. These "wicked" New Agers disobeyed him.

Time and again, whether due to editing, data compression or a language barrier, we see Bible stories that are not what they seem. In the New Testament there is a Christ and there is the Anti-Christ. (Likewise there is the Buddha and there is the Anti-Buddha.)

The Old Testament, however, is never clear which Lord it is talking about. Sometimes when we pull the face off the Old Testament Lord, the one everyone goes to Church to believe in, we find the Anti-Lord (Enlil) is the real subject of the story.

Likewise, once we put this story up to our Atlantean mirror, we discover an anti-Sodom in the story of the biblical Sodom.

Strangely, the book of Revelation (11:8) inexplicably, but explicitly, states that Sodom was where Jesus was crucified, connecting this place with salvation. When we take the face off Sodom itself, does it turn out to be a New Atlantis in the making whose progress was halted by a ruthless and violent slave-master?

• Were the "wicked" citizens of Sodom considered wicked because they were rivals to Enlil's power?

• Were these "wicked" citizens of Sodom human beings of lesser genetic value than Abraham who, we are told, lived *before* the Flood and possibly was a Shining One?

• Was this an organized killing designed to wipe out a particular unwanted genetic thread?

• Was the Lord holding the people of Sodom hostage in return for the power tools in a New Age power grab?

Realizing that Lord Enlil despised his brother Lord Enki's attempts at lifting humanity to the level of the gods, we must ask if Sodom was possibly a new "Garden of Eden" where the advanced teachings of salvation were being lived ala the Cathar settlement in Southern France?

Strangely, the circumstances leading to the elimination of the people of Sodom are virtually a carbon copy of the story of the elimination of the Cathars (which is a carbon copy of the attempted elimination of the Jews during WW II).

The Cathars lived simple lives in the Languedoc region of Southern France in AD 1,200. Simple, save for the fact that they claimed possession of the Secrets of Jesus. These Secrets were encoded in a special language. The Cathars insisted the Gospels be read in this language.43

In 1934, Heinrich Himmler sent Otto Rahn to the Cathars stomping grounds in search of the Atlantean power tools.44 Rahn, a best-selling German author and mythologist, returned convinced that the Cathars had been in possession of all four treasures.

Moreover, he was convinced the Nazis should drop their global ambitions, convert to the Cathars brand of Christianity and live lives of peaceful simplicity.

Rahn disappeared under mysterious circumstances soon after.

THE CATHARS AND THE FIRST EUROPEAN GENOCIDE

One of the proofs the Cathars had "the goods" Hilter was seeking was the event that had occurred 700 years before.

In 1209 AD, the Church sent 30,000 soldiers to eradicate the Cathars. One reason may have been to reclaim the power tools that had been stolen from Rome in 410 AD and ended up in the care of the Cathars. Rome had stolen these power tools from the Jews back in AD 70 when they ransacked Solomon's Temple. Did they want them back?

Here's the story;45 One dark and stormy night in 410 AD, someone "mistakenly" left the front gates of Rome open (another excellent example of one person doing one thing to alter history). Waiting was Alaric, the leader of the Aryan Visigoths, whose men terrorized the city, and ransacked the temples and state treasuries and vaults, including the Vatican vaults, until they found what they were after: the treasure of the Temple of Solomon and the power tools of Atlantis.

They did not leave empty handed. A large part of this treasure of Solomon, including the solid gold seven-branched candlestick fashioned under orders of Moses and belonging to the Jews, as well as the Ark of the Covenant, left Rome with the Visigoths. These and the other power tools were last seen in the vicinity of Rennes-le-Chateau, France (in Cathar country) where the Visigoths built a well-fortified community in this area.

Rennes-le-Chateau you say?

Numerous Rennes-le-Chateau theorists claim Jesus and Mary Magdalen once lived in this mysterious Camelot-esque mountaintop village or its environs. In addition, they say at Rennes-le-Chateau the power tools at last returned to the bloodline of Jesus, the Merovingians.

Merovee (died 438 A.D.), the father of the Merovingian empire, was believed to be a descendent of the royal line established by Jesus and Mary,46 but which originated with the Benjaminites, Mary Magdalen's clan, and one of the Twelve Tribes of Jacob.

This family's lineage has been traced by some to the original god beings who founded Egyptian civilization and claimed to have come from Sirius. These are the same beings whose logo F.D.R. stamped on the one dollar bill and who landed on Mount Meru, which is the source of their name, Merovingians.

Marriage with beings from other worlds appears to be a trademark of this remarkable family. A clue to their origns may come from lingusitic roots of their name. *Mer* (a reference to Tiamat) is derived from both mother and sea, and *ovee* is derived from the root word for egg.

There is a very interesting legend attached to birth of Merovee,47 the man who founded the modern Merovingian dynasty. One day his mother went swimming in the ocean while already pregnant with her son. There, she encountered a fish-man who abducted, seduced, raped her and grafted his own genetic material onto Merovee's developing fetus.

According to the legends, when Merovee grew into manhood, he possessed extraordinary supernatural powers, gaining fame as a sorcerer/magician/king.

An early Latin version of this legend describes the sea creature as "resembling a Quinotaur." The *quin* root catches our attention. Quin is the root for five and for *quintessence*, the elusive, purer-than fire fifth element.48

As we have seen, the Dogon tribe of Africa and the Babylonians depicted Enki or Oannes in a half-man, half-fish form. One ancient seal carries the inscription describing Enki as "god of the pure life."

It has been suggested that the story of Merovee being the miraculous offspring of a fish-man is a symbolic way of saying he was a descendent of the offspring of Mary Magdalen and Jesus, who was symbolized by the fish. However, we may now extend this family tree back to the Garden of Eden, to Tula or Atlantis when Enki came to earth from Sirius, or before.

The Merovingians, who ruled most of France and Germany during the 5th and 6th centuries, were priest-kings and were often called sorcerer kings. They were famous as healers and recognized by their trademark long hair which they believed gave them strength, and were forbidden to cut. Their magical blood was known as the "sang raal" or "sang real" -- *holy* or *royal* blood.

The Merovingians were not required to do any of the normal royal activities. In fact, they weren't required to do anything at all except be there. Still, they were in the way of the Church's grand scheme.

The Church is accused by some historians of knowing full well that Jesus had married his beloved Mary Magdalen (a star woman) and covered this fact up by promoting erroneous versions of the Gospels to further its political ambitions.

In addition, the Church is accused of knowing that Jesus' bloodline continued with the Merovingians and taking steps to enlist their cooperation or exterminating them altogether in order to insure that its version of history was the only one.

The Thule Society's early mission was to put a member of Jesus' family (a Merovingian) on the throne of Europe. When Hitler came along he dismantled this operation.[49]

In 496 A.D., Merovee's grandson, Clovis I (456-511) made a fateful deal with the Roman Church promising to keep the Aryan Visigoths and the pagan Lombards off the Pope's back as long as the Church promised to name him the "New Constantine" who would rule over the "Holy Roman Empire."[50] The Church agreed.

Dagobert II (652-679) was the next Merovingian king who seems to have been informed about the power tools his family possessed. With a name like Dagobert, so close to the fish-god-man Dagon who brought the power tools to earth, what does one expect?

He moved to Rennes-le-Chateau and married Giselle de Razes, the local beauty, who just happened to be the niece of the King of the Visigoths.[51]

Suddenly, Dagobert became very rich and the new King of the Visigoths. It is claimed that as a wedding present he was given a cache of sacred texts (which once belonged to Jesus) and a collection of power tools including a cup, a staff, a stone and a sword.

Dagobert was quickly and ritually assassinated by Pepin the Short, ending Clovis' deal with the Church. Dagobert was murdered by a lance stuck through his eye (or poison poured in his ear) while he lay sleeping. His skull became a sacred relic.

The power tools remained hidden in Rennes-le-Chateau, in the care of the Cathars, awaiting the next claimant with one foot in Atlantis to come along and discover them.

KILL THEM ALL. GOD WILL KNOW HIS OWN

In 1209 the Pope's march on the Cathars began at Beziers, where 222 Cathars lived amongst a population of thousands. When the Pope's army arrived, the citizens refused to open their gates. The axe-wielding butchers addressed the locals -- all of them Catholics -- and with threats of death and burning in hell, demanded that they either leave town or turn over the Cathars to them.52

The citizens of Beziers chose to stay put and protect the Cathars. One local commentator, writing in 1213, said they would rather "die as heretics than live as Christians." On the morning of July 22, Mary Magdalen's Feast Day, six thousand citizens packed themselves into the cathedral at Beziers. The Pope ordered the extermination of every man, woman and child within the city gates of Beziers.

One French crusader of conscience was said to have asked a superior how they were to tell Cathar from Catholic. The reply was direct and chilling; "Kill them all. God will know his own." A hundred Catholics died for each Cathar at Beziers.53

Estimates place the total Cathars and Cathar sympathizers murdered between 300,000 and 1,000,000 people.

Throughout forty years of carnage, report after report from the Crusaders substantiated an amazing testimony. The Cathars rarely displayed fear, terror or pain even after the most hideous cruelties were inflicted upon them. It was said their example caused many a crusader to undergo profound spiritual transformations. Later, at the siege of Montsegur -- the Cathars famous last stand, crusaders actually converted to Catharism and fought along side them.

What secret knowledge could the Cathars have possessed that caused this spiritual transformation?

What baptism could possibly transform a cold-blooded, axe-wielding murderer into a holy man fighting for a New Kingdom?

By all accounts it was a secret Science for transforming homo sapien into homo angelis, a human to an El. After the demise of the Cathars, this science went underground. A few of the remaining Cathars became paper manufacturers. They embedded the sacred hieroglyphic symbols of their secret for posterity in secret watermarks embedded in paper used by those "in the know."54

This symbology also reappeared in the four suits of the Tarot deck: the cups, swords, wands and pentacles,55 which may encode the secrets for the soul's return journey to the Galactic Core (Today, the United States Secret Service, in its quest to combat counterfeiting, has amassed the world's largest collection of watermarks. Is it possible they are "in the know" concerning the Secrets of the Cathars?)

50 RIGHTEOUS SOULS

Let us suppose the Sodomites were "pure ones" like the Cathars in the process of turning themselves into homo angelis who intended knock a hole in space to Tula. Were the Shining Ones working with Abraham or guiding this process? Did this rebellious activity show up on the Anti-Lord's (Enlil's) security screen provoking his picnic with Abraham?

Evidence for this important point may be cleverly concealed within the Biblical story: Abraham negotiated with the Lord. Abraham asked the Lord to spare the cities if he could show him there were 50 "righteous" souls there. Abraham, a crack negotiator, actually bargains him down to ten. That was still too high.

Biblical numbers were rarely chosen by chance. Numbers conceal deeper occult meaning. The number 50 sends up a flag, alerting us that this story may have a hidden meaning or point to another story. In Sumerian mythology, for example, An had fifty sons. Jason loaded 50 Argonauts on his ship, the *Argo*, when he sought the Golden Fleece of the ram.

In addition to concealing deeper occult meaning, the story of Sodom and Gomorrah has a political agenda. It is to make the Lord out to be a good guy. His spin doctor would like for us to see this as a story of a regular guy (Abraham) who was out to change the mind of God.

In fact, Abraham is routinely cast as the role model for faith and obedience to Yahweh. The Lord is about to exterminate the inhabitants of a pair of cities, yet has the compassion to consult Abraham first (or listen to his irritating spiel), and will even change his mind if Abraham can show him just *one* righteous soul in Sodom. Praise the Lord.

Not so fast! In our Atlantean mirror, stripped of its political spin, is this actually the demented story of a sick being trying to pass himself off as a god who planned and implemented a holocaust, and then had the nerve to brag about it?

Is there a horrible corruption of history, or a dark occult secret of psychological warfare, buried in the Bible's tale of Sodom and Gomorrah?

Substitute the words "the Lord" and "the wicked" in the story for "Adolph Hitler" and "the Jews," and do we see the same corrupt story replayed in our New Age?

Is this Biblical story the same as Nazi story of turning of brother against brother, neighbor against neighbor in a bloodthirsty campaign to exterminate a group of people who refused to obey a messiah wannabe?

Or as happened in the case of the Catholics in AD 1209, to turn over a group of Planetary Healers?

Hitler as exterminator of the Jews (among whom Rabbi Gershom argues were the Planetary Healers) showed exactly the same psychological dementia as the Anti-Lord in the Old Testament who exterminated the citizens of Sodom, and the Pope who ordered the extermination of the Cathars and his brother and sister Catholics.

Could it be that the precious souls who were marked for elimination in each of these horrifying genocides was the same soul group reincarnated, the Planetary Healers brought to earth by Enki to save humanity?

With each appearance do they ratchet up the intensity of the battle between light and dark for control of earth? Today, preachers and doomsayers wail about the final destruction of these pure ones. They call it Armageddon.

Ironically, Christian theologians and preachers frequently point to Abraham's negotiation with the Lord as an example of a powerful Christian concept. Is it actually the smoking mushroom cloud proving the chilling theory that the Lord Abraham is tangling with is not such a good guy after all?

That concept is the possibility that sinners could be saved from extermination by the presence of a small percentage of righteous souls.

What's so special about these righteous souls that makes them human shields for the "wicked" souls? We are asked to believe the righteous souls are souls who live in fear of the Lord. Translation: the righteous are obedient slaves who have no spiritual vision, ask no questions, and obey the commands of the Lord (Enlil).

However, our occult study has revealed the possibility that, during Atlantean moments such as this, the 50 *righteous* souls are those who, in the model of Jesus, are seeking to become gods -- if they are not gods already. They are the Planetary Healers who are rivals to the power of the Lord, Enlil.

Like Abraham's wife, Sarah, they laugh in the face of this Anti-Lord. As did the Cathars, and later the Jews during Hitler's time, did Sarah realize this being who proclaimed himself "god" is actually a sick little man pretending to be God who is after their power tools and seeks to create a racially pure master race and spiritually enslaved humanity?

The negotiation between Abraham and the Lord strongly suggests the possibility that the Planetary Healers, the higher vibrational soul group who are the offspring of Enki, were incarnate in Sodom.

As long as the righteous Planetary Healers (who are also Atlantean) were in Sodom, Enlil the Anti-Lord might think twice about blowing the city to kingdom come and risking a confrontation with Enki.

Is there a different interpretation of this story? Instead of demonstrating his obedience and faith in the Lord in his negotiation to save the handful of righteous souls of Sodom, was Abraham in fact Enki, the Gardener's point man, leading a revolt *against* the Anti-Lord?

Does this explain why the Anti-Lord (Enlil) could not find *any* righteous souls in Sodom? Had he had enough of these god wannabes in Atlantis before the Flood? Had he decided he was not going to put up with their unruliness in the New Age? Is this why, deploying his number one management technique, a show of sheer force, he destroyed Sodom?

Was the destruction of Sodom and Gomorrah the first Aryan-led (read "Enlilian") genocide of the Planetary Healers after the Flood? Was the pattern set in place for future genocides of these souls?

FIRE FROM HEAVEN

In a scene reminiscent of the obliteration of Hiroshima and Nagasaki, at dawn the next morning, as Abraham looked upon the valley below, fire came from "the Lord out of heaven" (Genesis 19:24). "The smoke of the land went up like the smoke of a furnace" (Genesis 19:28).

Sodom and Gomorrah were no more. Everything -- the cities, the farms, the children -- were destroyed by *fire* and *brim (s)tone.*

That the wicked of Sodom and Gomorrah were destroyed by some form of nuclear explosion is claimed by many and attested by the fact that Lot's wife, ignoring the angel's advice not to look back as they were fleeing from Sodom, turned to a "pillar of salt".

The traditional view has it that Lot's wife turning to salt was a bad thing. She disobeyed the Lord's command not to turn around. We now realize there is something fishy about this whole story.

If we pull the golden thread, and put this story up to our Atlantean mirror another heart-stopping occult Secret is revealed. The story of Sodom and Lot's wife reverses itself.

Brimstone, it turns out, is derived from Brimo, a title of Athene, or Athena and An-at. Both are names for Isis, the wife of Osiris, the Gardener.56

Because of her magical ability to cleanse and purify, Isis' stone was supposed to prevent disease. Also called the Tet, it was sometimes shown as a loopy red object – similar in shape to the ankh or Key of Life – which transformed the blood, giving the person "holy blood". It was used in the process of cleansing and purifying the souls in order to connect them with God. Alchemists tried to "marry Hermes and Athene," by combining mercury with brimstone, which they thought might create occult "gold" -- the holy blood of the gods.

Do fire and brimstone turn out to be occult references to the process of mating the two soulspheres, and salvation?

As was discovered by linguists in 1918,57 and reported to the American Oriental Society, a crucial mistake had been made in translating the Sumerian term for the pillar of salt -- the result of combining fire (frequency, vibration) with Isis' brimstone. It is actually a *pillar of vapor.*

This mistake was devastating.

We know of three dimensions: solid, liquid, gas. However, in the occult tradition, there is a fourth dimension: vapor, which has several of its own dimensions. Vapor, says Sitchin, was the form the soul took after death by the hand of a god.

Lot's wife's transformation into a pillar is significant as well. After Prometheus (Enki) brought fire (the higher vibrational souls?) down from heaven, he, like Atlas and the Greek savior Hercules, held the life force energy on his shoulders -- on his Pillars of Hercules, the gateway to Atlantis. Hercules stood Y like, upholding the world, with his (s)word, the vril or Life Force energy. As noted, this is the same body posture used by Moses and Jesus to channel the Holy Spirit.

In the Atlantean mirror, does it look suspiciously like the anti-story of Sodom is the story of the opening of a gateway to Tula?

Could Lot's wife turning to a pillar of vapor reflect her ascension into a higher dimensional being? Is this what the book of Revelation means when it says Jesus was crucified in Sodom? Did a Shining One, possibly Lot or his wife, appear in Sodom only to be crucified by Enlil?

Did Enlil's (the Anti-Lord's) negotiations with Abraham turn out to take place on the eve of another of his brother Enki's attempts at teaching the secrets of ascension? As the person in control of the power tools, was Abraham caught in the act of firing up the stargate? Was Lot's home, Sodom and Gomorrah, ground zero?

Is this what the Anti-Lord was out to stop?

Could this explain why all future generations were taught to fear the combination of fire and brimstone -- the light of heaven and the empowering stone of the goddess Isis -- which as the reader has by now certainly suspected is the (S)tone of Destiny?

As the prophecy on the back of the one dollar bill attests, the light of heaven, the Shining One of Tula, may be about to land on top of the pyramid in our New Age. He or she is forecasted to deliver exactly the kind of knowledge we are discussing here. When this happens, will we want to look out for a reprisal from the present caretakers of the world order?

Is this why Nostradamus called this figure the King of Terror?

A postscript: Following his flight from Sodom, Lot and his two daughters went and lived in a "cave," (aka the Great Pyramid) believing they were the last humans on earth. Did Lot take the Stone to the cave with him? Is this the (s)tone Jacob later acquired in Haran?

Inquiring Nazis would like to have known.

Notes:

1. Genesis 12:1, 5
2. Genesis 12: 6-8
3. Genesis 25:22
4. Genesis 28:11
5. Genesis 28:12
6. Genesis 28:13
7. Genesis 28:17
8. Genesis 28:17
9. Laurence Gardner *Bloodline of the Holy Grail* (Rockport, MA., Element, 1996)p. 298
10. Blanche Merz *Points of Cosmic Energy* (Saffron Walden, C.W. Daniel Co., Ltd., 1983) p. 53
13. Genesis 29:3
14. Rene Guenon *Fundamental Symbols: The Universal Language of Sacred Science* (Cambridge, Quinta Essentia, 1995) p. 121
15. W. Edward Mann *Orgone, Reich and Eros* (New York, Simon & Schuster, 1973) p. 140
16. Dr. Joseph R. Jochmans *Giza One - Keys to the Hall of Records*, p. 61
17. Lionel and Patricia Fanthorpe *The Secrets of Rennes-le-Chateau* (York Beach, Maine, Samuel Weiser, 1992) p. 178
18. Michio Kaku, *Hyperspace* (New York, Oxford University Press, 1994) p. 70
19. Ibid. p. 75
19. Ibid. p. 227
20. Col. Howard Beuchner *Emerald Cup: Ark of Gold* (Metarie, LA, Thunderbird Press, 1991)p. 169
21. Peter Moon *Black Sun* (New York, Sky Books, 1997) p. 67
22. Genesis 13:18
23. Genesis 14:6
24. Zecharia Sitchin *The Wars of Gods and Men* (New York, Avon Books, 1985) p. 305
25. Ibid. p. 305

26. Ibid. p. 308
27. Genesis 14:11-14
28. Reader's Digest *Who's Who in the Bible* (Pleasantville, NY, Reader's Digest, 1994) p. 271
29. Ibid. p. 528
30. Genesis 14:12
31. Genesis 14:14
32. Genesis 14:19
33. Genesis 18:6
34. Genesis 18:8
35. Genesis 15:5
36. Genesis 18:11-12
37. Genesis 18:14
38. Genesis 18:22
39. Genesis 19:1
40. Genesis 19:3
41. Genesis 19:5
42. Genesis 19:11
43. Genesis 18:23-25
44. Genesis 19:12-13
45. Margaret Starbird *The Woman With the Alabaster Jar* (Santa Fe, Bear & Co., 1995) p. 75
46. Col. Howard Beuchner *Emerald Cup: Ark of Gold* (Metarie, LA, Thunderbird Press, 1991) p. 78
47. Ibid. p. 58-60
48. Michael Baigent, Richard Leigh and Henry Lincoln *Holy Blood, Holy Grail* (London, Crowns, 1982)
49. Ibid. p. 24
50. Ibid. p. 25
51. Michael Howard *The Occult Conspiracy* (Rochester, VT, Destiny Books, 1989) p. 125
52. Ibid. p. 63
53. Ibid. p. 64
54. John J. Robinson *Dungeon, Fire and Sword: The Knights Templar in the Crusades* (New York, M.Evans & Co., 1991) p. 222
55. Ibid. p. 224
56. Harold Bayley *The Lost Language of Symbolism* (New York, Carol Publishing Group, 1993) p. 3
57. Ibid. p. 104
58. Barbara G. Walker *The Woman's Encyclopedia of Myths and Secrets* (New York, HarperCollins, 1983) p. 118
59. Ibid. p. 313

CHAPTER TWENTY TWO

THE BLACK STONE

On January 6, 1929, Heinrich Himmler, the tall Nazi with the big round head, pink face, and little wire-rimmed glasses, was appointed Reichsfuhrer SS. He was put in charge of three hundred well-trained thugs who were to be the nucleus of a spiritual/military force on which the Nazi-altered state could depend to carry out all orders. As Himmler was keen to point out, his dreaded Black Order, the inner sanctum of the *Schutzstaffel*, or SS, was born long before Hitler's accession to power.

Himmler claimed to be the reincarnation of the infamous German Emperor Henry I,[1] who was known as the "Bird-catcher". He had one foot in Atlantis, Hitler's fanatical devotion, and a burning desire to become the creator of Hitler's dream of the Third Reich. Of course, he sought to acquire the power tools of Atlantis.

Funded in part by the Big Three profiteers of WW II -- the German chemical conglomerate I.G. Farben, and the German subsidiaries of I.T.T. and Edison's General Electric -- the SS was an independent terrorist organization. As their leader, Himmler was as feared as Hitler. He was even feared by Hitler himself.

Hitler may have claimed to be the German messiah, but it was clearly Herr Himmler who was responsible for putting the dreaded "SS" in Hitler's messianic delusion.

Himmler was as renowned as the little sick man Hitler for his obsession with the occult. He envisioned the SS as an elitist occult secret society, modeling it after the Society of Jesus. Hitler liked to joke that Himmler was "the Black

Jesuit," comparing him with the order's founder, Ignatius Loyola.2 (Interestingly, some Jesuits envisioned the inner earth as a perfect cube a mile in diameter.)

Himmler was an avid reader of the *Mahabharata,* which contains the story of the Rama Empire's war with Atlantis. If he had the intelligence attributed to him he would have connected Abraham with Brahma, as did Voltaire,3 the Renaissance big brain who said that Plato (the founding father of Atlantology) should have been made a saint by the Christian Church for being the first promoter of the *Christos* mystery.

THE ORDER OF THE BLACK STONE

The inner core of the SS called themselves the Knights of the Blood,4 the Order of the Black Sun,5 the Black Order,6 or the Order of the Black Stone.7 Historians say they took their name from their notorious black uniforms.

That may be so on the mundane level. However, here is where our extensive questioning of the occult history of Abraham and Lot pays off.

The alchemists used the curious word VITRIOL to stand for *Visita interiora terrae rectificando invenies* **occultum** *lapidem.* "Visit *the interior of the earth*; through *purification* thou wilt find the **hidden stone**."8

Occult is Latin for "hidden." It has the same meaning as Lot ("covered"). The alchemist's occultum was called the "black (hidden) matter," "antematter" or "prematter." It is the original substance of creation. Mystics believe it is capable of rearranging matter at the atomic level.9 It is said to have the ability to transmute lead into gold, and quite possibly, normal human blood into holy blood.

When we connecte these dots, it appears the hidden or black stone of the goddess is the symbol for the gateway to the inner earth and the way to purify one's soul or blood for entering this gate.

Translation: possession of the black stone transforms a wannabe into a master of the universe. It is the Stone of Destiny of Tiamat.

The story of Abraham and the legends of the Black Stone offer valuable insight to explain why *an altar of black marble with two silver SS runes inscribed upon it was housed in the Holy of Holies of Wewelsburg, Himmler's Grail Castle.*10

Is it conceivable that Himmler's goose-stepping Nazi bird-men wannabes discovered this Black Stone?

Did they know copies of it were carted around the ancient world and installed in sacred precincts as the symbol of the power and authority of those who lived by (or sought to live by) the (s)tone?

Did they realize some of these sacred precincts were favorite fishing grounds of the heron? Or that the black stone of the SS is symbolically equivalent to:
- the brimstone or black stone of Isis in the story of Sodom,
- the black stone of the temple of Inanna (who is Isis) near Ur,
- the secret black stone, *cubical in shape*, which is preserved in an all-white temple called the *Caabaha* at the conclusion of the Mayan *Popol Vuh,*
- the sacred black (s)tone of Allah housed in the *Kaaba* in Mecca, worshipped by millions of Muslims who turn thrice daily to pray to this stone no matter where they are on earth, and who make a pilgrimage to Mecca to pray to Allah (Allat, Lot or Tula),
- the artificially cut *perfect (s)tone cube* (like the Ark) whose top remains, protruding from the ground beneath the sacred 8-sided Dome of the Rock structure in Ur-Salem or Jerusalem. [Nearby the Dome of the Rock is the Dome of the Tablets (Stones of Destiny?) where Jesus is supposed to judge (or balance) the world in the last days.],
- the black stone tomb which marks the grave of King Arthur and his Queen Guinevere at Glastonbury Abby in England? (Interestingly, (*Arthur* comes from *Asur* or Osiris)

THE MORNING OF THE MORONS

As Grail knight wannabes, the Himmler and the SS would have perhaps found the greatest benefit focusing on the Grail legends of the Black Stone over all others. According to the legend, when the Grail knight Perceval enters the Grail castle, he is entering the mystery world of the human body, the brain. It is there that "the stone of light" resides.

The stone is thought by occultists to be the pineal gland, the center of human consciousness (which the Aryans call the cave of Brahma). Is it possible the pineal gland is the same as "Penial," the place where Jacob found himself "face to face" with God in his vision?

In the Grail legends Arthur became king by pulling the covered (S)word Excalibur from the mysterious (S)tone of Camel-Lot. Once understood, the hidden "stone of light" (*aka* the occult "Stone of Lot") is said to ignite clairvoyant powers of perception lightning quick.

As one gazes upon this stone, mystical awareness arises from the heart and, faster than you can say lightning rod of blue fire from Tula, a total transformation of consciousness occurs.

The awakening of the latent powers of the pineal gland is identical to the transformation symbolized by the two twisting serpents or kundalini energies represented by the Key of Life. Hitler subscribed to the claims in the stories of the single-eye Cyclops, believing an early race of humanity once had an all-seeing eye or "magical vision" which had become atrophied to form the pineal gland.

In the *Spear of Destiny*, Trevor Ravenscroft states that one receives the all-seeing eye at the moment when the human soul becomes the living vessel of the Christ-consciousness.

"The human species" Hitler said (echoing HPB's occult evolutionary theories), "has been through a prodigious number of cycles since it made its first appearance. Throughout the ages it has traversed many stages of advancement, and was now coming to the end of its solar period". This would be a time when the Sun's influence would be at its maximum. At that time, a new and improved human being would appear.

"Christ," Hitler wrote in his autobiography *Mein Kampf* (*"My Struggle"*), "was the greatest early fighter in the battle against the world enemy, the Jews". Then he said, "the work that Christ started but could not finish, I - Adolf Hitler - will conclude".

Not quite. As history has shown, Hitler's megalomanical "Twilight of the Gods" was the "Morning of the Morons".

WEWELSBERG CASTLE: THE BLACK CAMELOT

Deep in Germany is Himmler's strange medieval castle, Wewelsberg, the home of the Nazi's Black Stone. This castle captured the imagination of Himmler for its shape (a triangle, the only one if its kind in all of Germany), its location (built atop a huge limestone rock next to the town of Herron), and its heritage (it was a Germanic stronghold for over a thousand years).

Under Himmler's direction Wewelsberg was to become the hub of the sprawling New Atlantis. Plans called for expanding the complex into a semi-circle of buildings one mile in diameter.11

The heart of this New Atlantis was to be the Supreme Leader's Hall, which Himmler ordered built in the north tower of the Grail Castle. This tower was to be used for ritual funerals of elite SS officers. The room had twelve windows and twelve pedestals which held the urns containing the ashes of the dead (presumably for some occult ritual).

Through the SS's Heritage program, Wewelsberg the Castle was quickly transformed into Wewelsberg the occult fortress library. As part of his New Atlantis vision, Himmler envisioned this castle as a repository where all the world's most important pieces of world art, culture, archaeology and scientific endeavor would be housed under one roof.

arrived, the townspeople had already stripped the castle of its
16,000 priceless occult books, 40,000 bottles of wine, and its
astounding collection of paintings, rugs, statues, tapestries,
porcelain, silverware and other treasures the SS had looted
from Europe's wealthiest families.

The black stone of the Nazis was nowhere to be found.

THE BLACK STONE AND THE UNITED NATIONS

Nazi Germany was not the last the world was to see of a
black stone. Should we be surprised to find this mysterious
stone's present location is the center of New Age politics?

In 1953, as his first official act as Secretary General of the
United Nations, *Dag* Hammarskjold ("Hammer shield") a
man who was world-renowed as "the Peacemaker," traveled
to Sweden. There he supervised as workmen hauled more
than sixty six-and-a-half ton black iron ore blocks from the
ground.

Finally, he found the stone he was looking for.

Hammarskjold ordered the stone shipped to New York
and installed in the pyramid-shaped Meditation Room of the
United Nations, "the Holy of Holies of the UN," which he
also had constructed.

Hammarskjold's "(s)tone of light" is a six-and-a-half ton
rectangular block of iron ore. This massive black stone is
polished on the top so that it brings forth a sheet of minute
lights that sparkle like billions of tiny stars. It is a natural
magnet emitting magnetic waves.

One wonders, what was it about this particular black stone
that caught Hammarskjold's fancy?

PROPHECY FULFILLED

The black stone's placement at the very center of the base
of the UN -- which was formed immediately following WW II
in 1945 and is based upon the ideals of the Iroquois
Peacemaker Deganawidah -- is meant to emphasize its occult
role as a "cubic stone" or "foundation (s)tone".

As F.D.R. is reported to have been the first person on
record to use the words "United Nations", this raises some
interesting questions. For instance:

• Is the black stone in the UN the missing capstone of the
pyramid F.D.R. stamped on the one dollar bill?

• Mystically speaking, is the UN the fulfillment of the
Peace project begun by Thoth and Abraham after the fall of
Atlantis, nurtured and cared for until 1,000 AD when the Tree
of Peace was planted in America by Deganawidah, and
pruned by George Morgan in 1776?

• Is the Tree of Peace on the verge of blossoming in the UN?

• With the Stone of Destiny installed in the UN, can we expect to see not just the eye, but the entire face of God, as in the experience of Jacob?

• Occult literature suggests we see the face of God in Tula or Atlantis. Does this mean the UN is the center for the New Atlantis and that we'll soon literally see God's face at the UN?

C.S. Lewis may have the answer. He was a Professor of Theology at Oxford University and popular Christian author of the 1930's and 1940's by day, and secret master of occult symbolism and storysmith or shaman by night.

Lewis was also one of a trio of geniuses which included J.R.R. Tolkien and Charles Williams who called themselves "The Inklings." These occult storysmiths wrote profusely in the Language of the Birds about magical parallel worlds, stargates, doors to unknown worlds, and the occult means to gain access to these realms.

At the heart of the enigma the Inklings devoted their lives to was the same mystery Nikola Tesla, Thomas Jefferson, King Solomon, and even Jesus -- in fact, all thinking men and women we have discussed so far -- have devoted their lives to: how to find, open and enter these doorways.

In 1937, Lewis announced in one of his books, *The Silence of the Earth*, that a war for the possession of the human soul would soon be fought. While most paid attention to the bloody exoteric aspect of this war, it was actually a "war between the gods," said Lewis.

Of course. He was talking about WW II.

In *Till We Have Faces*, Lewis gives a prophecy that "the gods will not speak to us face to face until we ourselves have a face."

Does this mean the gods won't talk to us again until we grow up and become gods?

Most interesting, to me, is professor Lewis' last known work *The Dark Tower*, a sixty-four-page fragment of a story rescued from a bonfire by his gardener immediately after his death. The work tells the story of a bizarre parallel universe to which human beings can gain access.

What do you suppose C.S. Lewis would say were he alive today? Has the human race gained its face?

Notes:

1. Dusty Sklar *The Nazis and the Occult* (New York, Dorset Press, 1977 p. 85
2. Ibid. p. 86

3. Leon Poliakov *The Aryan Myth* (New York, Barnes & Noble, 1971) p. 186
4. Col. Howard A. Buechner and Capt. Wilhelm Bernhart *Adolph Hitler and the Secrets of the Holy Lance* (Metairie, LA, Thunderbird Press, 1988) p. 82
5. Peter Moon *Black Sun* (New York, Sky Books, 1997) p. 172
6. Ibid. p. 82
7. Ibid. p. 172
8. Barbara G. Walker *The Woman's Dictionary of Symbols and Sacred Objects* (New York, HarperCollins, 1988) p. 162
9. Ibid. p. 250
10. Ibid. p. 118
11. Ibid. p. 119

CHAPTER TWENTY THREE

THESE LONG, HUNGRY YEARS

In 1930, the full effect of the Great Depression was yet to be felt across America. Before decade's end 40 million Americans would know poverty as a way of life. During these long, hungry years the soul of America was frozen as misery, doubt, cold, hunger, fear, and natural disasters including merciless floods, droughts, plagues, and dust storms, seized the land of the free. Like an iron fist from a rolling black cloud that sat over the nation and refused to let go, the Depression held America in its grip.

By March 4, 1933, when F.D.R. was sworn in as President of the United States, America was trembling from fear. That same morning every single bank in America closed its doors.1 F.D.R., a man who radiated so much confidence one observer declared "he must have been psychoanalyzed by God,"2 looked the thousands of desperate people who gathered in the shadows of the Washington Monument in the eye.

Then, he began knocking holes in the black clouds above with the power of his words: "This Nation asks for action, and action now."3 At first, through tiny cracks, the light of heaven suddenly began to shine, then the tide of destiny began to turn, washing the iron fist far away out to sea. Love him or hate him (as millions did), F.D.R. saved America.

American kids and teens of the 30's badly needed a retreat from reality. They also needed encouragement. They received both from the storysmiths of the time. From out of Nikola Tesla's invention, the radio -- which popular 30's commentator E.B. White called "a pervading and somewhat godlike presence which has come into (our) lives and homes"4 -- popped heroes of Atlantean proportions who would have a dramatic, even magical, effect on American consciousness.

The All-American Boy! the brainy, brawny, awesomely pure-in-heart, Jack Armstrong was one fictional hero who had his own radio show. Jack Armstrong inspired millions of kids to begin to live a life of adventure, to play fair and to love America. In one of his adventures, he ends up talking with a Tibetan monk (who may have also been bending the ear of Nicholas Roerich, who was bending F.D.R.'s ear).

"Tell the boys and girls of the United States this world is theirs. If they have hearts of gold, **a glorious new golden age awaits us.** *If they are honest, riches shall be theirs. If they are kind, they shall save the whole world from malice and meanness. Will you take that message to the boys and girls of the United States, Jack Armstrong?"*5

Does this message sound familiar?

Were American children being fed a healthy dose of Atlantean occult theology through fictional radio characters?

The 1930's also witnessed the arrival of Dick Tracy, Tom Mix, Tarzan, Flash Gordon, and above all, Buck Rogers to America. With his personal arsenal of Thermic Radiation Projectors, Electrocosmic Spectrometers, Disintegrator Guns, and the Super Radiating Protoreformer, Buck Rogers and the rest of his cosmic friends would help Americans of all ages blast off from their soul-ensnaring depression.

THE HITLER YOUTH

While American children were pulling themselves out of despair, the Nazi recipe of occult, racist and romantic idealism was effectively targeted at German children: the Hitler Youth, many of whose fathers had been killed in WWI, and who were brainwashed into seeing Hitler as god.6

The Nazi propaganda aimed at the Hitler Youth stressed the link with Germany's ancient ancestors -- the Nordic god-beings of Atlantis.7

Beginning with fairy tales, the young were brainwashed to believe Hitler had been sent from heaven to kill the wicked enemy who was bent on eating little children (as mentioned, Hitler's favorite movie was *King Kong*). The Hitler Youth were trained to fight in a holy war against "the evil enemies" of the Nazi-altered state: Freemasons and Jews.8

By the end of 1934 the Hitler Youth included six million members. Innocent children were brainwashed step-by-step to accept Nazi ideology. In addition to worhsipping Hitler as the Messiah, vegetarianism, abstinence from sex until marriage, physical fitness, and genius-level intellectual accomplishment were stressed.9

The Hitler Youth were enraptured by the uniforms and mesmerized by the pageantry of the Hitler movement and his famous torch-lit rallies under the stars. To be left out was perceived as punishment.

Like all cult leader wannabes, Hitler turned child against parents and family, brainwashing them not only to worship but also to obey Hitler as god.

In the end, the Hitler Youth movement turned into organized terrorism led by children who laughed at the sight of corpses.10

THE 1939 NEW YORK WORLD'S FAIR

From 1934 to 1939, life was all uphill for many Americans. However, as an alphabet soup of Federal works programs began to put people back to work, the long, hungry years ended, the nation's self esteem returned. The desperate children grew up.

By 1939, hope had triumphed over fear. America reached the top of the mountain. The Great Depression was over. It was time to celebrate. New York City was the place to be.

The 1939 New York World's Fair was by far the biggest, gaudiest, and most bewildering assortment of technological marvels the world had ever seen (at least since the time when reporters hung out in Tesla's lab). "*Here is the magnificent spectacle of a luminous world, apparently suspended in space...,*" said the official Fair guide book.11

The smash hit at the Fair was Billy Rose's *Aquacade*, an Atlantean-themed water musical where eight million awed visitors saw a team of "Aquafemmes" splash to waltz music.

28,000 people a day ponied up a whopping ten bucks each to see the Fair's sensational "World of Tomorrow" exhibit, which featured a scale model of a wide-eyed futurist's conception of the American landscape in the year 1960.

This Atlantean vision featured raindrop-shaped liquid air powered cars driven by handsome, tanned, well-toned couples whom, the guide book said, may have been on their two-month long vacation. The happiest people live in one-factory farm-villages producing one small industrial item and their own farm produce.

Most of the surface of the earth is lush forest and park. Airports and industry are subterranean. Great telescopes fill the sky. Microscopes literally see everything. Cancer is cured. The average life-span is an astonishing 75 years.12

On New Year's Day of 1940, though Nazi Germany had smashed its newly acquired iron fist through Europe's plate glass window, and Europeans were wondering where the hell Hitler and his ugly goose-stepping monsters came from, most

Americans were getting used to the good life at the top of F.D.R.'s mountain. Who cared if Hitler's Panzers were parked victorious in Poland, provoking war with defenseless France and Britain. So what if Japan was raping China. Americans were focused on themselves. And they wanted more, better, now! Besides, two great oceans separated America from the black cloud that had parked itself over Europe and Asia.

Though there was talk of America entering the gathering storm, as far as America was concerned, Europe was on its own. "I have said this before, but I shall say it again and again," said F.D.R. on Halloween (originally a sacred holiday to commemorate the sinking of Atlantis) of 1940, "your boys are not going to be sent into any foreign wars."13

But then, things began to change. The gods were restless.

In January 1941, Pearl Harbor was still twelve months away. "That Man in the White House," as he was now called by many because of his controversial social programs, asked Congress for $1.8 billion in his State of the Union address. His goal was to finance the largest peacetime military build-up in the entire history of the United States.14

By Christmas 1941, Pearl Harbor was in ruins. The oldest of the American kids of the 30's, who grew up listening to Buck Rogers, were now 18 and 19 year olds with one foot in Atlantis and the other in a draft line. They were getting ready to do cosmic battle with the arch-villains of earth -- the Japanese and their relatives, the Atlantis-brainwashed Nazis -- and hoping to blast these bad guys running wild on their planet back to the planet they came from, wherever that was.

It was that, or let the Nazis have the promised Golden Age and their way with Shirley Temple and the Little Princesses, the eleven-year-old Princess Elizabeth and six-year-old Princess Margaret Rose who were the international heroines and subjects of popular story books.

THE MARK OF COURAGE

One of the most fascinating occult aspects of WW II were the arm-patches worn by the GIs and officers of America's major military forces as they marched into battle to defend the free world and to make the world safe for Micky Mouse to build his magical promised land. With each insignia came instruction on its legend, lore and inspiration. Many of these arm patches may be astonishing to us for their surprising occult meaning elucidated by our study.

• The arm of General Dwight Eisenhower, the Supreme Commander of the Allied Forces, sported a flaming Sword of Destiny surmounted by a rainbow.

• The headquarters of the Southeast Asia Command was symbolized by a dragon emerging from the sea.
• The U.S. Army Forces, South Atlantic's emblem shows three Egyptian-style pyramids sitting inside a gateway.
• The European Theater of Operations was signified by a star-guided lightning bolt.
• The XVIII Airborne Corps who jumped into Normandy on D-Day and jumped into Germany did so with patches featuring spear-spitting dragons.
• The 45th Thunderbird division who bravely stormed Sicily, Salerno, Cassino, Anzio and Belfort Gap -- and were the most feared by Rommel -- took the symbol of the phoenix bird of the American Indians into battle with them.
• Multiple Army Air Force divisions wore golden patches with winged stars or circles identical to the ten thousand-year-old symbols of the gods of Sumeria and Egypt.
• The feared Seventh Army, destined to invade Sicily, southern France, fight up the Rhone, and take Munich did so sporting a golden Mayan stepped pyramid.

As the armed services demobilized, every discharged GI was awarded a bronze lapel button decorated with a spread eagle that appeared to be standing. It was irreverently dubbed "the ruptured duck." As eagles, they took on the totem bird of the An-nun-aki who were also called eagles.

THE WAR OF THE PROPHETS

Historians say WW II was a race war. Conspiracy buffs say it was a war of profits. Both are correct. By 1943 the U.S. economy had fully recovered. The U.S. standard of living was a full one sixth higher than in 1939.15 Business was booming, none more than big war business, whose titans married America's big industry, permanently, to the military.

For many, the race and profit motive are not enough, for the past fifty years the world has been asking itself the question: why the Nazis?

Four hundred years ago, it is possible a man asked that question too. His name was Nostradamus, the French prophet.

Nostradamus' prophecies had remained obscure since the time of his death in the sixteenth century. Then, one cold winter evening in 1939-1940, while his homeland of France was recovering from a massive beating from the German blitzkrieg that resulted in the fall of France, Magda Goebbels, the insane wife of Josef Goebbels, Hitler's morally-challenged Minister of Propaganda and Enlightenment, happened to be reading Nostradamus' prophecies in bed.

Suddenly, she gasped with excitement and amazement. "Did you know that Nostradamus said that in 1939 Germany would declare war on France and Britain over Poland?"

Goebbels most certainly was aware of this. He soon exploited Nostradamus' prophecies of Nazi victory, and even the appearance of Adolph Hitler as the second Anti-Christ, in a psychological warfare campaign.

In 1555 Nostradamus, writing in the occult Language of the Birds, prophesied the rise of a "bird of prey flying on the left," an Anti-Christ named "Hister," and also the ravaging effects of the war on his home.

Nostradamus saw beyond the war, predicting that in July, 1999, "the King of Terror" would come out of the sky and resurrect "the King of Angolmois," an anagram for Mongolia. As mentioned, this prophecy may relate to the return of Jesus. Why F.D.R. believed this would happen in 1934, decades ahead of Nostradamus' prophecy, is still a mystery to me. Could he have been fulfilling a task for a future event?

In France, Nostradamus' prophecies were distributed in handbills dropped from German aircraft by Nazi propaganda agents predicting Germany's victory.

In response, at Winston Churchill's urging, movie-going Americans were treated to "Movietone" news clips featuring the Allied interpretation of Nostradamus' prophecies and their predictions that the Allies and America -- the New Atlantis -- would win the war.

IAN FLEMING

Start spreading the news: England also launched an all-out occult and propaganda war. This effort was aimed at playing occult mind-games with the superstitious Hitler. Its headquarters was Rockefeller Center, the New York City office and shopping complex, which was a beehive of spies during World War II. Sir William Stephenson operated suites of offices containing the British Secret Services -- British Intelligence in the United States. These offices comprised secret occult counterintelligence and propaganda, undercover operations and coordination with OSS and FBI for operations against Germany and Japan.

One intelligence officer assigned to Stephenson was Ian Fleming, the creator of James Bond.[18] Fleming was the man chosen to lead this occult propaganda effort aimed at influencing Hitler's mental state. Fleming's undercover team of astrologers and psychics successfully infiltrated Hitler's inner circle of astrologers, feeding him bogus predictions.

Several famous English occultists played a key role in the psychic opposition to Hitler, including Alestair Crowley, a psychotic English black magician who claimed he was an agent for MI6 (the British Intelligence Agency).

Crowley was entangled in the attempt by British Secret Service to lure Rudolph Hess to Britain on a peace mission in 1941. Fleming was in charge of laying this trap which, if successful, would be a propaganda coup for the Allies.

Hitler deployed occult groups to raise psychic power to block the radar of RAF aircraft flying over Germany. A similar operation was used by the British occult services to deflect the Luftwaffe during their raids of Britain.

Early in the war the British attached well-known occultists, including Dion Fortune, to the newly created Psychological Warfare Department. Fortune used remote viewing to spy on the Nazi High Command. She also performed ceremonies to invoke the ancient guardian angels of Britain to protect the Isles from invasion.

In 1940, with the Nazi invasion of Britain imminent, a coven of witches and pagans gathered to form a Great Circle. This emergency rite, which involved invoking the spirits of dead witches to protect Britain, was called only twice before in British history, in 1588 to combat the Spanish Armada (which was defeated with the help of a "great storm"), and in the 1800's to prevent Napoleon from crossing the Channel.

Notes:

1. TIME-LIFE BOOKS *This Fabulous Century 1930-1940* (New York, Time-Life Books, 1969) p. 116
2. Ibid. p. 141
3. Ibid. p. 116
4. Ibid. p. 262
5. Ibid. p. 82
6. Dusty Sklar *The Nazis and the Occult* (New York, Dorset Press, 1977) p. 111
7. Ibid.
8. Ibid.
9. Ibid.
10. Ibid.
11. Ibid. p. 110
12. Ibid. p. 268
13. TIME-LIFE BOOKS *This Fabulous Century 1940-1950* (New York, Time-Life Books, 1969) p. 21
14. Ibid. p. 22
15. Ibid. p. 142

CHAPTER TWENTY FOUR

THE SPEAR OF DESTINY

Earlier, I mentioned that the Thule Society believed *their* ancestors, not the Israelites, had been keepers of the secret Atlantean science for entering the inner earth, the Land of the Living. As Hitler's propaganda declared there is a Nordic and National-Socialist science and religion which is opposed to Judeo-Liberal science and religion.

Further, the Thulists claimed the early leaders of Judeo-Christianity had destroyed this. In his search to rediscover this science, and its Pandora's Box full of magic, power tools and unlimited vril power, Hitler began with the Spear of Destiny.

AT THE GATE BETWEEN GOOD AND EVIL

For more than 2,000 years the spear alleged to have pierced the side of Jesus during the crucifixion – the Spear of Destiny -- is said to have captured the imagination of rulers of the western world.[1] Warriors have also been captivated by its message. General George "Blood and Guts" Patton, for instance, who is allegedly the only American military person said to have understood the occult power of the Spear.

In legends, the Spear is the symbol of the magical powers inherent in the blood of God's "chosen people". It stands at the gate between good and evil. Our interest in it stems from the fact that the Spear may be the blade attached to the Staff of Destiny, one of the four Atlantean power tools.

In Hebrew lore, the Spear of Destiny was "made" under the direction of an ancient prophet named Phineas (c. 1400 B.C).[2] "Made" is routinely taken to mean manufactured. However, since the Spear was possibly already in existence (it is claimed to be the property of the Atlanteans or Tuatha de'

215

Danann), the term "made" could also be understood in the sense in which the police use the term: identified, understood.

Phineas was Moses' older brother Aaron's grandson.3 In Acts 6:22 we learn that Moses was trained in all the wisdom of the Egyptians including the mystery school at Heliopolis. In fact, says the wisdom tradition, Moses became a High Priest of Heliopolis. Growing up, Phineas likely heard amazing stories of the exploits of his grandfather and his brother, Moses.

Moses lived at the time when An was said to have made its last rendezvous with earth, c. 1500 B.C. The Bible's troubling tale of seven long years of plagues, crop failures, increased earthquakes, volcanic eruptions and other natural disasters and phenomenon that preceded the Exodus are all tip-offs to the intense, earth-jolting magnetic and gravitational effects of the approaching planet An.

Things get worse when the planet heads on its way back into the deepest recesses of our solar system.

Usually, when An is close to earth, Anu, its ruler, would come down and have a look see. Coinciding with An's visit during the time of the Israelite Exodus, for example, the Lord came down and proclaimed at pivotal his summit with Moses at Sinai that his covenant with the descendents of Abraham meant "ye shall be unto me a *kingdom of priests.*"

This interesting statement gave the official job description of Abraham's family: a royal priesthood. If "the Lord" who appeared to Moses on Mount Sinai was Anu, it also suggests Anu continued to be impressed with Enki's genetic results, and that the priesthood formed in Atlantis to benefit Enki's creation was back in business.

From here, things get a little twisted. Phineas' first notable act, a murder, is recorded in the Old Testament. He ran the Spear through an Israelite man and his sex partner, a woman who worshipped a Baal god, who were accused of performing sex magic. (Is this episode similar to the two twisting serpents that Thoth separated with his staff?).

Unfortunately, space does not permit us to explore the titillating questions concerning the true nature of this event, however, in recognition of Phineas' zeal, Yahweh (Enlil? or Enki?) lifted a plague he had sent, which had killed 24,000 people. Yahweh rewarded Phineas and his descendents with "a perpetual priesthood" (Numbers 25:13).

A perpetual priesthood you say? Like the kind which is in contact with higher beings and passes secrets and power tools along down the ages (perhaps even Atlantean knowledge)? This priestly dynasty, which preserved the writings of Moses, was called the Levites, the sons of Leviathan (which happens to be a Hebrew name for one of the satellites of Tiamat).

According to the apocyryphal *Assumption of Moses*, some of this secret library was given to Joshua to hide where it would be safe until the time of the "end days". These writings were to be deposited in a sacred repository "in the place which He made from the beginning of the creation of the world".

To the Egyptians, this place would have been underneath tthe Egg of Creation, the twelve-acre megalithic rock platform upon which sits the Great Pyramid in Egypt.

To the Jews, the sacred place was the rock beneath the Holy of Holies of Solomon's Temple in Jerusalem. (Which is one reason why the Temple Mount is one of the hottest pieces of real estate on earth.)

Jewish secret doctrine states Phineas was reincarnated in 850 B.C. as Elijah, a one-man wrecking crew who raised hell with the existing world order on behalf of Yahweh. He also led a priesthood (the same priesthood founded by Phineas?) which confronted and defeated 900 prophets of Baal,[4] and then climbed aboard a mysterious space vehicle the Bible called a "Whirlwind,"[5] and achieved immortality.

Elijah, said Jesus, reincarnated as John the Baptist.[6] He is expected to return today as the Peacemaker, the King of Terror. Like Elijah and John the Baptist, he's bound to upset the apple cart of New Age politics.

A BONE OF HIM SHALL NOT BE BROKEN

Herod the Great is said to have possessed the Spear of Destiny before Longinus. Herod used it as the symbol of his power and authority when he ordered the death of every male child in Judea. This was done in order to eliminate the Christ child who would become the King of the Jews.[7]

The Spear was later carried by the head of the Temple Guard assigned to order the breaking of Jesus' legs as he hung upon the cross. Longinus, a near-blind Roman Centurion, snapped it out of his arms and then pierced Jesus' side with the Spear, an act which restored Longinus' vision, gave him spiritual sight and changed the history of the world.[8]

When Longinus pierced the side of Jesus on the cross he did so to save him from the mutilation which was certainly to come. It was customary for the bones of crucified men to be broken as a way to hasten death.

Longinus became an early hero of the first Christians for his actions that Good Friday in April, 2,000 years ago. If Jesus' legs had been broken, his body weight would have crushed his lungs, causing him to die from asphyxiation. The breaking of the legs was viewed as a far-from customary coup d'grace since it saved the crucified person from days of agony. (Curiously, Jesus' legs were not broken, yet he died within hours anyway.)

If Jesus' legs had been broken, the prophecy of Isaiah, "a bone of him shall not be broken," would not have been fulfilled. In that moment, by his single action, Longinus may have held the destiny of the world in his hands. When he made the decision to pierce the side of Jesus, proclaiming his death, Longinus altered history.

Today, an artist's conception of the Spear is on display in the Habsburg Treasure House in Vienna. Long and tapering, the Spear is made of iron now black with age.

One of the first things one notices is that the Spear is full of contrasts. Its wide base with menacing metal flanges depicts the wings of a dove. A cuff threaded with soft gold, silver and copper wire secures a nail to a central aperture of the blade. Crude golden crosses are embossed on the lowest part of the Spear's base.

The Spear's iron blade stands out of place compared with the golden crowns, scepters and other, frankly ugly, treasures on display in the Habsburg Treasure House. Still, it radiates spiritual power compared to which the other objects appear lifeless. As well it should, the Spear marks the boundary between yesterday and today, this world and another.

Could this really represent the Key of Life that permits one to get past the Flaming Sword that guards the gate to Atlantis? Hitler, Spear enthusiasts tell us, certainly seemed to think so. He had been foaming at the mouth to acquire the Spear since his teen years.

When he removed the ancient Spear from its resting-place Hitler recalled going into a trance, whereupon a "Superman" hovered over and possessed him. In light of the myth of the guardians of the power tools this may be no joke. Henceforth, Hitler claimed the Spear and set into motion a chain of tragic events.

Spear enthusiasts maintain that the night Hitler stole the Spear in 1938 was from then on known as the "Night of Terror". This is interesting given that in Hebrew myth the shape-shifting Shining Ones were also known as the Terror.

However, the truth is, Hitler didn't remove the Spear for a year. Why?

In order to given an answer to this question we must pull on another strand of the golden thread.

CALLING SATAN ON THE OUIJA BOARD

In the spring of 1941, Hitler was systematically squashing neighboring Denmark, Norway, Belgium, Luxembourg and the Netherlands (and figuring out how the Luftwaffe could make it rain German bombs on Britain and turn the rest of

Europe into a smoking ruin). In anticipation of the crushing of France (their last known repository), Heinrich Himmler was busy tracing the rest of the Atlantean power tools in anticipation of the crushing of France.

All during the hungry years, while Germany suffered a self-esteem crushing economic depression after its loss in WW I, Himmler and the Thule Society focused on searching for the secrets of Atlantis and the mysteries of Teutonic lore. Now, with an unlimited Nazi budget, his search was escalated.

Teuton or *Teutonic*, like the Mayan Teotihuacan, comes from the base word teuta (pronounced *tay-oo-tay*), a word which rings of Tahuti ("he who balances," pronounced *ta-hoo-tay*).10 Tahuti is better known as Thoth, the Egyptian scribe of the Gods.

It is ironic that Himmler would have to master Thoth's lore, as the Egyptian Thoth is identified as the same person as the Jewish super-heroes and key-holders, Enoch ("righteous one") and Moses. The Book of Enoch tells of the pre-Flood civilization and its hero, Enoch, and his trip to heaven to meet with the Lord and his return to earth with instructions for the construction of the Great Pyramid.

The Mayan and Egyptian myths suggest Thoth was also Atlas, the first priest-king of Atlantis. So, Thoth's lore could actually be Atlantean in origin. Nothing would have suited Himmler better.

On the other hand, what might Himmler have made of the statements in the Egyptian Book of the Dead which substantiate Thoth's Atlantean heritage and also reinforce the idea that the Jewish people may also have been Atlantean or Aryan?

Compiled from Egyptian funerary documents written on temple walls, and attributed to Thoth himself, this remarkable 6,000 year old Egyptian text depicts Thoth as the Lord of Divine Books, Scribe of the Gods and Lord of Divine Speech (aka the Language of the Birds).

Sprinkled throughout its pages is Thoth's story of being raised in a distant land in the west, which was across a body of water. This land was sometimes called the "Island of the Flame" which is in the sea. When a cataclysm occurred which *blackened the sun* (which no doubt would get Himmler's attention for its association with Order of the Black Sun), Thoth led his people across the ocean to an eastern country: Egypt.11

This story is remarkable when viewed dualistically:

• Could the *black sun* refer to a tunnel or gate through the sun revealing the hidden Central Sun?

• Was the *ocean* Thoth led his people across (through this tunnel) the cosmic ocean?

• Is the mysterious *eastern country* Thoth led them to the heavenly Egypt or Tula?

By this rendering, could Thoth have created a tunnel in the sun to lead a mass exodus of souls off the planet? Was the place of departure the Great Pyramid in Giza? (In a moment we will explore the device he may have used to open the gateway: the Ark of the Covenant.)

Indeed, in Chapter 183 of the *Book of the Dead*, Thoth is credited with uniting upper (heavenly) and lower (earthly) Egypt, a feat for which he is called the Peacemaker. In Chapter 85 of the *Book of the Dead* it says Thoth then took up residence in the "field of peace". Was this the docking station on earth or its mate on the other side of the cosmic ocean, in heaven?

Interestingly, Jacob's son Joseph, (whose name meant "he who was brought to life by the word of the Goddess") was placed into a Pit during a death-rebirth initiation. The Pit, the land of death, (or earth) was the training ground where knight wannabes of all Ages have beheld the Black Sun or hidden Central Sun, and saw the gods of the upper and lower worlds "face to face."

HELIOPOLIS IS A TULA

At the very center of Thoth's lore, we must remember, is the ben ben stored at his city Heliopolis, the City of H*elios* or City of 8. Remember the ben ben?

The ben-ben was a sacred conical-shaped stone which was credited with cosmic origins (ala the Stone of Destiny). It was the "celestial chamber," the ark, in which the gods landed on earth. At one time it may also have landed at Baalbek (a second Heliopolis), or even Ur-Salem (Jerusalem) where the Muslims built the Dome of the Rock to conceal their sacred "(s)tone".

The Egyptian ben-ben was the forerunner of the Christian phoenix, the legendary cosmic bird of resurrection, rebirth and calendrical cycles, which was said to have come from Tula, the place of herons. It was believed that the heron came to the City of 8 at the dawn of each New Age. From here, the heron radiated light and delivered knowledge concerning the means for the soul to make its transformation into a cosmic bird, a higher being which may be called homo angelis.

According to the Copts (early Egyptian Christians), the baby Jesus was given shelter at Heliopolis at the time of the Flight of the Ark (Mary) into Egypt after his birth in the "manger".

This would make sense.

It would have meant the heron (Jesus) had returned to announce the New Age of Pisces.

As scholars are now beginning to question whether or not the town of Nazareth existed during the time of Jesus, it is leaving many at a loss to explain why Jesus was called the Nazarene.

Further, while the little town of Bethlehem is given credit, scholars cannot definitively identify the actual location of the manger of the messiah either.

It may be helpful if they consult the sky-watchers of the ancient Chinese, Egyptians, and Babylonians who made the crucial observation, as did the later Christians, that the Three Wise Men of Orion's belt *point directly to*, or are tipped by, Osiris' star in the east, *Sirius*. In Syrian, Arabian, and Persian astrology Sirius was *Messaeil* -- the Messiah.

Many traditions, including the Egyptian and the Dogon of Africa, believe Sirius was the actual home of Isis and Osiris. Could this be the true "manger" Jesus came from as well?

Sirius is in the constellation Canis Major, meaning "the Greater Dog." This is why it is called the Dog Star. In the world's oldest known zodiac found painted on the ceiling at the ancient Temple of Denderah in Egypt, Canis Major is shown as a hawk, the natural enemy of the dragon.

The name of this constellation is *Naz*, meaning "Caused to Come Forth". Sirius comes from *Sar* or *Seir*, which means the Prince.

It is very interesting to note that when the names of this constellation, *Naz* (hawk or bird) and its brightest star, *Seir*, are combined we get the word *Naz-Seir*. Together, they define Jesus as the Nazarene, or the Prince who came from Sirius. As these Sirius folk settled in Mongolia, F.D.R. would have been correct in looking for the reincarnated Jesus there.

In the nineteenth century, mythologist and linguist Godfrey Higgins sought to uncover the Ur-relgion and Ur-language by tracing word meanings. In his book *Anacalypsis* he writes that Nazareth, the town of Nazir, or *the flower*, was situated in Carmel, the vineyard or garden of God.

Jesus was a flower, he says, from which came the adoration, by the Rosicrucians, of the Rose and the Cross. The rose, he says, comes from *ras*, or knowledge or wisdom. Higgins says this rose was stolen from the garden, and was crucified. That is why his emblem is the emblem of the Rosicrucians -- a Rose on a Cross.

Do these astrological and mythological interpretations of "Nazareth" create a picture of Jesus as a "flower" or "flower-er" who is somehow linked with Sirius?

If so, can we locate the "garden" in which this flower blossomed?

How about Heliopolis? Located just north of Cairo in Egypt and directly across the Nile from the Great Pyramid, Heliopolis was the Egyptian headquarters for the Children of An.

This makes Heliopolis one of the most sacred and mysterious places on earth. It is known in the Bible as *On* or *An*. However, according to renowned French mythologist Rene Guenon, the true ancient name for Heliopolis was *Luz* (light), *Salem* (Peace) or *Tula*.

Now we are getting somewhere.

Heliopolis is a place just strange enough to be an ancient Tula, and another possible earthly manger of Jesus, as well.

In Thoth's time the ben ben -- the heron's ark -- was housed in the Holy of Holies of the Temple of the Phoenix in Heliopolis. In his Emerald Tablets Thoth states: "Deep neath the rocks (at Heliopolis) *is buried a ben-ben*, waiting the time when man might be free."

In ancient times Egyptians made pilgrimages to the shrine at Heliopolis to view and pray to the ben-ben. The original ben-ben has long since disappeared. However, it was depicted on Egyptian monuments as a conical chamber within which a god or a goddess could be seen.

Archaeologists have unearthed a stone scale-replica of the ben-ben. It shows a god or goddess standing at its open hatch-door in a welcoming gesture. The striking similarity in appearance and, no doubt, function, to a command module for a modern Saturn rocket is certainly thought provoking.

What most catches our attention here, and fires the imagination, is the Sumerian symbol for Heliopolis: a tall spear, or what could symbolically represent a rocketship on a launch tower. It is said to mark the location of the ben-ben, the Ark of the heron.

A spear, you say, symbolizes Heliopolis? A moment ago, we noticed Hitler foaming at the mouth for years over the Spear of Destiny, and then when he has the chance to possess it, he passed.

Hitler was mad. However, he was no idiot. Did he realize the story of the Spear that pierced the side of Jesus is just that, a story, a nice story, but a street legend nonetheless?

Similar to the way "Lot" may have been used as a literary cover in the story of Abraham, is the relic in the Habsburg a cover for something else?

Is attaching the Spear legend to Hitler like saying Hitler was calling Satan on an ouija board when in reality he may have had a satellite link?

Is the Spear legend designed to point us to something else?

If so, what?

Suppose the Staff or Spear of Destiny is one and the same as the Key of Life, a device for opening gateways into other dimensions? Now, add the fact that the Egyptian city of Heliopolis was symbolized by a tall spear, and the Spear or Staff of Destiny suddenly takes on an added dimension.

Could it be that the *real* Spear of Destiny is in Heliopolis, the possible Tula complex in Egypt?

Is the real Spear of Destiny the obelisk, needle or spear, marking the location of earthly dots where heaven and earth connect? Is the Spear the projectile (spiritual, biological, mechanical, or otherwise) which propels a human into the heavens?

In March 1942, Field Marshall Erwin Rommel ("The Desert Fox") was awarded the Knight's Cross with Oakleaves for his victories in North Africa with his legendary Afrika Corps.

There is little mystery as to why the Nazis might have sought to control this area. As we have seen, the H represents the gate to heaven. As depicted in *Raiders of the Lost Ark*, the Nazis were in a race to capture the power tools of Atlantis. Egypt was among their favorite digging grounds.

Did the Nazis recover the Ark in Egypt as depicted in the movie? Or was the Ark in some other form?

Let us now turn to this question.

THE ARK OF THE COVENANT

The Bible tells us the Ark is a cranky, all-purpose, golden *box-shaped* device between four and five feet long and two to three feet in both breadth and width. Moses and Aaron built it per original instructions that came directly from heaven. The Ark was used by the Israelites, the Lord's chosen few or "army," to contact ("have a Covenant with") Yahweh until they made it back to headquarters ("the Promised Land").

Aaron was also ordered to construct a magical staff of power. This staff "blossomed" only while in the presence of the Ark. Moses possessed and was trained to operate a similar "rod of God" (Exodus 17:9). He acquired it in Heliopolis. It may well be a component of the Spear or Staff of Destiny.

Like the Spear, Moses and the Israelites are unlikely to have made the Ark. Proof of its earlier existence is the Egyptian description of Ra's golden box, which was preserved by the priests of Heliopolis and precisely matches the Ark.

In Psalm 29 we learn there were actually *four* places on earth where the Voice of Yahweh is heard. Does this suggest that there was either more than one Ark or there are four sacred repositories and the Ark is alternately stored in one of these places?

Psalm 29 lists Lebanon (Baalbek) as one of those four places. Baalbek was originally called Heliopolis, "the City of the Sun God," and was the sister-city to the Heliopolis in Egypt. As I mentioned, local legends claim Adam and his son Cain built this temple in cooperation with the "giants" (the Shining Ones) who were later destroyed by the biblical Flood. This would make it an Atlantean power place.

Like its designer, Yahweh, the Ark of the Covenant appears to have a split personality. Generally, it provides a cornucopia of benefits. Then, on other days it more closely resembles Pandora's box, the magical chest which Zeus (who shares many negative traits with Enlil) maliciously sent to mankind with Pandora. Like the Ark, Pandora's box bore a blessing, but also evil curses: strife, pain, death, sickness, etc., which Pandora released among the wrong men.

The Ark is described as a sacred golden throne designed so that a person could sit in the "mercy seat" between two cherubim and communicate with "the Lord". The cherubim catch our attention. These winged guardians often appear in religious contexts, especially around the Tree of Life, the link between heaven and earth. The Winged Gateway at Paran, for example.

In Genesis (3:24), these winged beings were placed by Yahweh east of the Garden of Eden (Atlantis?) -- "*to keep the way of the Tree of Life*" -- meaning either as guardians or as intermediaries between the human and divine realm.

Either way, the cherubim stand between humanity and the mysteries that lead us to Atlantis/Tula. At the gate to Eden, these cherubim are beside a *Flaming Sword*, which may be, the (S)word of Destiny. It if is, it appears the Ark of the Covenant works in conjunction with the Sword of Destiny or is set-up in the same locale, i.e., Eden, the Great Pyramid, the New Atlantis.

The (S)word of Destiny is a companion power tool to the (S)tone of Destiny. The (S)tone appears to adjust our brain waves. The (S)word, like the word Jesus will have on his thigh during the Second Coming, is a magical word of power which may open the gate guarded by the cherubim.

After his summit on Sinai the Lord instructed Moses to build a Tabernacle, a portable sanctuary to house the Ark, and place copies of the Ten Commandments (or the Stone of Destiny?) in the Ark. This Tabernacle was carried for forty years by the Israelites in their wanderings in the wilderness of the Sinai.

Yahweh led the Israrelites by day, visibly appearing as an enormous "cloud". By night he appeared as a "cloud of fire". Wherever the cloud went the Israelites followed. Every now and then, the Shekinah ("spirit of glory") of Yahweh

224

would beam from the Ark (like something straight out of *Aladdin*), filling the tribes of Israel with awe and wonder.

After forty years of wandering in the wilderness, Joshua finally deployed the Ark. On its first mission, the Israelites carried the Ark to the Jordan River. When the priests stepped into the river with their gleaming device, the Ark, the waters miraculously stopped flowing so that the tribes of Israel could effortlessly cross over into the Promised Land on dry land.

Viewed dualistically, where earthly rivers are copies of heavenly originals, could the "river" Joshua is said to have parted actually be the Milky Way? Could the Promised Land the Israelites crossed into be Tula?

In another intriguing Old Testament military engagement, the battle of Jericho, the Ark was used as a weapons system. The Israelites carried it seven times around the city. The walls fell and the Israelites conquered the city.

Is there any wonder why the wide-eyed Adolph Hitler would dispatch Himmler and his crew to ruthlessly seek to include this decisive weapons system in his own arsenal 3,500 years later?

Interestingly, occult knowledge concerning the Ark of the Covenant and the Egyptian ben ben would come together in the Nazi flying saucer program.

NAZI FLYING SAUCERS

Under the direction of Himmler, the Nazis are believed to have implemented an advanced flying saucer program. The program was based upon the work of Viktor Shauberger, an Austrian scientist who, it is claimed, mastered anti-gravity and anti-matter (or is it ante-matter?).

Shauberger met with Hitler in 1934. However, he despised the Nazi regime. In fact, he despised all regimes. He was later discredited by the Nazis, had his apartment blown up by the Russians, and was robbed and confined for one year for his knowledge of atomic energy production by the CIA.

Shauberger is reported to have had access to the secret science of sound and vibration of Pythagoras and the secret teachings preserved by the Knights Templar.

The Knights Templar you say? The Templars, we know, got all their stuff from Solomon's Temple -- where the Ark of the Covenant was stored after it left Heliopolis.

After allegedly discovering the Secret of the Temple, these warrior monks constructed Chartres Cathedral in France, encoding the Secret within the amazing masonry of Chartres. Mysterious stone reliefs show the arrival of the Ark of the Covenant at Chartres, but strangely, not in the traditional form of a box, but in the form of the Ark of Ezekiel, the fiery airborne chariot of the gods. Surely the Templars were not that confused.

There are two schools of thought concerning what *exactly* the Ark of the Covenant is. A box? An energy source from a command module of a star ship?

Two alternatives, however, do not make a choice. So, I'll introduce a third possibility here. What the Biblical figures who could operate the Ark are actually ancient ocult trained big brains who knew the secrets of hidden power words (or tones, frequencies or vibrations) that could activate such space craft? Or, more profoundly, what if they possessed the alchemical key of life and transformed *themselves* into a shining body of light, a space vessel, ark or boat capable of traversing the Milky Way?

If we think about it, isn't that what the Spear of Destiny is truly pointing to?

Wasn't the blood of Jesus holy because of what the crucifixion did to him?

Wouldn't the Spear be more valuable if it pointed to or symbolized the key of life, a sacred Science, revealed by the crucifixion, which enabled *anyone* to achieve the holy blood and travel the universe, completing the looping 8 between earth and Tula?

What if the Ark of the Covenant was actually a science *and* device which:

• when housed within a specially designed tabernacle or cosmic egg (read "the Great Pyramid, Solomon's Temple and Chartres Cathedral"),

• designed to encode a sacred goddess geometry (Phi geometry) that aligns this earthly egg with the Cosmic Egg,

• and empowered by the (S)tone of Destiny,

• can open a stargate or portal leading into other regions of the galaxy.

Does this explain the Nazi fascination with this device?

THE GOLDEN EJECTOR SEAT

As evidenced by the stargate story found in the annals of the An-nun-aki's kin, the Tuatha de' Danann, the Ark's stargate-opening ability is nothing new in mythology. In the Beltane appearance of the Tuatha de' Danann *a golden image* is erected and a star being emerges.

In *When Time Began*, Zecharia Sitchin tells of a Sumerian recollection of a state visit to earth by Anu and his wife Antu, the ruler of An via a similar device.

During the morning-time ceremony in which the royal couple departs earth after their look see, Enki and Enlil, two sons of Anu, await Anu at what is called the "*golden supporter*". They hold several objects: "that which opens up the secrets" (the Spear of Destiny or Key of Life which was used as the "remote control" for the Tree of Life), "the Sun disks," and the "splendid shining posts".

If the same doorway created by these golden pillars is anything like the Pillars of Hercules leading to Atlantis, the pillars of Solomon's Temple, and the archway Jesus and the Essenes were renowned for possessing, we are talking about a life-altering technology.

When Anu and Antu climb aboard the "ejector seat" of the golden supporter, which may be the golden throne seat of the Ark of the Covenant, above them they see the golden needle, the Pillar or Tree of Life.

Perhaps like riding a bull, cowboys who ride this device lean forward, because if you lean back you fight the spin instead of rolling with it. The device comes alive, the gate swings open and Anu (and presumably the Ark) is hurled into the Abyss (sometimes called the Fish of Isis) like a missile, twirling through hyperspace.

LOOK, IN THE SKY...

Could the Ark really be a UFO? What if the Ark is a pod from one of the evacuation vehicles of Tiamat, even the vessel Jesus' mother Mary rides around in? Should we look in the sky for its return? Or, what if this vessel is the Moon?

After Solomon ("Sun God of On") built a permanent temple to house the Ark, Yahweh's Shekinah glory continued to speak from upon the Mercy Seat upon the Ark and guided Israel.

The Ark, with the (s)tone Tablets of Destiny inside, became a "(s)tone that whispers" or a rune (s)tone.

In this way the Ark symbolized the phoenix, the heron or the Messiah, the bird-man who spills cosmic secrets in the Language of the Birds. Is this why the Jews consider the Ark the most important occult artifact in history, and hold the site of Solomon's Temple sacred?

Whatever it is, the Ark appears to be a technology, which allows humans to have a covenant with God, or even become a god. The key word here is covenant, or contract.

Let us suppose the technology that enables this covenant changes forms. The reason I ask is because the symbol of the New Covenant of Jesus is the Cup containing his blood.

What if the Ark and the Cup of Destiny are actually the same thing?

In the next chapter we shall discover that it looks as if Henry A. Wallace, and possibly F.D.R., pulled the golden thread of this pivotal question.

Notes:

1. Trevor Ravenscroft *The Spear of Destiny* (York Beach, ME, Samuel Weiser, 1973)

2. Col. Howard A. Buechner and Capt. Wilhelm Bernhart *Adolph Hitler and the Secrets of the Holy Lance* (Metairie, LA, Thunderbird Press, 1988)p. 61

3. Reader's Digest *Who's Who in the Bible* (Pleasantville, NY, Reader's Digest, 1994) 357

4. Exodus 22:20

5. 2 Kings 2:1

6. Matthew 11:13-15, 17:10-13, Mark 9:11-13

7. Ibid. p. 62

8. Col. Howard Beuchner *Emerald Cup: Ark of Gold* (Metarie, LA, Thunderbird Press, 1991) p. 126

9. Trevor Ravenscroft & T. Wallace Murphy *The Mark of the Beast* (Secaucus, NJ, Citadel Press, 1992) p. 9

10. Peter Moon *Black Sun* (New York, Sky Books, 1997) p. 69

11. E.A. Wallis Budge *Papyrus of Ani*, Chapter CLXXV

CHAPTER TWENTY FIVE

THE CUP OF DESTINY

*Today is Good Friday, and they wait
there a Dove, winging down from heaven.
It brings a small white wafer, and
leaves it on the (s)tone.*

According to legend, it was from the wound by the Spear of Longinus that Joseph of Arimathea (or possibly Mary Magdalen) caught the blood of Jesus with the Holy Grail.

There is a critical debate as to what, exactly, this Cup is made of: silver, gold, emerald, wood, copper? Let us suppose it is made of the same material as its companion object, the (S)tone of Destiny.

Recall, this was the (s)tone upon which Jacob lay his head when he saw the vision of the angels ascending and descending a ladder which reached into heaven (an event which may have taken place at a Tula).

As noted, star sapphires are called (s)tones of destiny. The sapphire is a vital link to uncovering the secrets, ancient mysteries and long ago legends of the holy blood and the Holy Grail. In *The Woman's Encyclopedia of Myths and Legends*, Barbara Walker notes that the Bible called lapis lazuli *sappur* or "holy blood."1 It was the substance of God's throne (Ezekiel 1:26).

As we know, God's throne sits upon the Ark of the Covenant.

The Authorized Version inaccurately translates sappur as "sapphire". Does this indicate that the Bible is in agreement with what the Tuatha de' Danann meant to say? That is, together the (s)tone of Destiny, Cup of Destiny and the Key of Life or Spear of Destiny contain the secrets and means for creating the "Holy Blood" required for walking through the doorway or being hurled into the Abyss like a missile.

According to lore, God sent the archangel Raziel, whose name means "Secrets of God," to give Adam the operating directions for the Holy Grail and the Key of Life. These secret instructions were written in a book known as The *Book of the Angel Raziel*, which was inscribed on a *sapphire* (s)tone. The (S)tone of Destiny.

As we have learned, these Edenic texts were written in the Language of the Birds. From another point of view, is it possible that what the Tuatha de' Danann meant to say was that, along with the Holy Grail or its companion, the Spear of Destiny and its instruction manual inscribed on the sapphire (s)tone of Destiny, all who possess these objects receive the ability to transform their blood into the holy blood?

Does this help to explain why Himmler sought to master this lore? Did he realize there is nothing special or "pure" at all about Aryan blood? Did he understand the Germans were Aryan in name only unless, like Moses, they could wave the Spear or Key of Life and turn their blood into holy blood?

CUP OR ADVANCED MEDICAL DEVICE?

Here, we have to ask: is this just a Cup and Spear or are these some form of advanced soul or blood transforming medical devices which prepare us for travelling via arc or stargate? Is the Cup a high-tech container?

This may not be as far-fetched as it sounds. Symbolically, a cup is a receptacle, like a jar, vase or a flowerpot. Jars or vases are a common icon in the myth of the Sun god. The Egyptian *Pyramid Texts* even state the sun-god dwells in a vase. Likewise, the Hindu Vasishtha was "born from a jar".

Similarly, Muslim tradition has it that the soul of Allah's prophet Mohammed preexisted in a vase of light in the world of spirits before his incarnation on earth. This symbolism is also found in China where the "True Man" lives in a vessel.

Likewise, among the Mayans, the vase symbolized the divine essence of light, and life proceeding from the "Heart of Heaven," (which is another name for Tula and its prophet Osiris, the Egyptian name for Enki).

Eerily, the Egyptian priests claimed that Osiris (Enki) was a potter. The resurrected dead ancestors received "the fresh water (souls?) in a *jar* which Ptah (Enki) had fashioned". In between bodies, the essence, or likely, the soul of this sacred son was kept in a jar. The symbol of the sacred marriage of Osiris with the Mother (Tula) or Moon Goddess was the *menat*, "moon charm". This was depicted in hieroglyphics as a phallus-shaped jar pouring fluid into a wider pot or vase.

The phallic water jar represented the soul of the Savior in all the religions of the Middle East and Egypt.

This may allow us to venture an explanation as to why the mysterious man with the water jar awaited Jesus in the upper room on the evening of the Last Supper (Luke 22:10).

Here, it is interesting to ask: was it truly a jar this person preceding Jesus was carrying, or was it possibly some form of advanced soul-transfer device? As Jesus was prepared to give up the ghost, was this person preparing to capture (or set free) the soul of the Savior for a future incarnation? Is this why this person was following him around?

Let us look closer at this "jar". A key to unlocking the secrets of this phenomenal jar may lay in unlocking another meaning of the word *pithos*, which was misused to describe the jar. "In Christian custom," says Barbara Walker "the pithos was transformed into the *pyx* or "box" that enclosed the body of Christ; and Erasmus confused the two vessels (jar and box) in translating the patriarchal version of the Pandora's box myth."2

The Ark of the Covenant is described as a "box". Is it really?

Could it be that the Ark, which houses the Messiah, and the Grail -- the Cup of Destiny, which symbolizes his blood -- are interchangeable? That is, once one achieves the Holy Blood is it not possible they see the Rainbow Bridge, an arc, from earth to the Moon to the Pleiades to Tula? Does drinking from the Holy Grail create the Holy Blood capable of transporting the soul to higher dimensions?

These age-old questions take on astonishing modern proportions momentarily. First, let us take a more detailed look at the legends of the Cup of Destiny.

GRAIL KINGS AWAITING THE (S)TONE

After the Crucifixion, the Cup and Spear of Destiny did not remain together long. Joseph was said to have taken the Cup of Destiny to Britain (or "Bright An or On"),3 where he and his offspring became the Grail Kings or Guardians of the Grail, the forerunners of the Knights Templar, that strange priesthood of warrior monks who claimed to guard the Secrets of Jesus.

Does the story of King Arthur (from Asur or Osiris) and his wife Guinevere mark the return of the Atlantean power tools to Britain (which claims to be descended from the Atlanteans)?

Interestingly, Glast-On-bury was transformed into the Isle of Ava-l-on. Is this because *ava* or *avi* is the Latin root for angel or bird, making Ava-lon birdland? Further, could this be one reason why Arthur is called the legendary "once and future king" who will rise again like the phoenix and lead Britain in its hour of utmost peril?

Guinevere fled Arthur's court after it was revealed that she had an affair with Lancelot, (or is it Spear of Lot? or Spear of Light?) the father and reincarnation of Galahad. (It is said Arthur lost his sacred manna when Guinevere walked out on him.) Galahad was said to have descended from either Joseph of Arimathea, or through Guinevere, a descendent of Jesus.

Galahad, the pure Knight, was thought to be the last to possess the Holy Grail. Interestingly, after discovering it, he took a sabbatical at the Central Sun (Tula) returning to earth with Catherine, the dancer at the fiery wheel at the central point in heaven, who became the namesake for the Cathars, the Pure Ones.

AWAIT THE STONE

We began our search for the occult secrets of WW II with Henry A. Wallace and F.D.R.'s search for the reincarnated Jesus in Mongolia and a question: did they find him? This led us to the power tools of the Atlanteans, which I proposed were used to open gateways for the Messiah to enter the earth plane. One of these power tools may even be a special container that stores the soul of the savior.

It would be nice to conclude this book with a smoking gun, concrete proof that F.D.R. and Wallace did find Jesus and were waiting for the proper moment to introduce him to the world. We may have that very thing in one of Henry A. Wallace's letters (dated March 12, 1933) to Nicholas Roerich.4 "Dear Guru," it said:

"I have been thinking of you holding the casket -- *the sacred most precious casket.* And I have thought of the *New Country* going forth to meet *the seven stars under the sign of the three stars.* And I have thought of the admonition '*Await the (s)tone.*' (My emphasis and parenthesis added)

We await the stone and we welcome you again to this *glorious land of destiny*, clouded though it may be with strange fumbling fears. Who shall hold up the compelling vision to these who wander in darkness?

In answer to this question we again welcome you. To drive out oppression. To drive out fear. We think of the People of Northern Shambhalla and the hastening feet of the successor of Buddha and the Lightning flashes and the breaking of the New Day.

And so I await your convenience prepared to do what I am here to do.

May Peace, Joy and Fire attend you always.

G "

According to Wallace's biographers, Graham White and John Maze, the initial *G* with which Wallace signs his name stands for Galahad, the nickname given to Wallace by Helena Roerich.5

Beyond this the letter is open to interpretation. Based upon our study, however, we may make some informed speculations as to the secret subject matter behind Wallace's code.

What if the *sacred casket* is the Grail, the jar (or advanced medical device) possibly holding the soul of Jesus?

Could the *seven stars* be the seven stars of the Pleiades?

Are *the three stars* the three belt stars of Orion?

If the *New Country* is America, the New Atlantis, wouldn't this mean the (s)tone Wallace awaited is the (S)tone of Destiny?

Isn't America *the land of destiny*, and the *New Day* referred to by Wallace the new Thousand Years of Peace introduced by Jesus, which are as a day in the eyes of the Shining Ones?

Does this letter prove Wallace, and his compatriot F.D.R., were Grail Kings awaiting the Cup and (S)tone of Destiny? (They would not be the last in New Age politics.)

If so, and Roerich did deliver "the goods" to F.D.R. is it possible Jesus did reincarnate in 1935?

Or was F.D.R's. a link in the golden chain of events leading to Jesus' return soon thereafter?

TO THE MOON

F.D.R.'s Administration would not be the last to be touched by the light of the Moon or the Grail legend. J.F.K's Administration would soon follow.

After his assasination John F. Kennedy's wife Jacqueline ("noble in truth") dreamily referred to her late husband's Presidency as "Camelot". It has been claimed that Camelot is derived from *Camulodunum* -- or "City of Mars". However, as I have shown, Camelot is also related to Sodom, Lot's city of salvation.

It was President Kennedy who pointed us to *the Moon* as a symbol of our salvation. On July 20, 1969, at the beginning of the Dog Days of Summer when the light from Sirius was brightest on earth, humanity landed on the Moon.

It is ironic that numerous former Nazi scientists, including former honorary SS officer and rocket scientist Werner Von Braun, were instrumental in rescuing and developing NASA's fledgling rocket program, saving the U.S. enormous sums of money, and probably saving a few American lives.

Perhaps this was the first lesson to be learned from working together instead of devising ways to kill each other.

Our landing on the Moon raises a question that perhaps only future generations can answer. If the (S)tone of Destiny represents a contract for the allegiance of a group of souls going back to the times of Thoth, Abraham, and Moses, does it mean that this contract was altered in some way when we landed on the Moon?

Interestingly, on the Great Seal of the United States the eagle holds thirteen arrows in one talon, an olive branch in the other. To the Hopi (the Peaceful Ones), the thirteen arrows represent the bondage of the Planetary Healers. When the eagle on the Apollo 11 insignia was shown landing on the moon without the arrows, it represented to the Indians the release of the Peaceful Ones from bondage. Perhaps, their rescue is complete.

Notes:

1. Barbara G. Walker *The Woman's Encyclopedia of Myths and Secrets* (New York, HarperCollins, 1983) p. 890
2. Ibid. p. 767
3. John Matthews *The Grail Tradition* (Dorset, Element, 1990)
4. Graham White & John Maze *Henry A. Wallace: His Search for a New World Order* (Chapel Hill, The University of North Carolina Press, 1995) p. 65
5. Ibid. p. 66

CHAPTER TWENTY SIX

THE NEW ATLANTEAN MOMENT

When an alien civilization set up camp in Germany in the 1930's the world had no idea it was about to have one foot in Atlantis. The Nazis, with their blond ambition, acted like they were Enlilians from Mars, hell bent on tightly focusing the precious human gene pool. It wasn't until the sleeping giant of America stirred its melting pot that the Enlilians were beat back.

Today, as An is anticipated to make an appearance, we find the politics of ages past is the politics of our New Age.

In American New Age politics, are the philosophical children of Enlil represented by the Republican Party? White and conservative, they, more than any party epitomize the elitist and militarist Enlilite tradition in America.

Does the Democratic Party, then, represent the anti-military children of Enki? As American politics enters the New Age F.D.R's party represents the melting pot party of pacifists, scientists, intellectuals, homosexuals, ecologists, gnostics, artists, Jews, Latins -- those who have been barred from the highest ranks of the military.

The children of Enlil cut educational programs. Enki's children want to slash the military budget.

Despite the conflict, America is on the brink of fulfilling every possible dream. Perhaps both sides are sensing it is time for the newly emerging consciousness, which some call the Third Way.

The Third Way is the way of compromise or synthesis between right and left, Enki and Enlil. It is tech-tinged, but heart driven. The new political leaders who are embracing the

Third Way, are molding themselves into politicians who scrap big spending, big government and look to the people for solutions.

The Third Way stresses balance, individuality, self-reliance and the restructuring of planetary resources. Could this be the face of New Age politics and spirituality we have been looking for?

AS BELOW, SO ABOVE

The main question as we look about the New Atlantis concerns balance. How do we bring the four billion people on earth who do not have access to a toilet and are two and a half days walk from the nearest telephone into the 21st century at the same time we have people vacationing on the Moon?

Below us is mud, above us the stars. How do we achieve balance?

The Third Way suggests we create it by the union of human and god on earth. The choice we make for creating this balance in these days is the greatest choice in the history of the world.

Earth is our cradle. This cradle is composed of a balance of forces: environmental, spiritual and material. These forces form an interconnected grid work or Planetary Grid in which each of us live.

Because the forces which keep our cradle steady are showing signs of being out of balance, our cradle is rocking. Obviously, the early signs are the weather changes that are attributed to global warming.

We also have imbalances in our common thoughtsphere. Until humanity learns to disarm its self-loathing belief system, our children will have to deal with messiahs and madmen who kill others and themselves for their beliefs.

Only with self-love will we create heaven on earth.

To align ourselves with this lofty goal, our energy, our every thought, must be directed toward lifting humanity above its usual material concerns and directing it toward the realm of the transcendent or spiritual, the Third Way.

We must be giving and loving enough to open to the positive changes currently unfolding on earth. We must be willing to accept the light and the greatness within us.

We cannot be stubborn seeds, locked in the shadows of obsolete belief systems which for *their* survival demand that we stay the same when the universe is giving us the opportunity to grow.

THE NEW HEAVEN AND EARTH

As the New Atlantis unfolds, humanity and the earth are on the brink of blossoming. Like a flower reaching out to the sunlight, humanity is in the process of opening up to our newly emerging reality.

Higher human spiritual evolution has been accelerating in the last few centuries. As planned by the ancients, we big brains of the New Age of Aquarius are on the fringe of the scientific and spiritual harvest that will follow once this acceleration explodes.

In a single magical moment, like a seed that changes into its flower form, humanity may break free from its existing state and emerge in a changed form. The pace of change is now unprecedented for our species. Could it be that a new species is about to emerge? Are we the last of homo sapiens?

It may be up to our children to decide.

Would you feel defensive if suddenly you met an aquatic child -- who lives in the sea and breathes with a set of gills?

What about A star-man, whose body is genetically adapted to life in space?

Would meeting a hybrid between an earth man and an alien species alter your lifestyle?

If scientists and prophets are correct, we may very soon be meeting these, or possibly other, new humans. It is therefore worthwhile to begin to familiarize ourselves with a few concepts being tossed about for the possible forthcoming redesign of our favorite species, homo sapien.

As we do so let us bear this question in mind: Would any of these "possible humans" be more adequately suited to storm the (star) gates of heaven than the present model of earthling?

OFF TO SEE THE WIZARD

In 1939, America stood at the gate to the New Atlantis. That same year L.Frank Baum's *The Wizard of Oz* was in the movie theaters. Those of 1999 and beyond can take a lesson from Mr. Baum.

In this masterful story a lost or voyaging soul named Dorothy is swept up into an ascending spiral of spiritual evolution represented by a whirling tornado. In what could also be a tale of initiation, she meets an angelic Shining One who sets her "off to see the wizard, the wonderful Wizard of Oz" and the way home.

Like Dorothy we are on the Yellow Brick Road looking for, or waiting for, the gate to the New Atlantis to open.

On her quest Dorothy meets a wicked witch, flying monkeys, the Munchkins, the Lollipop Kids and others. Most importantly she meets three seekers:

A Cowardly Lion in search of courage.
A Tin Man who is looking for a heart.
A Scarecrow who wants a brain.
On their journey to the mythical Oz (a Hebrew term meaning "strength is within"), each of these seekers in their own way achieves a spiritual insight or acquires wisdom. They overcome obstacle after obstacle enroute to finding the exalted wizard of Oz and self-actualization.

Have you ever considered that each of these characters represents an aspect of humanity's present unfoldment?

When we watch these four seekers set out on their metaphysical journey we are watching them model the four main pathways in which humanity may choose to remake itself in the coming years, the totality representing the blossoming of humanity. They are:

• The Genetic Blossoming (The Cowardly Lion)
• The Cosmic Blossoming (Dorothy)
• The Hallucinogenic/Morphogenetic Blossoming (The Scarecrow)
• The Cybernetic Blossoming (The Tin Man)

It is interesting to note that the four members of the rock group KISS (with the SS lightning bolts in their logo) also represent these four characters *and* the four beasts of the Sphinx.

• the Lion (Peter Criss)
• the Bull or Dragon (Gene Simmons)
• the Eagle or Space Man (Ace Frehley)
• the Star Human (Paul Stanley)

Perhaps my favorite of all the fictional characters who represent these four pathways, are the four main characters from *Star Trek, The Next Generation*:
• Lieutenant Worf. The warrior of a genetically pure race who, like the Cowardly Lion, searches to overcome his genetic limitations.
• Deanna Troy. The beautiful goddess who, like Dorothy, is the cosmic/empathetic space cadet.
• Commander Data. The cybernetic proto-human or Tin Man looking for a heart while floating in a tin can at warp speed.
• Captain Picard. The cosmic Scarecrow turned space voyager seeking belief systems that will expand human consciousness.
Each character represents the soul's fuller expression or flowering through the sensory system of human DNA. When

these sensors unfold they will bring a more complete awareness of the multidimensional reality in which we live. A new Heaven and a new earth will emerge, fulfilling the prophecies of the ancients.

Let's briefly explore each possible blossoming.

THE CYBERNETIC BLOSSOMING -- HOMO ROBOTIC

As human beings we build machines to extend consciousness. The astrophysicist *becomes* the machine orbiting Jupiter. The oceanographer *becomes* the submersible exploring the ocean floor. In this way man and his civilization become his machines. In this way the civilization of Atlantis did rise off the coast of Florida as prophesied by Edgar Cayce. The space shuttle *Atlantis*, that is.

In our Cybernetic Blossoming humanity is choosing to activate our powers technologically through miniaturized circuitry. We may turn ourselves into consciousness extending machines like Data. This vision is also depicted in such popular movies as *Robocop* and *The Terminator*, which, incidentally, are designed to appeal to children.

When Dorothy meets the Tin Man in *The Wizard of Oz* he needs the human touch to bring him to life. Likewise, Commander Data, the android on *Star Trek*, desperately seeks to be human by acquiring emotions. Captain Picard and Data often talk of this quest.

Like the Wizard, who tells the Tin Man he doesn't know how lucky he is not to have a heart, Picard is supportive of Data's quest, but cautionary. (In the 1996 *Star Trek* movie *First Contact*, Data finally acquires human emotions and it spells trouble.)

"Hearts will never be practical until they can be made unbreakable," says the Wizard of Oz. Still, Data and the Tin Man realize they need a heart to be fully human. Ironically, cyberneticists believe we may never be fully human unless we are part robotic.

Computer research is directed in this area. Virtual reality machines in which synthetic worlds are created and experienced through a three-dimensional helmet and body suit are now available in university research centers and video arcades.

There is no question cybernetics will play a part in the evolving New Atlantis. Technology called "neurochips" or "biochips" to "download" the entire contents of one's brain onto computer chips will be available within 20 years. Hans Moravec at MIT believes he will be able to download the contents of a person's brain onto a chip, then send it off into space with instructions to self-replicate. This would create the technological equivalent of immortality.

Is the point of all this technology to create a suit of armor to protect our human feelings and to enhance our ability to fulfill our life's quest --the return to Home?

The Cybernetic Blossoming raises many ethical problems, as do each of the other blossomings. Who will control the technology? Will everyone have access to it, or just an elite few? Will a person with neurochips and a bionic heart be more or less human?

THE GENETIC BLOSSOMING

The laws of nature permit biological forms well beyond what now exist, and engineering such new forms is rapidly becoming technically feasible. The focus of this research is to give us more courage to overcome the obstacles, fears, vulnerabilities and shortcomings of life.

Scientists will soon have a complete map of the genetic code, which may permit designers to genetically change any and all aspects, including the appearance and disposition, of humanity.

Like the tornado in *The Wizard of Oz*, the science of biology is centered on the swirls of the helixes of the DNA strands. As life evolves it does so through an ascending spiral.

How many readers would like to change the way they look or genetically insure their children are physically beatiful (whatever that means)?

Is this our true source of strength and power?

At the end of *The Wizard of Oz* the Cowardly Lion was crowned with a wreath signifying glory. Is the present form of the human body the most glorious?

As we reach out to receive the higher "blossoming energies" we can assume our DNA will change to enable our physical bodies to access and accommodate these energies. It is clearly a two-way energy flow.

Would you feel defensive if suddenly you met a man with a tail -- who lives in the jungle and swings from tree to tree?

What about a ten foot tall "stuff man" -- adapted to life on the basketball court?

What about meeting a child who is the first to be released from aging? A genetically enhanced child born today could conceivably live to be 400 years old.

What if a Brain Race develops where some of us get larger brains than others?

Will things really be much different than they are today?

One thing is a virtual certainty, all of these questions and even more fantastic ones will be addressed by humanity in the New Atlantis.

HALLUCINOGENIC/MORPHOGENETIC BLOSSOMING

The Hallucinogenic Blossoming refers not just to drugs but to the mind's image creating ability. The mind's natural state, when it is allowed to express itself from within is to hallucinate, to generate images. The mind is thus naturally hallucinogenic. This is why suddenly we have music videos and the War on Drugs is a farce. Within our lifetimes music and image will become one. We won't just hear, we will simultaneously, seehear.

I refer to the Hallucinogenic Blossoming alternately as the Morphogenetic Blossoming. *Morphogenetic* comes from "morph" meaning change and "genetic" meaning genesis.

The Scarecrow in *The Wizard of Oz* is not fully human, but neither is he an android like the Tin Man or Data. The object of his quest is the ability to think for himself, or to create images. As the story progresses, the Scarecrow learns. He acquires data. In modern parlance he is creating and manipulating a Morphogenetic Field or Planetary Grid. The Morphogenetic Grid is a form of collective memory by which similar beings can tune into each other across space and time.

The Morphogenetic Field is manipulated by the Els, the intermediaries between man and the gods. At the end of *The Wizard of Oz* the Scarecrow is the one who has mastered this Field and can see into another realm. He sees the good witch, another Shining One, emerging from the invisible realm, another Field and alerts Dorothy of her presence.

Physicists and astronomers are now working in the area of wormholes, passageways linking one part of the galaxy with another. Are there dimensions beyond our own? Is time travel possible? Can we change the past? Will our children take a scientific odyssey through a gateway to parallel universes?

THE COSMIC AWAKENING: THE HUMAN BLOOMING

What if, as mystics claim, earth is a garden where, if we desire, all of us can achieve higher consciousness and "blosssom"? What if this blossoming is the first step in welcoming us into the Cosmic Garden?

For millions of years humanity was raised in Mother Earth's lap. Now we are leaving. Can each of help plant the thoughts of things that are to come? Can each of us participate by holding within us an image of greatness, of universal concerns, and of helping the earth itself?

Mystics claim we can utilize the energy that is here now. In order to tap it we will need to develop such soul qualities as peace, clarity, love and joy. We must recognize that each of us has been given an opportunity to utilize the energy and transitional atmosphere of our times to propel ourselves into a higher consciousness. Such thoughts enable the human blooming.

Many parents and teachers are seeing signs of this blossoming daily in their homes and classrooms: children are demonstrating psychic abilities, communicating with angelic guides, and even recalling past lives. Other extraordinary experiences are offering clues of things to come.

Millions of children, and adults, have been tapped by the energies of Near Death Experiences and encounters with UFO's. All of these profound experiences are potentially soul blossoming cosmic occurrences that deliver much the same message to all who receive them: WAKE UP! You are loved! Live abundantly! God wants us to be happy.

If humanity chooses the Cosmic Blossoming we will activate our psychic powers by naturally awakening the latent power of our big brains. Could this begin simply by promoting rather than fearing the power inside each of us?

In addition to including such concepts as clairvoyance, psychokinesis, telepathy and precognition, the idea of things Cosmic now tends to include such things as vastly enhanced performance in sports, concentrated studies in intuition, creativity, awareness, and empathetic communication.

Is it possible to teach these cosmic abilities? The answer appears to be a resounding, "yes". The key is willingness to learn them. Their development is most dependent first on how one thinks of oneself and then on how one perceives the rest of the universe.

When one knows he or she is "plugged into" the deep reservoirs of human expression life begins to become excellent and exciting. A future appears in the form of growth, blossoming of potential, and knowledge that one will be able to succeed, to complete and achieve goals. Setting up negative thought patterns colors our life in grays. A positive cosmic self-image colors our thoughts in a brilliant combination of the colors of the rainbow.

Folks who have looked into the subject of Hitler and the Holocaust have routinely pointed to the psychological rather than the occult factors.

There is evidence that the roots of human conflict and suffering lie in our habitual and rarely challenged processes of decision making, in how we think of ourselves. Prior to any outer action is a thought process. Could it be that there is something inherently wrong with the way that we have been trained to use our minds?

Is there a new way we can think of ourselves?

Or, can we let our children teach it to us?

Does the new way to think of ourselves begin by seeing ourselves as Cosmic citizens? Is the erroneous premise upon which we have based virtually our every thought simply a mistaken way of thinking of our selves?

Mystics claim that as long as we see ourselves as separate, isolated individuals, our thought processes will never be truly logical because they will continue to spring from an illogical premise. Until we experience ourselves as integrated members of a single, interwoven, biological and spiritual family or garden, everything we think, hear, say and do will be subject to distortion.

A cosmic-centered view of our place in the Garden would awaken our souls by helping us remember a few things about ourselves.

• Our spiritual identity. Aren't we God-made immortal souls expressing ourselves through this biological/material form rather than bodies with souls?

• Our partnership with nature. Don't we live on a living planet, a being from a species all its own, and an intelligence of its own, rather than merely a planet with life on it?

• Our heritage. Are we brothers and sisters to beings on other planets or even dimensions of experience, some of whom have played a role in our development?

• Our powers and our future. Each of us has access to a storehouse of barely tapped mental, emotional and physical abilities. What would happen if we could tap abilities so that we can use them in service of the world?

THE PAYOFF

Individually or collectively, the possible ways humanity might blossom as described above offer immense benefits to humanity. The payoff is a New Atlantis, a new Garden. By altering our consciousness in the ways we are now doing and will do in the future we are guiding, designing or discovering a new consciousness, and with it a new species.

There are also unforeseen dangers awaiting us. As our species enters into the symbiotic relationship with the New Atlanteans, wonders of life all around us will be revealed. And, so too, undoubtedly, will new challenges.

Y2K
AND THE COLLAPSE OF THE CRADLE OF WESTERN CIVILIZATION

One strand of the golden thread running through this work has been the premise that one person can alter all of human history. In the 1950's, a computer programmer suggested leaving the first two digits off the date to save space on punch cards. He planted a time bomb of atomic proportions.

Did he or she know that when the year 2,000 clicked over, the Year 2,000 problem would debilitate the entire global brain?

Did a son of Enki or Enlil cause Y2K?

We may not want to think about this, but a new Atlantean moment is in the making with the year 2,000 or Y2K computer problem. The entire global brain of our techno-mad civilization may shut down if the Millennium Bug is not cured. Many reports suggest the entire global system must be year 2,000 compliant for the system and the Planetary Grid to be safe.

The domino effect is potentially catastrophic. As we turn the corner on the next one thousand years two questions remained to be answered. Can we solve the Y2K problem and its spiritual and genetic counterparts?

WE'VE HIT AN ICEBERG

In 1997, millions of people went to see the movie *Titanic* – the story of a ship going way too fast that hit an iceberg at sea and sank.

Y2K appears to be the tip of our iceberg that includes the disintegration of the family, spiritually bankrupt politicians, the rape of our environment, and anal commercialism. We have hit it already and are now feeling its effects.

The *Titanic* story is similar to the myth of Atlantis -- the story of a civilization that sank in the middle of night 10,000 years ago. Atlantis was supposed to have been destroyed when her scientists and shamans (smiths) got carried away with advanced technology based on light and genetics. Atlantis is named after Atlas, one of the Titans, for which the *Titanic* is named.

Is Y2K our Atlantis moment? Are our magical speed-of-light technologies on the brink of evaporating...again?

Aboard the *Titanic* panic set in. The ship sank. We must recognize we've hit the iceberg and are now parked just beyond it. Now, we must prevent the ship from sinking, or, our cradle from rocking further.

A teacher once asked his sixth grade class what they would do to keep the *Titanic* from sinking. The solution: turn the ship around and tie it to the iceberg and let it hold the ship until help can arrive.

This being the case, we must apply this too-late solution for the *Titanic* to our present situation regarding the glaring prospect of Doomsday.

We need to tie our ship, the earth, to an iceberg. If we could do this wouldn't it help bring order out of the chaos and avert panic?

WHAT IS OUR ICEBERG?

According to the remarkable Edgar Cayce readings, when Thoth arrived in Egypt he encountered a civilization in chaos, on the verge of massive earth changes. He stuck his staff in the ground and introduced the first Way. He united Egyptian civilization to build the Great Pyramid, which may be thought of as a five-sided iceberg, a giant mountain of rock. The Great Pryamid brought stability to his world.

We could benefit by taking a lesson from this episode. Most pyramid researchers disagree about how, why or by whom the Great Pyramid was built. Few, however, disagree that it is a testimony to the power of the imagination and the human heart.

A well-intentioned heart and imagination are our true stabilizing forces. This means our iceberg, our solution for Y2K or any other challenge, is within each of us.

Next, we must accept the case that the iceberg (Atlantean-esque technology) can assist us. By massively communicating the nature of our situation and possible solutions, technology can aid us in instantly preparing for what is to come.

In myth, Atlas' job was to hold the world up. We've each got to find a way to do this. Like Atlas, we've got to learn to hold the cradle (the ship) steady.

Each of us must take maximum personal action to lift the spiritual vibration of the earth and to physically prepare for the coming days. We've already hit the iceberg. What is to come is merely the aftermath. We must let everyone know we are safe and will survive. This is actually our chance to make a quantum leap forward into a new Golden Age.

We must devise "ropes" to hold the earth steady.

A good rope would be: to always keep a balance between your logic and your emotions. Choose love over fear. And, remember, Love is giving. Keep your spiritual lines open.

Above all, we must keep a pure heart. Each of us is part of the solution. We must draw from the knowledge that we are spiritual beings.

One other thing: WW II taught Americans to renew their relationship with the earth. During the war Americans planted Victory Gardens. Why not revive this beautiful tribute to our selves and our future. Within that garden we can all plant seeds for the future. If we nourish them we will be nourished in return.

PLUS ULTRA

Nostradamus claimed the King of Terror would appear in July 1999. In another quatrain he said this would be "after plus ultra". *Plus ultra* means more beyond. It is said that the Pillars of Hercules carried an ominous warning to all who dared go beyond them: *Ne Plus Ultra* or "No More Beyond". What secrets lay beyond the Pillars?

Could it have been, as many speculate, a reference to the sunken continent of Atlantis? Hardly a soul dared find out.

Many centuries later the same cryptic warning appeared on the coat of arms of the ruling family of Spain, under a depiction of the fabled pillars. The motto remained intact until Columbus successfully reached the shores of America. From that point forward the motto read: *Plus Ultra* -- "More Beyond".

After Columbus, *plus ultra* became the inspiring motto of the early pioneers of science led by Sir Francis Bacon whose *New Atlantis* was the "bible" of the founders of America.

As plus ultra represents the gateway to the New Atlantis, the occult meaning of "Y2K" may represent a similar gateway for Generation Y. We get past it and we're home free.

Synchronistically, Y symbolizes the body posture used by Atlas, Hercules, Moses, Jesus, Thoth, Quetzalcoatl and the goddess religions to channel the Holy Spirit, lifting one world on top of another. When standing with our outstretched arms, palms flat, we create a pillar within.

Welcome back, my friends, to the show that never ends.

Resource Guide

Earthpulse Press
P. O. Box 201393
Anchorage, Alaska 99520 USA

24 Hours a Day
VISA or Master Card Accepted
Voice Mail Ordering: 1-888-690-1277
or 1-907-249-9111
http://www.earthpulse.com

<u>A free catalog of all of our products and books is available
on request.</u>

1. <u>The Peacemaker and the Key of Life</u>, by William Henry is a controversial book that explores and challenges the ideas surrounding the end of the present age. Through careful research, and a new perspective, the author describes the religion, philosophy and archeology of the end times. The book is $22.95 shipped airmail in the U.S. or $27.95 internationally.

2. <u>The Keepers of Heaven's Gate: The Millennial Madness, The Religion Behind the Rancho Santa Fe Suicides</u> by William Henry is an attempt to elucidate the mystical and prophetic happenings which are fueling the furor of new millennial cultists. The end of the last millennium brought suicides and a rash of prophetic ideas surrounding "the end of the world." Today history is again repeating this pattern. Is this the "age of the end" as some are suggesting, or the beginning of a "new heaven and a new earth" as others believe? Only history will reveal the actuality of future events as yet unwritten. Available shipped airmail in the U.S. at $15.95 or internationally for $17.95.

3. <u>Pyramid Power, The Millennium Science</u> is the first paperback edition of this title which sold over a million and a half copies in hardcover in the early 1970's. This book ahead of its time remains a classic. The book is $17.95 Air Mail in the U.S. or $19.95 Air Mail internationally.

4. Earthpulse Flashpoints is a Microbook series edited by Dr. Nick Begich. Microbooks cover four major areas: government, frontier health sciences, earth science, and new technologies. The goal of the publication is to get hard-to-find information into the hands of individuals on their road to self empowerment and self discovery. For six issues send $19.95 in the U.S. and $26.95 internationally.

5. Towards a New Alchemy: The Millennium Science is book about the Neurophone™ and other inventions of Dr. Patrick and Dr. Gael Crystal Flanagan. This book will awaken readers to areas of new science which will change the way we live. The book is $17.95 Air Mail in the U.S. or $19.95 internationally.

6. The Coming Energy Revolution was written by Angels Don't Play this HAARP: Advances in Tesla Technology co-author Jeane Manning. The book is about some of the more interesting new energy systems just on the horizon which could revolutionize the production and uses of energy. The book is $15.95 Air Mail in the U.S. or $17.95 internationally.

7. The Secret Life of Plants, by Peter Tompkins and Christopher Bird is a classic on plants and early work in sound stimulation of plant growth. This product is shipped air mail in the U.S. at $19.00 or internationally for $24.00.

8. Living Energies, by Callum Coats. This inspiring book could help unravel Nature's mysteries, rewrite science textbooks, revolutionize politics – and safeguard Earth's future. This book is 320 pgs., has 72 photographs, 36 charts and tables and 321 line illustrations. Available shipped in the U.S. at $22.95 or internationally for $27.95.

9. Secrets of the Soil, by Christopher Bird and Peter Tompkins, is the most important book ever published on new ideas for more productive agriculture. Faster growing rates and greater yields without using petrochemical based fertilizers are revealed in this incredible work. The book is of great use to home gardeners and commercial growers alike, an important book for all private collections. Available shipped in the U.S. at $22.95 or internationally for $27.95.

10. <u>Bringing the War Home</u>, by William Thomas is a controversial book which explores and challenges the ideas surrounding the events in the Gulf War. Through careful research, and a new perspective, the author describes the problems leading to the conflict and the startling results. The U.S. government's cover-up and military personnel's exposure to biological weapons is detailed in the most incredible exposé ever written on the subject. But it doesn't stop there – in the 448 pages of this book a cure for some of the diseases is detailed. The book is $22.95 shipped airmail in the U.S. or $27.95 internationally.

11. <u>Scorched Earth: The Military's Assault on the Environment,</u> by William Thomas is a detailed account of how the military has exposed Americans and people around the world to toxic risks they never disclosed. Every page contains well footnoted evidence of how our lives have been negatively affected by the lack of concern for the impact of military technology. The book is $19.95 Air Mail in the U.S. or $21.95 Air Mail internationally.

12. <u>Angels Don't Play this HAARP: Advances in Tesla Technology</u> is a book about non-lethal weapons, mind control, weather warfare and the government's plan to control the environment or maybe even destroy it in the name of national defense. The book is $17.95 Air Mail in the U.S. or $19.95 internationally.